INTEREST GROUPS
AND
EDUCATION REFORM

The Latest Crusade to Restructure the Schools

Veronica Donahue DiConti

University Press of America, Inc.
Lanham • New York • London

Copyright © 1996 by
University Press of America,® Inc.
4720 Boston Way
Lanham, Maryland 20706

3 Henrietta Street
London, WC2E 8LU England

Library of Congress Cataloging-in-Publication Data

DiConti, Veronica Donahue.
Interest groups and education reform : the latest crusade to restructure
the schools / Veronica Donahue DiConti.
    p.   cm.
Includes bibliographical references and index.
1. Education and state--United States. 2. Pressure groups--United
States. 3. School management and organization--United States--case
studies. 5. Educational change--United States. I. Title.
LC89.D53   1996   379.73 --dc20   96-25405   CIP

ISBN 0-7618-0435-8 (cloth: alk. ppr.)

For Superman

Contents

Foreword

For more than a decade now, Americans have agonized about the state of public education -- concerned that the nation's school children might not be good enough for the nation's economy. Since the publication of *A Nation At Risk* in 1983, a succession of committees, commissions and foundations has generated a veritable library of reports criticizing the performance of American students, teachers and schools. Most have expressed apprehension whether today's students will be adequately prepared to face the rigors of competition in a global market. A few have proposed school reforms to remedy faults that they have found. Proficiency testing, tougher graduation requirements and merit pay for teachers have all been recommended as steps toward scholastic improvement. But one of the most distinctive features of the current education reform movement is the extent of its concern with the structure of school governance. Many of today's reformers are convinced that they can change the process of teaching and learning only by completely overhauling the institutional architecture of public education.

Veronica Donahue DiConti has subjected these educational reforms to the same kind of searching scrutiny that their proponents have focused on the schools themselves. Her examination of Public School Choice and School-Based Management looks behind the reform proposals to the interest groups that supported them, their political strategies and their intentions. The detailed case studies that she has conducted of school reform politics in Minnesota and Baltimore provide compelling evidence that what is at stake in these episodes is not simply the quality of education but who will control it. In the process, Dr. DiConti reminds us that public schools are political institutions.

Matthew A. Crenson
Johns Hopkins University

Introduction

Changes in American Education Policy

In the United States, changes in public policy most often occur when difficulties are presented to the government in the hope of solving them. Some problems become issues and receive the government's attention because they are immediate and of enormous scope (as in the case of a natural disaster). Other issues, however, are less visible and may require the strategic efforts of groups and individuals in order to bring about a change in public policy by the government.[1]

The agents of such change are various. Political parties were once the great catalysts for change in government policy. When a new party arrived in Washington, some modification in overall government policy would almost always occur. Some of these changes were quite dramatic. The Democratic administration of Franklin D. Roosevelt illustrates this point. In 1932, Roosevelt began his first term in the Oval Office by greatly increasing the government's role in the provision of services to citizens in an effort to relieve widespread suffering from the Great Depression.

Roosevelt's four terms as president contrasted sharply with that of his Republican predecessor, Herbert Hoover. The Hoover administration embraced a laizzez faire philosophy in its response to hard times. Hoover believed that the appropriate answer to the nation's escalating ills could be found in the competition of the free market. As a result of its attachment to this conservative doctrine, the Hoover administration followed a course of limited government intervention in the economy despite the worsening economic conditions of the United States.

But the strength of the political party as a catalyst for change began to weaken during the post war period. Changes in the presidential nominating rules by the 1960s diminished the centralizing force of the party apparatus for both the Democrats and the Republicans. As a result, political parties began to focus almost all their resources and attention on elections and the selection of candidates to fill public offices.[2]

As the importance of the political party in the policymaking process declined, interest groups began to take over many of the responsibilities that the two major parties had abandoned. Ordinarily, interest groups arise when people coalesce around an issue of shared concern and attempt to gain influence in the decision making process. Once they achieve this access, interest groups then focus their activities mainly on the lawmaking phase of the government process.[3]

It is not surprising that interest groups should flourish in the United States as a way to bring about new ideas and changes in government policy. Even in the earliest day of the new nation, James Madison argued that people tended to organize in some way to further their common interests. Madison, however, perceived a negative influence inherent in interest groups. In *The Federalist*, Essay Number 10, he warned of the dangers of interest groups or, as he referred to them, temporary factions. Such factions, he argued, would unite either a majority or a minority of citizens around a common goal. A crisis could arise when the goal being sought adversely affected individuals or society.

For Madison, there were two important mechanisms that would correct the "evils of factions." The first mechanism was the design of the new federal government. With its system of checks and balances, the new democracy would compel the various selfish interests to check each other so that no single interest or group of interests could control society. Secondly, Madison argued that the natural diversity of interests would prevent particular groups from dominating politics.[4]

Madison's view of the diversity of interests found a later incarnation in American social science of this century when the primacy of groups in the policy process was emphasized once again in the literature of political science.[5] Pluralist scholars argued that there were many -- or plural -- interests in society that found representation in the policymaking process through lobbying by private organizations. Pluralist theorists were reacting to a current strand of political thought put forth by elite theorists who found power concentrated in among society's elite. Pluralists, on the other hand, argued that power lay in the complex combination of many groups and governmental officials and structures. In fact, Pluralists supported the Madisonian ideal of groups freely participating in the policymaking process. They argued that none of these groups would become too powerful because of the natural conflict of interests and that government would act as a moderator for competing interests.[6]

Competing Interests in Public Policy: The Case of Education

Nowhere is the impact of competing interests on public policy more evident than in American educational policy. Interest groups hoping to set the education public agenda for their own purposes have fueled the dramatic and numerous changes in the public education system since its inception in the early 19th century. In the educational policymaking arena, the alignment of various competing interest groups routinely defines alternatives for change.

In many instances, particular groups have successfully dominated policy development. For example, educators for quite some time have had a profound impact on the overall design of American public education. The effort of Horace Mann illustrates this point. In 1837, Mann, the first Massachusetts Secretary of Education for a newly created state board of education, sought to set up an overall education system in the state to educate children of diverse backgrounds which would be public, tax supported, and non-sectarian.[7] This organizational structure of public education became known as the common school.

The idea of the common school served as a catalyst for establishing public education in America and swept across the country during the early part of the 19th century. The movement itself was not a unified formal crusade but a loose coalition of local groups centered on educators. Boston, for example, established free elementary schools in 1818; New York in 1832. By the end of the Civil War, virtually all large American cities in the North and West had significant educational institutions providing free public primary schools for all potential voting citizens (and for many young women).[8]

In addition to supporting the creation of public schools in general, the earliest and most persistent advocates of compulsory schooling were school officials. For example, in Chicago, educators began to call for compulsory education as early as the 1860s.[9] Their efforts successfully attracted strong allies.   Labor unions supported compulsory education as a way to protect their interest in the work force.   Compulsory schooling would help to enforce child labor legislation passed in 1881.

Between 1890 and 1920, the comprehensive high school emerged in different states and became a normal extension of the common primary school.[10] Following the establishment of the high school, the interest of educators in the public education system as an institution intensified. The drive for teacher power, civil service reform, and professionalism arose in part from a widespread desire of teachers to gain more control over their destiny. Gradually, schoolmen developed ideologically and an organizational consensus ensued in their search for educational order.[11]   Convinced that there was one best system of education for urban populations, leading educators sought to discover it and carry it out in numerous school systems.

Education officials, such as school superintendents, also worked with business and civic elates in an effort to secure the future of public schools as a central municipal institution. Educators and civic and business elates believed that structural reforms, such as centralization, for example, were necessary to create efficient, rational, and non-political school bureaucracies.[12]

The interest of business and civic leaders in school reform, however, was part of a much broader municipal reform movement in many Northeastern cities. Reformers sought to remove politics from city service agencies by establishing agencies that would operate independently of City Hall. Instead of political patronage dominating the appointment process of city personnel, reformers hoped their efforts at municipal reform would place agencies in the hands of bureaucratic professionals. In order to achieve their objective in the public education system, reformers replaced ward elections with appointed school boards, granted autonomy to the superintendent, and developed a more specialized and well-defined hierarchical bureaucratic order for the improvement and control of the schools.

The Impact of Interest Groups on American Education

The efforts of educators and their allies were highly successful. The common school movement flourished in most of the country, representing the start of a national system of education controlled at the local level. The new system brought uniformity and integration to the schools through the creation of a system of political authority. What is more important, however, is that the common school movement established a distinctive American pattern of mass enrollments with little stratification.[13]

This pattern allowed the schools to play an important integrative role in society, especially for immigrants. In the process, the schools succeeded in creating a core of common values by absorbing great streams of immigrants which have, at various points in the history of the nation, flooded the United States, speaking different languages and observing different customs. For example, following the Irish potato famine of the 1840s, thousands of Irish workers settled in the cities and towns of the Northeastern United States. At that time, schooling became a means of integrating an ethnic working class into the social fabric of American life.

In fact, progressive historians identify schools as democratizing institutions that opened opportunities to all social classes. One progressive historian in particular, John Dewey, argued that the schools helped integrate America's youth into various occupational, political, familial and other adult roles required by an expanding economy and a stable polity. For Dewey, education became "the means of the social continuity of life."[14] As one of the few social institutions which people encountered daily, the common school both reflected and shaped a sense of community.[15]

Progressive historians also argue that public education has helped to fulfill an important egalitarian role in American society. To support their assertions, they examine the role of interest groups in the public education system during the 1960s when the schools became central to the civil rights movement as a way to achieve racial integration in society.

At that time, civil rights activists successfully shifted the focus of school policy from the Kennedy administration's earlier emphasis on excellence in math and science in the nation's high schools and universities. Following the launch of Sputnik in 1957, the Soviet space success awakened public interest in education, its goals and operations.

The Kennedy administration subsequently sought excellence in education as a way of guaranteeing the preeminence of the United States in world politics.

In response to the civil rights movement, however, the focus of public education changed dramatically. The schools became defined as a mechanism of social mobility for African-Americans in particular, a group routinely excluded from the educational design that sought a unifying influence of common learning under one roof of the common school. The Great Society programs of the Johnson administration made public education a central feature of dramatic federal programs for social reform. For the first time, the federal government intervened strongly in elementary and secondary education. Such programs as compensatory education and school desegregation existed on financial and other types of federal support.

In its egalitarian role, schooling centered on the notion of equality of opportunity. From this new perspective, the schools needed to serve the redistributive function of elevating the status of poor people and giving them access to the mainstream economy, a policy that would enable poor and minority children to achieve social and economic advancement, subsidized by the tax revenue of the community at large.

But education reforms that centered on demands for integration and equality of opportunity brought turmoil and conflict in many American cities. Central-city schools came under increasing scrutiny from African-American and neighborhood groups. School boards in cities such as Chicago and New York were subjected to a wide variety of redistributive demands, including demands for racial integration, increases in school funding, the relocation of teachers, complete equalization of educational resources, and compensatory educational policies that would allocate extra resources to the schools serving low-income areas.[16]

Despite frequent good intentions and abundant rhetoric about "equal educational opportunity" the public schools have rarely taught the children of the poor effectively -- and this failure has been systemic and idiosyncratic.[17] Nonetheless, progressive historians argue that the aggressive political participation and the challenge to authority that came out of the civil rights movement energized a traditional democratic interest group that had grown passive and complacent. At that time, the schools brought African-Americans together as a group with particular political demands and a distinct history of political practice centered around education issues in an effort to achieve

equality.[18]   In addition to African-Americans, the schools have, from
time to time, galvanized parents, students, worker organizations, ethnic
minorities, women and others to use the public schools for their own
objectives: material security, culture, a more just distribution of
economic reward, and a path of personal development conducive to a
fuller, happier life.[19]

Questioning the Premise of One Best System

Although school observers agree that in many instances the features
of intervention in school politics -- educators, business, politicians --
are the same, there has been a significant difference of opinion as to
their intentions as policymakers in American education.   In fact,
dissenting intellectuals criticized the one best system of urban
education that sprang from the common school movement for its
mechanical routines and its deadening effect on children.[20]

For example, revisionist historians offer a different, or revised
perspective from the progressive historians.   Most closely identified
with Marxist scholars, revisionists argue that schooling has reflected
the need of industrial capitalism for mechanisms to control labor, to
discipline the working class, to create proper work attitudes, and to
block the growth of a socialist ideology.   Revisionists point to the
creation of the Massachusetts public school system during the early
19th century to illustrate their point.   As the public education system in
Massachusetts began to take shape, conservative leaders, fearful of the
social dangers posed by a period of rapid industrialization and
urbanization, looked for ways to impose upper and middle class values
upon poor and uneducated communities.   The public school system,
say some of its critics, became an essential mechanism for creating a
submissive and skilled work force that was essential to the capitalist
system in general and local economic growth in particular.[21]   The
progressive era also supports an example of the imposition perspective
advanced by revisionists.   In sharp contrast to the progressive
historians, revisionists argue that the progressive era reformers,
composed of educational professionals, business leaders and civic
elates, imposed an agenda on an education system to further their own
interests.   These reformers successfully shaped the public school
system by concentrating their efforts on the curricula and introducing
vocational education into American high schools.   A vocational
education, business and civic elates argued, would help students

develop the proper business and social skills as well as the right economic beliefs. To achieve their objectives the progressive era reformers offered school administrators and teachers the promise of an enlightened partnership with business. Together the two forces would work for change based on enlightened self interest.[22]

Contemporary Reforms in Education

Recent changes in educational policy provide a further illustration of the influence that interest groups can exert on the public schools in the hope to change the function of education. The quest for educational opportunity that began with the civil rights movement and dominated the educational policy and reform agendas for more than 20 years, quickly receded into the background. The most recent reform effort presents the schools as a mechanism for economic development and employment. This new reform effort, popularly referred to as the "excellence movement" followed almost two decades of overall decline in educational achievement and a growing demand for greater economic productivity and national prosperity.   Excellence in education, business and political leaders argued, would guarantee America's preeminence in world markets.

The reforms of the 1980s, however, served the interest of business and political leaders and imposed on a schools' constituency that had grown inactive and ineffective. But the 1980s efforts to change educational policy in the nation's schools stagnated largely because business and political leaders could not mobilize the necessary degree of support from the educational establishment for their reform initiatives. The public school bureaucracies themselves -- the school boards, the central administration staff, and in many instances the school superintendents -- strongly resisted new reforms. Instead of joining this movement for change in the early part of the 1980s, the education establishment became an interest group in its own right and strongly supported protectionist policies that were obstacles to reform.

A negative response on the part of the bureaucracy to new reform initiatives is not unique to the education establishment. Bureaucratic organizations rarely support policies that would diminish their own powers and autonomy. More often than not they resist such changes.[23]

The chief administrators of such organizations often believe that the changes sought by reformers will involve them in a complex, uncertain series of managerial tasks.[24] For these and other reasons, bureaucratic organizations commonly resist changes in policy that outsiders try to impose.

As the 1980s progressed, and the bureaucratic interest could not be engaged in reform debate, reformers began to turn their attention away from elevating educational standards to restructuring the schools. Restructuring the schools, reformers argued, would be a necessary precursor to achieving excellence in the classroom.

Two restructuring proposals became extremely popular in the reform debate. Both proposals sought to minimize or eliminate the potential for bureaucratic influence on new educational policies by shifting functions away from the central administrators and down to the students and schools themselves.

The proposals, however, stemmed from two entirely different premises about the best way to restructure the public schools. The first, School Choice, centers on the idea that students should have the right to exit their assigned schools and attend a school of their choice. Through the use of this exit option, reformers argued, the schools would be forced to improve largely because they would have to compete with one another to retain and attract students.

The second restructuring proposal, School-Based Management, looks at the merits of strengthening the voice of parents, students and teachers in the management of their neighborhood school as a way of stimulating academic improvement. Through the use of school-based councils or committees, those most deeply involved in the education process would assess the needs, resources and development of local schools.

The Forces behind Exit and Voice

During the 1980s, exit and voice formed the basis of public policies designed to reverse a deteriorating educational system. Albert O. Hirschmann, an economist, first observed the dependence of organizations upon exit and voice as mechanisms for their reform.[25] The exit option, Hirschmann argues, allows a dissatisfied consumer to "vote with his feet" by switching to a firm or product that he likes better. Thus, the unhappy consumer is sending a signal to the organization for the need for change. In recent education reform debates, exit option proponents argue that recovery on the part of the school system will come by way of the invisible hand, or market forces, as a by-product of the consumer's -- the student's -- decision to exit.

Whereas the exit option is more closely attuned to economics, the voice option, on the other hand, is political action. In fact, voice is just the opposite of exit. Voice is the articulation of critical opinions rather than a private, "secret" vote in the anonymity of the marketplace. What is more important, however, is the fact that voice can be graduated all the way from faint grumbling to violent protest.[26]

Like the exit option, the use of the voice option has been a central component of the American education reform debate since at least the 1960's. Both reforms, however, have done little to improve the overall quality of American education. In fact, Hirschmann points out in his argument that the use of exit usually prevents a declining firm from ever recovering. Nonetheless, education reformers still actively support some form of exit as a way to improve the schools. As a result of this support, the education reform debate continues to polarize around these two recovery mechanisms.

But the two recovery mechanisms, exit and voice, are not mutually exclusive categories. Hirschmann argues that there are institutions in which perfecting the exit option is also compatible with improving the operation of the voice option. American education provides one example of an institution in which perfecting the exit option is also compatible with those designed to improve the effectiveness of the voice option. Under some conditions, however, the exit option will prevail over the voice option and vice versa. The evolution of Public School Choice and School-Based Management as strategies for reforming the public school system provides a perfect opportunity to discover a.) under what conditions and b.) the problems that arise when either of these options comes to the forefront of the education debate.

Format of the Discussion

This analysis begins with a discussion of the "excellence movement" and the subsequent calls by business and political leaders in the mid-1980s to restructure the nation's schools. Chapter two then explores the exit and voice options that dominated the restructuring debate. Chapter two also includes a brief history and synthesis of the options that have been adopted across the country. Then two case studies are presented in chapters three and four. Chapter three looks at the implementation of an exit option reform, Public School Choice, in

Minnesota. The second case study, presented in chapter four, examines the strategy of providing more voice to the teachers, parents and students with the implementation of School-Based Management in the Baltimore City Public School system. From these two case studies, the techniques of reformers become apparent.

In chapter five, three important conclusions are drawn. During the 1980s, the education policy agenda and reform debate proceeded from a public consensus reached by the business community, politicians and educators. To a considerable extent, these three groups were able to shape the restructuring debate. Although it is an oversimplification to collapse the interests and centers of power in educational policymaking into three categories, in the late 1980s these forces in school politics not only provided most of the fuel that generated school controversy but also the balance of power among them went far to explain the political settlements shaping educational policy.

To begin with, this study argues that the alignment of interest groups in the policymaking arena consistently defines the alternatives for change. The same is true for recent reforms. In fact, the influence that the business community, political leaders and educators bring to the policymaking arena explains why a deterioration in some school systems generates a demand for the exit option offered by the Schools of Choice concept while deterioration in other school districts led to pressure for School-Based Management systems that would strengthen the voice of parents or teachers. Despite decades of evidence that either the practice or threat of exit or voice has done little to improve the quality of education, reformers in the 1980s proceeded to advance yet another model of exit and voice. These new forms of exit and voice, School Choice and School-Based Management, they argued, would bring about fundamental and systemic changes in the school system. The power alignments in the local setting will determine whether exit or voice will prevail as the preferred strategy of reformers for bringing about change and improvement in the educational system. In essence, the group that acts as the catalyst for reform will strongly influence the kind of reform adopted in a given school system.

Secondly, the research will provide two models that will alert reformers to the problems they will confront as they seek to bring about systemic change in the schools. What is more important, however, is that it provides a way to examine the political context of recent decentralization efforts. In general, the education reform movements of the 1980s differ significantly from those of the 19th century, which were interested in building up institutions like the schools. Contemporary reforms spurred by interest groups challenge these public institutions and try to make them more responsive to forces outside the local administrative structure through the mechanisms of exit and voice. The desired result is to remove authority from a centralized administrative structure and to fragment decision making.

Finally, although this work is about educational policymaking, much of the debate in reform circles had very little to do with teaching and learning, educational philosophy, or the functions of schools beyond economic development and preparation for employment. Although education reform touched upon certain important systemic issues, in general it has remained peripheral to what goes on in the classroom. In fact, the proposals for structural reform were not serious attempts to improve the quality of education. Instead, the design of the proposals would serve educationally extraneous interests that sought to weaken a central administrative authority in order to advance their own interests.

Notes

[1]   Charles O. Jones, *An Introduction To The Study of Public Policy.* (Belmont: Duxbury Press, 1984), 42.

[2]   Ronald J. Hrebenar, R.K. Scott *Interest Group Politics in America* (Englewood Cliffs: Prentice-Hall, Inc, 1982), 3.

[3]   Hrebenar and Scott, 5.

[4]   James Madison, Essay Number 10, in *The Federalist Papers* (New York: Bantam Books, 1982), 42.

[5]   See Robert Dahl, *Who Governs?* (New Haven: Yale University Press, 1969).

[6]   Jeffrey M. Berry, *The Interest Group Society.* (Boston: Little, Brown and Company, 1984), 3, and Dahl.

[7]   S. Bowles and H. Gintis, *Schooling in Capitalist America: Educational Reform and the Contradictions of Economic Life.* (New York:Basic Books, Inc., 1976) 167.

[8]   See Ira Katznelson and Margaret Weir, *Schooling for All: Class, Race, and the Decline of the American Ideal.* (New York: Basic Books, 1985), 70.

[9]   Katznelson, 10.

[10]   Lawrence A. Cremin, *Traditions of American Education* (New York: Basic Books, 1977).

[11] David B. Tyack, *The One Best System: A History of American Urban Education* (Cambridge: Harvard University Press, 1974), 7, 97.

[12] Tyack, 148.

[13] Richard Rubinson. "Class Formations, Politics, and Institutions: Schooling in the United States." *American Journal of Sociology.* 92 (November 1986): 533.

[14] John Dewey, *Democracy and Education* (New York: The Free Press, 1966), 20.

[15] Tyack, 17.

[16] Paul Peterson, *City Limits*, (Chicago: The University of Chicago Press, 1981), 181.

[17] Tyack, 11.

[18] Katznelson and Weir, 190.

[19] Bowles and Gintis, 101.

[20] Tyack, 83.

[21] Michael Katz, *The Irony of Early School Reform: Educational Innovation in Mid-Nineteenth Century Massachusetts.* (Cambridge, Massachusetts: Harvard University Press, 1968), Colin Greer *The Great School Legend* (New York: Basic Books, 1972), Joel Spring *Education and The Rise of The Corporate State* (Boston: Beacon Press, 1972) and S. Bowles & H. Gintis.

[22] Peter Sola, "The Corporate Community on the Ideal Business -- School Alliance: A Historical and Ethical Critique," 75 in *The New Servants of Power: A Critique of the 1980's School Reform Movement*, ed. O'Shea, Christine M., (New York: Greenwood, 1989), 75-83.

[23] There are, of course, exceptions to every rule. See Martha Derthick and Paul J. Quirk, *The Politics of Deregulation* (Washington, D.C.: The Brookings Institution, 1985.) In their analysis, the authors find staff members of the Civil Aeronautics Board actively and enthusiastically supported changes in deregulation that would strip them of much of their powers.

[24] Paul R. Schulman, *Large-Scale Policy Making* (Westport: Greenwood Press, 1980).

[25] Albert O. Hirschmann, *Exit, Voice and Loyalty: Responses to Decline in Forms, Organizations, and States.* (Cambridge: Harvard University Press, 1970) 62. Hirschmann takes this schism one step further. He argues both options reflect a more fundamental schism, the one that exists between economics and politics. Exit belongs to economics and voice belongs to politics.

[26] Hirschmann, 16.

Chapter One

The Excellence Movement

At the start of the 1980s, a nationwide movement began in the United States to address the shortcomings of the country's public school system. This latest in a number of modern crusades to improve the quality of the public schools centered on the notion of excellence. The "excellence movement," as this reform effort became popularly known, followed almost two decades of dramatic declines in the performance of American school children. The concern over excellence in education stemmed in large part from the belief held by business and political leaders that the skills and expertise of a country's work force are the essential ingredients needed for greater economic productivity and national prosperity.

As the 1980s progressed, the excellence movement continued to gain momentum. By 1983 the Reagan administration effectively pushed education reform to the top of the country's agenda with the release of *A Nation at Risk* by the President's National Commission on Excellence in Education. That report detailed the practical problems that would face the United States if the quality of the public schools did not significantly improve. Too many students, the report found, were leaving high school and college without having mastered skills necessary to participate fully as workers in an increasingly technological society. Without a skilled and educated work force, the report concluded, the United States would risk forfeiting its competitive edge in domestic and world markets.

Many of the most outspoken critics of the nation's public schools came from the business community. Business leaders warned that deteriorating schools were undermining the nation's economy. American business executives pointed overseas to Japan, where they attributed an economic bonanza during the early 1980s in part to a work force that was highly skilled, disciplined and educated.

Low levels of student performance, business leaders argued, were having a profound impact on the ability of United States industry to compete internationally. Declines in mathematical ability have become increasingly troublesome in this country with the growth of science, technology and industry. On the Scholastic Aptitude Test (SAT), for example, one measure of student achievement, there has been a slow and long term decline in overall pupil performance since 1967. In 1967, American students averaged 466 on the verbal portion of the exam and higher on the math section with a score of 492. By 1983, however, both scores dropped by 40 and 30 points, respectively. Although there was a slight increase in SAT scores from 1983-1987, by 1988 the scores reversed their slow upward climb. By 1990, student performance on the SAT reached its nadir with a 424 average on the verbal section and 476 on the math.[1]

With test scores dropping since 1963, American students in the 1980's could no longer compete with their counterparts in other industrialized nations. Critics started pointing to international assessments which reveal United States students lagging far behind their Asian counterparts. For example, in Korea, 78 percent of thirteen year old students can use intermediate mathematics skills when solving two step problems, compared to only 40 percent of their counterparts in the United States.[2]

Although the overall pattern suggests that American students have lower test scores than comparable students in Asian and some European countries, the data comparing United States students to other countries are generally quite limited and can be misleading. For example, in the United States, a comparison to other nations in overall achievement is inappropriate, largely because a higher percentage of all age cohorts in America are in school than is true in other countries. Although South Koreans score higher on standardized tests than students in the United States, compulsory schooling in that Asian nation stops at age 12. In the United States, on the other hand, compulsory schooling ends at age 16.[3]

Even *A Nation at Risk*, which warned of a "rising tide of mediocrity" threatening the future of the country, recognized that more Americans were going further in school than ever before. By the 1980s, three in four teenagers graduated from high school (compared to fewer than one in two at the end of World War II), and nearly half of those graduates went on to college.[4]

A similar comparison with European nations is revealing. In fact, the American educational system contrasts sharply with Europe in two ways: the amount of schooling is much higher, and the degree of stratification is much lower. England, for example, did not develop a public primary system until 1870 when it passed the Education Act that year. A secondary school system did not follow until 1902. Since the inception of British schools, both primary and secondary systems remain highly stratified by class. In the United States, on the other hand, the common school movement established a greatly expanded and uniform system of primary and secondary schooling by the 1840's for all Americans regardless of class.[5]

The Cost of Inclusiveness over Excellence

Despite the fact that more Americans were staying in school longer, the overall quality of education declined as the decades progressed. By the 1980s, corporations increasingly assumed the cost of teaching fundamental skills, which the public schools should have taught. Not only had the nation's schools failed to teach the three R's, said business leaders, they had also begun producing "technologically illiterate" graduates. Business leaders maintained that the current generation of students would need to work with larger and more complex bodies of information in performing even the most basic tasks as employees. But more than half of the nation's 17 year old graduates were inadequately prepared to perform competently at jobs that require technical skills or to benefit from specialized training.[6]

Not only was the quality of labor declining, but corporations have begun to feel the effects of a shrinking labor pool. For the first time in American history, business faced a shortfall in the availability of labor so widespread that it threatened the well-being of hundreds of companies. "Youth 2,000," a study published by the United States Departments of Labor, Education and Health and Human Services in the mid-1980s, indicated that by the turn of the century there will not be enough adequately educated workers to fill entry-level jobs in the United States.

With fewer young people entering the work force, companies are frequently dependent on immigrant labor. Between 1980 and 1987 immigrants accounted for 22 percent of the growth in the United States labor force, more than double their contribution in the 1970's. Many companies expect that percentage to rise during the 1990's. But most of these new workers will need instruction in English, and about one-third have only elementary education. If current demographic and economic trends continue, American business will hire a million new people a year who will not be able to read, write or count.[7] The National Alliance of Business estimates that the $30 billion spent annually by corporations for worker training and retraining could increase dramatically and become an insurmountable obstacle to U.S. international competitiveness.[8]

Due to the declines in both the quality and availability of labor, the business community in several localities across the country began to increase its involvement in the public schools. Although the private sector has traditionally played a key role in education, business involvement in the schools began to diminish over 20 years ago when the education policy agenda -- civil rights, school finance, and collective bargaining -- became increasingly bitter and confrontational. By the 1980s, however, corporations began to forge links with central city schools in an effort to improve the employability of school graduates.[9]

At that time companies and civic minded business organizations started to sponsor a variety of activities in the public schools including experimental schools and programs. For example, the business communities in cities such as Memphis and Los Angeles formed partnerships with schools which linked individual schools with business firms in their areas. These partnerships attempted to raise student achievement levels by allowing business to contribute funds, personnel and resources to the adopted schools. Business firms also focused their attention on the curriculum in public high schools. Business involvement in curriculum development, reformers hoped, would result in a better prepared work force, lower training costs for industry, and increased communications between educators and business people. By 1983 according to the National School Volunteer

Program, some four million volunteers were working in the schools, and approximately 18 percent were from the business community.[10] During the excellence movement, state politicians also took note of the growing public perception that economic development was becoming increasingly intertwined with the quality of the public schools. State after state across the country responded to an increasingly competitive business environment by examining the status of their educational systems. A sound educational system, state lawmakers argued, would help ensure the existence of a highly trained and motivated work force. A competitive and competent work force would in turn attract new industries to the state and help retain existing business.[11]

To advance economic development objectives, politicians began working with the business community on new education initiatives. This powerful coalition succeeded in enacting numerous reforms. A brief overview of the state level reforms shows that all 50 states made important changes in their public school systems during the period of the excellence movement. Fourteen completely reorganized their education systems and more than 40 states raised their requirements for graduation at all levels, with 19 adding a minimum-competency test for high school graduation.[12]

Lawmakers also focused on teacher pay and quality. Forty-six states mandated competency tests for new teachers, and 23 allowed teachers alternative routes to certification. States also raised teachers' salaries dramatically, with top pay surpassing $50,000 a year in many districts. To carry out these new reforms, state governments substantially increased their spending levels on education. By the late 1980's, education became the number one expense in every state.[13]

By elevating educational standards, governors, state legislators and reform minded business people argued that students and teachers would be forced to work hard to meet the new goals.[14] But after almost six years of shifting from local to state control, increasing monitoring and accounting activity, student performance remained stagnant. Changes that were introduced by business leaders at the school site and politicians at the state level from 1980 to 1986 were not enough to achieve improvement. A nationwide survey conducted in 1986 by the Business Roundtable, a powerful organization made up of the chief executive officers of the nation's largest 200 corporations, found that as many as 60 percent of high school graduates were not prepared for entry-level jobs.[15]

Even worse, more than half of the nation's public high school students were still not taking chemistry or advanced algebra before graduating. Nationally, student science achievement remained well below the levels of 1969.[16] Increasingly education reformers realized that simply requiring more courses for graduation was not enough to stimulate student improvement and to raise the quality of high school graduates. Arkansas, for example, is one state with the most rigorous graduation requirements for high school students. But the state allows students to fulfill science and math requirements by taking introductory courses. Despite the new requirements for graduation, the state continued to rank last in the percentage of high school students taking upper-level science courses and near the bottom in the percentage of students taking upper-level math courses.[17]

By the mid-1980s, reformers began to turn their attention to the way in which educational services were reaching the classroom and the individual student. Excellence, business leaders and politicians began to warn, would remain an elusive goal unless reformers could find some way to hold the schools accountable for what they accomplish or fail to accomplish in the classroom. Reformers pointed to the present system of hierarchical accountability, which, they argued, prevented the sweeping legislative mandates of the excellence movement from achieving any measurable amount of success.[18]

The focus of the present system of accountability centers on the accomplishments of school officials, their collective goals and their adherence to standards and procedures set out by policymakers. Because policymakers and higher-level administrators are distant from the school site and cannot directly supervise decisions made at the schools, large educational bureaucracies emerged to enforce strict adherence to organizational goals. Bureaucratically mandated procedures and schedules are common as well as controls and aggregate measures of student performance.[19] But the result is that educational systems have become so overburdened with bureaucratic norms and standard operating procedures that they no longer respond effectively to client concerns and demands.[20]

In addition to the growth of the central educational bureaucracy, the rise of teacher unionism has done much to obscure accountability. Since the inception of collective bargaining in education during the early 1960s, the teachers' unions have concentrated on improving the economic and working conditions of their members. In urban school districts in particular, decision making tends to be heavily weighted in favor of the public bureaucracies and their unusually well-organized employees and their immediate beneficiaries.[21] Where teachers' unions are strong, they affect local school district policies and resource allocations and struggle for power with local administrators. Like any union organization, they are primarily concerned with the collective interests of their members and are nearly impervious to outside influences.[22]

Given the goals and structure of teachers' unions, their primary concerns are to pursue policies that enhance teacher power, protect jobs and seniority rights and increase wages. Since the beginning of collective bargaining, teachers' unions have frequently rejected educational policies that threatened these primary concerns.[23] In fact, the excellence movement provides one example of how resistant unions can be to reform. Reformers began to advocate a system of merit pay during the 1980s. Merit pay, they argued, was one way to encourage greater participation by teachers in the reform movement. A system of merit pay would relate pay to effectiveness rather than seniority.

Politicians in particular supported merit pay systems. In fact, the Reagan administration as well as several state governors proposed merit pay as a component of education reform packages. By basing teacher pay on job performance, politicians hoped to introduce a new system of accountability in the education system. But governors soon realized that education reforms would be difficult to carry out effectively without the active cooperation of teachers. Teachers, however, opposed a system of merit pay, which they saw as a threat to their bargaining unity. As a result, politicians abandoned merit pay proposals in many states in exchange for tightening up the curriculum and content.[24]

The insularity of the nation's educational bureaucracies and teachers unions, however, began to break down when reform minded business leaders and politicians started turning their attention to the basic governance structure of the schools. By 1986, the excellence movement took a turn toward the restructuring of school systems. Restructuring the bureaucratic organization of the schools, reformers argued, seemed necessary largely because the schools were no longer responsive to their political environments -- to the political system and the desires of the parents and the communities they presumably serve. Nor, say proponents of restructuring, do school conditions and practices accord with the schools' internal environment as defined by the nature and needs of the those who populate schools -- teachers and administrators as well as students.   Substantive improvements, reformers began to warn, would continue to be elusive unless the decision making process underwent some form of decentralization in order to increase the power and participation of families and communities in the educational system.[25]

Public School Choice and School-Based Management Emerge in the Reform Debate

By the late 1980s two broad strategies that sought to increase popular control and bring about improvements in the nation's public school systems began to surface in numerous school systems across the country. The two reform proposals, known as the Schools of Choice Concept and School-Based Management/Shared Decision Making, focus on fundamental changes in the delivery system to improve the quality of education. Both the Schools of Choice Concept, or Choice, and School-Based Management seek to redefine the social order within the school by introducing changes in the existing decision making structure that will redistribute roles and change the functions among students, teachers, administrators and parents. But the two reforms stem from entirely different conceptions of the best way to shift accountability downward in the educational system.

The first restructuring proposal, Choice, relies heavily on the idea of increasing local school autonomy as an effective means of shifting accountability away from the bureaucrats and down to the parents themselves. Choice advocates argue that local school autonomy is a key variable explaining student achievement. The Choice approach attempts to "deregulate" American education by freeing the schools from the present system of political and bureaucratic controls so that each school can create its own identity. This school reform concept stems from the premise that if parents and children have the opportunity to choose their public schools, they are in a position to "vote with their feet" unless administrators listen and respond to their complaints.[26]

Choice advocates argue that this exit option is the best method of reinvigorating the schools because public empowerment forces the schools to compete with each other. The individual school, in turn, will be forced to develop a school mission that a public accepts as valuable. The development of this mission will then spur the formation of such norms as collegiality between teachers and a sense of shared ownership, which includes everyone involved in the education process -- students, parents, teachers and administrators. In turn this should encourage the development of links between the school and the community, which may be a prerequisite to the amelioration of problems that plague both the schools and American society.[27]

Improving individual schools by encouraging citizen or parent participation in their affairs is the basis of a second popular reform proposal, School-Based Management, carried out in many school districts during the 1980's. School-Based Management, however, is not an alternative to the Schools of Choice concept. The two reforms have grown up side by side, and it is conceivable that a school system might adopt both of them.

Like Choice, the endorsement of School-Based Management by education reformers represents a challenge to the dominating bureaucracy and centralized control of the current school system. Yet there is a fundamental difference between restructuring proposals derived from parental choices and those derived from site management proposals. The difference lies in the organizational structure of the two systems. Choice proposals seek to change the incentive structure of public schools from an essentially bureaucratic model to one more closely attuned to client preferences, while School-Based Management models propose to reform the existing bureaucratic structure of schools by decentralizing some functions as a way of making school programs more responsive to the communities the schools should be serving.[28]

The top-down tradition of the public school bureaucracy, advocates of School-Based Management argue, stifles creativity in the classroom and prohibits principals from exercising professional judgment on decisions that are needed at the local level. Teachers, on the other hand, have only as much voice in the operation of a school as the principal allows and encourages. The rise of teacher unionism, meanwhile, has made the relationship between principals, who are management, and faculty members more adversarial, further weakening the cohesion of school staffs. School-Based Management attempts to alleviate both problems by inducing principals to become more effective leaders and involving teachers in key decisions about school policy. The underlying goal of this restructuring approach is to get principals and teachers alike to take more responsibility for the educational life of the school and to be accountable, as professionals, for the well-being and growth of their students.

But School-Based Management is not a singular concept and has come to mean many things to many people. The most encompassing definition is the one used here. School-Based Management is a process for decision making at the local school level that involves the principal and teachers in matters affecting school policy. School-Based Management also calls for school improvement by involving members of the community. Shared decision making is the vehicle that creates and sustains responsibility and improvement. Through the use of community councils, parents are encouraged to become partners in policymaking. The school site team or council meets regularly to assess the needs at the schools, sets its own goals and objectives to address those needs within school board policy, and then carries out its plan.

In the process, School-Based Management recognizes the democratic character and political nature of the public school system and provides a "voice" in the organizational structure for students, administrators, teachers and parents in an attempt to change the practices and policies of the schools. Supporters of School-Based Management argue that by changing the governance structure and decision making relationships of the school system, the individual schools will become more responsive to their students, more receptive to innovation and creativity, and more deserving of public support.

Choice and School-Based Management call for a reordering of school organization to enable the individual school to define itself to a far greater extent than is now the case.[29] Restructuring advocates on both sides of the debate agree that greater school autonomy is an essential ingredient for higher levels of academic achievement even though they disagree on whether an increase in exit or voice is the best way to reform the public school system.

The consensus on the outcomes of school reform policy arises principally for two reasons. The first is that the participants in the educational policymaking arena are the same when Choice and School-Based Management are at the center of the education debate. In the 1980s the interaction among business and political leaders and educators provided most of the ideas that pressured change in school systems across the country. The balance of power among them went far to explain the political settlements eventually shaping educational policy.

Secondly, restructuring proponents of Choice and School-Based Management agree that local school autonomy makes an "effective school." In fact, reformers on both sides of the debate use the Effective Schools research to support their assumptions. The Effective Schools movement, originally advocated in 1975 by the late Ronald Edmonds, drew on decades of studies of successful schools. From this research a list of five general characteristics associated with Effective Schools emerged: "Strong principal leadership, academic focus, high expectations, healthy and orderly environment, frequent monitoring of student achievement."[30]

From the research, Edmonds concluded that the most important factors in a student's education were the characteristics of the school itself.[31] Edmonds argued that social scientists, like James Coleman, professor of sociology at the University of Chicago, incorrectly concluded that family background determines pupil performance. Coleman and a team of social scientists in the mid-1960's reached this conclusion following their landmark study, *Equality of Educational Opportunity*, conducted for the U.S. Office of Education under a Congressional mandate to explore the issues surrounding desegregation. Coleman and his associates argued on the basis of extensive empirical data that background characteristics of students and their peers almost entirely determined academic performance.[32]

Following Edmond's assertions, Coleman subsequently conducted his own research about American high schools in the early 1980s. In *High School Achievement*, Coleman and his co-authors, Thomas Hoffer and Sally Kilgore, used the High School and Beyond data set, by far the largest data set of information ever gathered on schools, to carry out a comparative study of public and private schools. They concluded that private schools do a better job of educating students. This superior performance arises from important differences in school organization across all sectors. From that research, Coleman switched his position from family background as the key contributor to student performance and supported the idea of local school autonomy as an effective educational tool.

Coleman's research subsequently became a significant part of the exit option debate in the late 1980s when two political scientists, John Chubb and Terry Moe, expanded on his earlier work and conducted a nationwide survey of 400 American high schools and approximately 20,000 teachers. From their research, Chubb and Moe concluded that local school autonomy is an effective way to increase student achievement levels. To support their assertions, the two political scientists point to the superiority of private and parochial schools, which, they argue, offer a better education precisely because of their independence from democratic controls such as local school boards, superintendents, central office bureaucracies, and corresponding apparatus at the state and federal levels.[33] This independence from democratic controls provides the opportunity for each school to create its own identity to compete in the marketplace.

In general, Chubb and Moe successfully aroused the nation to debate the merits of School Choice. In particular, they advocated an entirely new structure for public education in the United States -- a market system of education. Under the market system all schools, both public and private, receive a charter from the state. The government's per pupil expenditure follows each individual student with the schools competing for dollars in the marketplace of students. Students are then free to "shop" for a school of their choice. In turn the competition for students, reformers argued, would stimulate reform by allowing good schools to thrive and bad schools to close.

Although the market system of public education brought new life to an old debate, questions of accountability and the potentially detrimental effect of competition on a public education system eventually removed the Chubb and Moe model from the education debate. In fact, in their analysis, Chubb and Moe avoided discussing political issues that would impede implementing a market system of public education. For example, state legislators consistently hesitated to enact into law any new measures that would fund private elementary and secondary as well as public schools. More specifically, politicians did not want to support a system that violated the constitutional principle of separation of church and state by funding religious schools. They feared that non-public, and particularly religious schools, would be able to promote their own private agendas with the support of state dollars.

Moreover, critics pointed to the potentially detrimental effects of market forces on the schools. To begin with, a highly deregulated system would remove any accountability in a system where school observers were already complaining of a lack of accountability.

Choice opponents also argued that such a system of public education would eventually cost the taxpayers more to operate. They based their argument on two assumptions. The first is that the market system of public education would result in a new set of appropriations of public expenditures for children already in private school without any change in the current education system. Secondly, they point to higher education to supports their concerns. Despite the fact that there is competition in higher education, the cost of a college education has outpaced inflation in the past twenty years.

Chubb and Moe also failed to address the overall decline in American education since the 1960s that has plagued both public and private schools. Although a Choice school may produce students that score higher, it is uncertain whether this is because Choice schools are better or because they tend to attract more motivated students and parents.

Finally, despite the decline in private school achievement scores, teachers argued that there would be elite academies for a few, and second rate schools for many. Even worse, the larger problem in public education would remain; namely two powerful constituencies -- well-informed parents and superior schools aggressively seeking the brightest children -- will combine to segregate the most promising students from the rest of the school population.

The Other Side of the Restructuring Debate

School-Based Management is also an outgrowth of the Effective Schools research. In addition to school autonomy, review of the Effective Schools literature draws attention to school-site management as one of the "most important organizational-structural variables" connected with Effective Schools.[34]

Like Choice, the Effective Schools research does not support the possibility of fundamental reform occurring with School-Based Management. This diverse body of research often contradicts itself. For example, Effective Schools research sometimes attributes success to strong instructional leadership by the principal. Yet, in the words of one critic, "Contrary to the traditional formula, the instructional leadership at most of the effective schools did not depend solely on the principal."[35] Others have gone even further in asserting that the research takes the most common form of school organization -- the hierarchical type -- as a given. "As a result, Effective Schools research and the school effectiveness movement that spring from it are primarily concerned with improving schools by making small adjustments rather than fundamental changes." This means that the assumptions at the foundation of traditional schooling remains unexamined and unchallenged.[36]

Even though it is clear that neither Public School Choice nor School-Based Management is capable of addressing the major problems facing U.S. society in the 1980s, reformers were able to convince themselves that these restructuring efforts might work for two principal reasons. The movement to restructure the nation's schools followed in the wake of a broad ideological shift to the right and a structural change in the economy.[37] With the support of the business community, a conservative agenda eventually moved to a belief in the free market to solve the nation's education problems. Secondly, decentralization remained attractive because Choice and School-Based Management, reformers argued, would redistribute scarce resources more effectively.

Methodology

Despite the extensive amount of research and publications on the latest wave of education reform, a comparison between the implementation of School Choice and School-Based Management has yet to be drawn. The goal of this study is to understand the processes by which the two reforms, the exit option or the voice option, began and continued.

Therefore, the focus of the investigation is on the issues of leadership -- initiative, assembly of resources and creation of consensus, rather than classroom practice. In an effort to assess correctly and understand the political forces that shaped the restructuring debate, the unit of analysis is on the level of the school system rather than on the individual school or classroom. The focus of the inquiry is beyond classroom practice and on the central political question of how authority over educational policy shifts in response to external demands. By examining the relationship between the political system and the schools, it then becomes possible to discuss the basic political issues underlying the restructuring movement.

The focus of the inquiry is due, in large measure, to the fact that Choice and School-Based Management are not education reforms, they are political reforms. In fact, the popularity of the two restructuring reforms stems from political reasons rather than educational ones. In an effort to clearly assess the educational policymaking process, chapter two traces the philosophical and intellectual beginnings of Choice and School-Based Management by exploring the exit and voice debate in American educational policymaking since the 1960's.

Chapter two also provides a broad overview of school systems undergoing reform in an effort to assess correctly the issues facing restructuring policymakers in general.

Through two case studies, an examination of the political process that transforms special interests into institutional patterns of change becomes apparent. The case studies provide a way to observe the educational policymaking process. The results of this process, however, are difficult to put into quantitative terms for two reasons. First, school district boundaries are political boundaries. More often than not the boundaries reflect the property tax distribution in a given county. Many times those boundaries change because of demographics or because of the need for a more equitable distribution of the tax base.

Therefore, the boundaries set for school districts have nothing to do with any uniform measure such as educational quality or achievement. As a result, it is difficult to empirically assess the impetus and outcomes of the policymaking process. Secondly, public elementary and secondary education in the United States occur in over 83,000 schools in approximately 15,000 school districts. The sheer volume of schools makes it difficult to assess trends in restructuring.

Therefore, interviews with policymakers form the basis of the research. Information was drawn from interviews with reformers conducted during two three-month periods from March to June 1992 and August through October 1992. Interview questions focus on defining the political context of the policymaking arena and tracing the genesis and development of the two types of educational policy. Respondents included representatives from each of the three interest groups that were involved in the policymaking process. More specifically, each case study included interviews with representatives from business organizations and politicians involved in the reform movement. This group consisted of state legislators in Minnesota and those involved in the Mayor's education initiatives in Baltimore City.

Respondents were also selected to include people who often take opposing positions on school policy questions. In many instances, these respondents were members of education associations. Educators interviewed for both case studies included the state superintendent of schools, representatives from each education association such as the teachers' and principals' unions, and members of the state school boards associations.

Finally, the interview process included persons identified as being involved in the policymaking process, such as concerned citizens,

Parent/Teacher Association representatives, community groups, and civic organizations. I report only findings that are substantiated through multiple independent interviews. Information from documents provided by school districts, as well as newspaper accounts and journal articles, supplement the interview data.

Selected for the examination of Choice is the state of Minnesota. Because we lack any working examples of a truly market-based system of School Choice, where public education for every student consists of schools that rely solely on vouchers given to the students by the state, the most comprehensive Choice plans in the United States are state mandated and voluntary Open Enrollment Plans. Although there are seven states with Open Enrollment, Arkansas, Idaho, Iowa, Minnesota, Nebraska, Ohio and Utah, Minnesota is the best possible representative of the exit strategy for two reasons. To begin with, Minnesota was the first statewide plan to offer students the exit option in the United States. Under the Minnesota Open Enrollment Plan, a student may attend any school district with state funding following the student. In turn, the receiving district does not charge the student non-resident tuition. Secondly, it is state-mandated and state-wide. This plan differs significantly from other Choice programs that are voluntary for school districts or restrict student withdrawal options to movement within a single district.

Finally, the implementation of Choice in Minnesota provides a rich history of educational policymaking as it spans over ten years of efforts and incremental movements toward expanding the exit option in the public schools. Chapter three examines the reform debate in Minnesota which centered on the notion of broadening the use of the exit option in an effort to improve the quality of the schools. During that debate policymakers achieved significant compromises. By 1988 a politically feasible School Choice model emerged, and at that time the Minnesota Open Enrollment Plan significantly influenced the education debate nationally and the Choice debate in particular. By 1989 the Minnesota model had been replicated in Arkansas, Iowa, Idaho and Nebraska, without controversy.

At the same time as Minnesota's state legislators started to debate the merits of Open Enrollment, several school systems across the country began to look at the merits of providing more voice to their constituents through School-Based Management. Reforms that would provide or perfect the voice mechanism, however, were initiated at the local level instead of the state level where Open Enrollment plans have their genesis.[38] Although there are sometimes significant differences between state policymaking and local policymaking, nonetheless, from the two case studies general patterns emerge that explain the role of interest groups in policymaking and the subsequent institutional patterns of change.

Chapter four examines the implementation of School-Based Management in Baltimore, Maryland. Baltimore City began to look at the merits of providing more voice to parents and teachers in a public school system that was not successfully educating a student body made up largely of the urban poor, many of whom are members of minority groups. Baltimore, however, was not the first school system to institute School-Based Management. Nonetheless, it was selected for this study because the effort met several criteria. To begin with, movements toward decentralization began and continued during the same time frame as those efforts in Minnesota, thus providing the same political context at the national level. Therefore, earlier School-Based Management movements that began in the 1970's, like those in Hammond, Indiana and Dade County, Florida, were not considered.

Secondly, Baltimore City was selected as a representative effort because of the type of School-Based Management model that was carried out. During the selection process for a School-Based Management case study, a state by state examination revealed that in the cities like Miami, Los Angeles and Cincinnati, the teachers unions became significant policymakers in the restructuring efforts. This was also true in cities like Albuquerque, San Francisco, Pittsburgh, Rochester, Toledo, and Baltimore where the unions were using collective bargaining as one way to advance School-Based Management. In Baltimore, as in other locations during the 1980s, restructuring proponents were dependent on the teachers' union for information, policy recommendations and policy implementation. As a result of this dependence on the Teachers' Union, the decision regarding restructuring in Baltimore heavily favored the collective interests of the teachers.

The school populations in these two case studies are quite different. Minnesota is mostly white with an affluent and largely middle-class population, and Baltimore City is mostly African-American and poor. But the two case studies were not selected to draw parallels between Minnesota and Baltimore City. Nor were they selected as a means of comparing the effectiveness of the two reform strategies. Instead, they were selected to demonstrate trends and institutional patterns of change in educational systems across the country.

Chapter five, the concluding chapter, examines the significance of restructuring beyond Minnesota and Baltimore City. The ability of interest groups to capture and redefine a public institution based on the mechanisms of exit and voice is persistent, long-term and continuing. Thus, the concluding chapter addresses the future of exit and voice in educational policymaking.

Notes

[1]   Table 123 "Scholastic Aptitude Test Score Average for College-Bound High School Seniors, by Sex: 1966-1967 to 1989-1990." *Education Digest*, National Center for Education Statistics. Washington: Government Printing Office, 1991) 123.

[2]   Archie E. LaPointe, N. A. Mead, G. W. Phillips, "A World of Differences: An International Assessment of Mathematics and Science." Report No. 19-CAEP-O1. (Princeton: Educational Testing Service, 1989).

[3]   Table 373. "Selected Statistics for countries with populations over 10 million, by Continent: 1970-1988. *Education Digest*, 396.

[4]   *A Nation At Risk: The Imperative for Educational Reform*, (Washington, D.C.: Government Printing Office) 36.

[5]   Rubinson, 536.

[6]   Nathan Stone, "Does Business Have Any Business in Education?" *Harvard Business Review*, 52.

[7]   "Mathematics: Are we Measuring Up? The Mathematics Report Card." Report No. 17-M-02 Executive Summary, National Assessment of Educational Progress. (Princeton: Educational Testing Service, 1989).

[8]   The Business Roundtable. Ad Hoc Committee on Education. *The Role of Business in Education Reform: Blue Print for Action*. (New York: The Business Roundtable, 1988).

[9]   Paul T. Hill, A.E. Wise, and L. Shapiro, *Educational Progress Cities Mobilize to Improve their Schools*. (Santa Monica: Rand Center for the Study of the Teaching Profession, 1989) 29.

[10]   The Business Roundtable, *The Business Roundtable Directory of Education Initiatives*. (New York: The Business Roundtable, 1990).

[11]   D.P. Doyle, & T.W. Hartle, *Excellence in Education: The States Take Charge*. (Washington, D.C.: American Enterprise Institute for Public Policy Research) 13.

[12]   Dennis P. Doyle, B. C. Cooper, and R. Trachtman, *The American Enterprise*, (March/April 1991), 32. See also, The Business Roundtable, *1991*

Status Report on the Business Roundtable Education Public Policy Agenda. Pre-publication draft. Washington: The Business Roundtable, 1991.
[13] Alexander Lamar, *Time For Results: An Overview Phi Delta Kappan* 68 (Nov. 1986): 202-204.
[14] M. W. Kirst, "The Crash of the First Wave," in *Education Reform: Making Sense of it All.* ed. S.B. Bacharach. (Boston: Allyn and Bacon, 1990), 20.
[15] The Business Roundtable. Ad Hoc Committee on Education. *The Role of Business in Education Reform: Blue Print for Action.* New York, New York: The Business Roundtable, 1988.
[16] Ina V.S. Mullis & Lynn B. Jenkins, Editors, *Science Learning Matters: The Science Report Card: An Interpretive Overview.* Report No. 17-S-02. (Princeton: Educational Testing Service, 1988).
[17] Bob Davis, "Science and Math Education in U.S. Fails to Make Grade." *The Wall Street Journal.* 29 May 1991.
[18] Mary Anne Raywid, "Rethinking School Governance," in *Restructuring Schools.* ed. R.F. Elmore. (San Francisco: Jossey-Bass Publishers, 1990), 154.
[19] Tweedie, 398.
[20] J. Tweedie, "Parental Rights and Accountability in Public Education: Special Education and Choice of School," *Yale Law and Policy Review,* 7, (1989): 398.
[21] See Herbert Kaufman, "Administrative Decentralization and Political Power," *Public Administration Review,* (January/February, 1969): Theodore Lowi, "Machine Politics Old and New," *The Public Interest,* 9, (1967) and Matthew Crenson, "Notes Toward A Developmental Theory," in J. David Greenstone, *Public Values and Private Power in American Politics.* (Chicago: University of Chicago Press, 1982), 209.
[22] W.L. Boyd & F. Seldin, "The Politics of School Reform in Rochester, New York," *Education and Urban Society,* 7, August 1974: p. 439.
[23] Joel Spring, *Conflict of Interests: The Politics of American Education.* (New York: Longman, 1988), 120.
[24] Samuel B. Bacharach, *Education Reform: Making Sense of it All.* (Boston: Allyn and Bacon, 1990), 14.
[25] David K. Cohen, "Reforming School Politics," *Harvard Educational Review,* 48, (November 1978): 429. The case for decentralization has been made by Chester E. Finn "Toward Strategic Independence, Nine Commandments for Enhancing School Effectiveness." *Phi Delta Kappa* (April 1984), and John I. Goodland *A Place Called School.* (New York: McGraw Hill, 1983).
[26] John Chubb and Terry Moe, *Politics, Markets and America's Schools.* (Washington, D.C.: The Brookings Institution, 1990).

[27]   Bacharach, 6.

[28]   Raywid, 6.

[29]   The recommendation that the school be recognized and treated as the primary unit of education is further supported by John Goodland. Goodland has urged it on the basis of his extensive study of schools (1984) and the Effective Schools research has underscored it.

[30]   Stewart C. Purkey and Marshall S. Smith, "School Reform: The District Policy Implications of the Effective Schools Literature" *The Elementary School Journal*, 1984.

[31]   Ronald Edmonds, "Effective Schools for the Urban Poor," *Educational Leadership*, Volume 37 October 1979: 15-42.

[32]   Chubb and Moe, 14.

[33]   John E. Chubb and T.M. Moe, "Politics, Markets and the Organization of Schools" *The American Political Science Review* 82 (December 1988): 1065.

[34]   See Ernest Boyer, President of The Carnegie Foundation for the Advancement of Teaching, John Goodland, Director for Educational Renewal at the University of Washington, and Ted Sizer, Chairman of the Coalition of Essential Schools at Brown University.

[35]   Steadman, 1987. See also Zirkel and Greenwood, 1987.

[36]   American Federation of Teachers, Center For Restructuring, *Radius* 1 (May 1988).

[37]   Katznelson, 3.

[38]   There is only one instance where School-Based Management was mandated by the state. That was in Kentucky following a court order to remedy disparities in educational spending between school districts. Thus, the manner in which Kentucky considered and implemented School-Based Management is an exception to the rule and not applicable to other case histories of School-Based Management.

Chapter Two

National Trends in Restructuring

It is difficult to argue that previous attempts at either the threat or the practice of exit or voice has in fact led to any major educational improvements. This is largely because behind the debate over exit and voice, as Albert O. Hirschmann describes these two reform strategies, lie deep philosophical disagreements in American education over how we govern, organize and operate public schools.[1]

In fact, restructuring the schools in an effort to improve students' performance has been an issue in American education for several decades. To a large degree, today's Choice and School-Based Management proposals are predicated on earlier restructuring attempts in the nation's schools. During the 1960s, in particular, education reformers advanced proposals such as vouchers and school decentralization in an effort to grant parents more opportunity to improve the education of their children. Reformers argued that vouchers would give parents the right to exit the public school system entirely, whereas school decentralization would provide parents with a voice in a child's education.

In order to understand the forces that would lead to the implementation of Public School Choice or School-Based Management as a recovery mechanism, we need first to examine the previous efforts by reformers to improve the schools through the mechanisms of exit and voice. In particular, the controversies surrounding vouchers and school decentralization will provide insight into today's reforms.

The Evolution of Exit and Voice in the Education Reform Debate

Much of the debate surrounding the use of the exit option began at the national level. Promoting Choice in American education is not a new idea either intellectually or legislatively and has been part of a much larger governmental reform strategy for quite some time. The notion of applying market principles to solve problems in public education follows a more general pattern promoted by conservative presidents and employed in public policy since the 1960's. President Richard Nixon, for example, supported a variety of policies that would bypass government agencies at the federal, state and municipal levels.

Milton Friedman was the theorist behind several of the Nixon administration's reform proposals, including education reform. Friedman's *Capitalism and Freedom* became the major popular expression among conservatives of the virtues of classical marketplace theory. Market principles, Friedman argued, would reform public education. As early as 1962, Friedman proposed to supplement the public schools with a system of state-subsidized private education.[2] The government's financial contribution would, under his proposal, go directly to parents in the form of tuition vouchers valued for a fixed dollar payment toward each child's education at public or private schools. The system proposed by Friedman would also allow parents to supplement the voucher, if they wished. Without tax support, the public schools would be forced to rely on voucher payments for support. In this way, parents could choose the kind of schooling they desired, and the schools in turn would have to compete for clients, thus creating a financial incentive to provide better education.

Following the nomenclature employed by Friedman, in the late 1960s and early 1970s, the Nixon administration launched a serious effort to establish several experimental voucher projects. The Office of Economic Opportunity (OEO) designed and sought to carry out a voucher experiment in a large urban area. By 1973, six school districts received OEO funds to study the feasibility of setting up full voucher systems. But the proposal stirred up tremendous opposition from teachers and school boards in almost all of the districts selected.

As a result of the opposition, of the six sites, only the Alum Rock Unified School District near San Jose in California attempted to establish a voucher system. But the program's initial mission, to use vouchers at public and private schools to stimulate improvement through the introduction of competition into the public school system, never reached fruition. Instead, the OEO program officers were forced to reach several compromises with educators in the Alum Rock district. During negotiations for the project, the different agendas of OEO officials and Alum Rock educators and staff became clear. Because OEO needed a test site for the Nixon program, and Alum Rock was the only potential site left, the superior bargaining position of the district quickly became evident.

For example, the aim of the district's superintendent, William Jeffereds, was to decentralize the schools, not introduce a voucher program. In general, Jeffereds argued that decentralization would improve a public school system that was failing to educate numerous African-American and Chicano students.[3] Jeffereds was able to convince OEO to produce some money for his decentralization program even before Alum Rock agreed to the voucher test.[4]

The teachers were also influential in negotiations. They agreed to support the voucher experiment only after they secured a pay raise and only if the plan, as designed by OEO, excluded private schools.

As a result of the concessions made by OEO program officers, the Alum Rock parents gained a measure of consumer choice within the school district, but school-level professionals gained even greater control of educational policy. Not only did teachers and principals inherit power from the central office as a result of decentralization, but they also acquired influence from the greater flexibility, uncertainty, and fiscal leeway that followed from parent choice.[5]

The plan, however, was fragile at best. It collapsed when Superintendent Jeffereds went on leave. Although the Alum Rock experiment was a disaster, Nixon effectively pushed the education debate in the United States to question whether the state should be the monopolistic supplier of schooling for the public.

President Reagan also questioned the role of government in education. Reagan, however, promoted a more limited federal role in education than Nixon had. During his first term in office, President Reagan condemned the Department of Education as a symbol of federal intrusion into matters that should be left to state and local control even though the historical role of the federal government has been to provide general aid within a few broad categories. For example, the federal government has provided aid for technical and vocational education to state and local districts without significant policy-shaping restrictions other than the customary prudential financial safeguards.

But during his campaign for the presidency, Reagan promised to abolish the Department of Education. Reagan's views were not unpopular. Local control and financing of public schools are a tradition that sets the United States apart from most other Western democracies, which have national curricula and national student examinations. In the United States, education is a state function by virtue of the Constitution. The U.S. Constitution makes no mention of education and, thus, education is one of those rights reserved to the states. The states, in turn, have farmed out this responsibility to local school districts, which now number roughly 15,000.

Following the release of *A Nation At Risk*, President Reagan began a reform campaign that would improve public education through the use of tuition tax credits to reimburse parents who wanted to send their children to private schools and by substituting vouchers for an existing federal program of remedial services to educationally disadvantaged children.[6] For the most part, members of Congress did not perceive the Reagan tuition tax credit and voucher programs as a way to strengthen public education but to provide a feasible alternative to it. Both proposals failed to win support from Congress because of fears that such a system would undermine the public school system by directing money to private schools. The Reagan proposals, however, gave new life to the argument that parents could obtain a better education for their children than the existing system of public education could provide.

In fact, a few states were already utilizing some form of the voucher model before Reagan advanced his reform plan. Many of the voucher models proposed in state capitals since the late 1960s have been variations of Friedman's plan.[7] Vermont, for example, has been using a voucher system for more than one hundred years in an attempt to avoid building schools in sparsely populated areas. Vermont students can use government funds allocated for their education at any school they want -- public or private.

But the effort of the Nixon and Reagan administrations to use voucher proposals as a method of regenerating public education stirred up tremendous opposition and found scant support in state capitals.[8] Vouchers were considered a radical form of "parent choice" because the concept would allow students to bypass the public system of education completely -- at government expense. As a result, a wide variety of organizations continued to oppose vouchers on the grounds that the plans undermine the public education system.

The education establishment in particular opposed the idea of vouchers. Teacher organizations viewed the competition introduced by vouchers as an invitation to union-busting. School administrators were afraid of losing control over budgets and appointments. Civil libertarians, on the other hand, were apprehensive that the flow of public monies to sectarian schools would represent a breach of the constitutional separation between church and state.

Civil rights advocates were in favor of allowing urban blacks to choose their own schools, but balked at the prospect of granting whites the same freedom of choice -- a disaster for desegregation.[9] The same phenomenon would occur, civil rights advocates argued, in the case of the public schools. Vouchers, they argued, would eviscerate one of the nation's few egalitarian institutions by paying for private education at the taxpayer's expense, leaving the public schools to become the alternative of last resort, reserved for those without the knowledge to go elsewhere.

Today, Choice continues to stir up opposition largely because of its unsavory past. Two decades ago Freedom of Choice was the rallying cry of segregationists seeking to block busing aimed at desegregating public schools. For example, in the South, open enrollment plans allowed school districts to fulfill their constitutional obligation to dismantle the dual system of public education ordered by the 1954 Supreme Court decision in *Brown v. Board of Education.* Open enrollment plans, which would permit students to attend any school in their district, existed in an intense environment of hostility and prejudice. As a result of the racial tensions surrounding the schools, African-American transfers to white schools were few and white transfers to black schools were non-existent. By 1968 the Supreme Court did not consider Freedom of Choice plans as an adequate remedy to court ordered desegregation.[10]

But at the local level the goal of desegregation has given impetus to the School Choice movement. In fact both federal and state governments promote magnet schools as a costly, although non-controversial way of accomplishing desegregation.[11] The magnet school is a unique reform in that it seeks to couple egalitarianism with the pursuit of excellence, two goals that often collide with one another in education reform. For example, cities like Chicago, Nashville and

Denver developed magnet schools to educate certain types of students: bright children, the artistically inclined or children who want a particular curriculum. Through the exercise of free choice, reformers argued, schools desegregate voluntarily. In 1976 an amendment to the Emergency School Aid Act (ESAA) provided federal funds for magnet school programs as a voluntary alternative to the desegregation of school districts. In 1985 all magnet school support programs were consolidated under Magnet Schools Assistance Program. The annual budgetary allocation has remained constant since then: $75 million in 1985, $71.76 million in 1986, and $75 million in 1987. In light of the Reagan administration's general budgetary cuts for education, a constant level of budgetary support suggests that there must be persistent political support for one form of Choice.[12]

At the state level, one of the earliest states to allocate specific funds for magnet schools to avoid the controversies of court-ordered busing was Massachusetts. In 1973 Boston's Mayor Kevin White sought to shift the focus from integration of the schools to the larger question of how to achieve "equal" education opportunity for every school child in the Boston metropolitan area. The mayor urged a mixture of "magnet" schools and "voluntary transportation" to and from the suburbs. In this way, White argued, poor people, both black and white, would have the same access to quality education as the rich enjoyed.[13] By 1974, the Massachusetts legislature repealed the provisions of the state's 1965 Racial Imbalance Act that gave the state Board of Education the authority to order comprehensive mandatory desegregation reassignments and substituted a program of generous funding incentives for magnet schools and voluntary transfers.[14]

The Popularity of Voucher Plans in the National Reform Debate

While Choice was spreading at the local level in response to court-ordered desegregation, voucher plans continued to be popular at the federal level. Despite decades of opposition to Choice in general and voucher programs in particular, while he was president, George Bush proposed increasing parent Choice through the use of vouchers as a solution to many of the problems in education. His support of vouchers, however, conformed to his overall approach to the problems presented to government in the hope of solving them.

To address domestic problems during his administration, Bush outlined a "New Paradigm" in 1990. The paradigm, or model, emphasized decentralized decision making, individual empowerment, market forces, personal choice and pragmatism. Bush's "New Paradigm" had its philosophical roots in the long-held Republican belief about the primacy of the individual, a distrust of big governmental institutions, and fear of centralized public authority.[15]

For example, Bush's housing commissioner, former New York Republican Congressman Jack Kemp, became the force behind the administration's public housing policies which focused on the notion of allowing individuals to purchase their own housing units. Kemp followed a public policy effort started in Great Britain during the 1980's. At that time, the British government attempted to solve public sector problems by privatizing government services. As a result of this strategy, the administration of Prime Minister Margaret Thatcher developed programs that would sell government owned council houses to their residents. In the Bush administration, the application of private sector principles to solve larger social problems, the president's advisors argued, would provide a more principled framework for his administration.

Bush's approach to education particularly fit this model. His Education Secretary, Lamar Alexandar, introduced several new education initiatives during the Bush administration. While most of them focused on accountability and efficiency, the hallmark of the Bush educational program was Choice.[16] To show federal support for this strategy, the United States Department of Education opened the Center for Choice in December of 1990 in order to provide information and guidance to teachers, administrators, and parents who want to explore the Choice approach to educational reform.

Bush also wanted to extend Choice to private schools. Like many conservatives, he envisioned education as a free market, with families choosing public, private or parochial schools -- all paid for with public money in the form of vouchers. Bush proposed giving $500 million in grants to state and local governments for demonstration programs in 50 cities across the country. Under the Bush proposal, the government would have distributed $1,000 vouchers to families earning less than the median annual income of $35,353. Students could cash in the vouchers at any public, private and parochial schools in the program.

Many of the voucher initiatives at the local level had their genesis in the national agenda.[17] For example, the governors of Colorado and Tennessee endorsed vouchers for pupils with low achievement levels. In Wisconsin, a 1990 voucher plan for low income students went into effect in Milwaukee. The program, sponsored by and widely identified with African-American State Representative Polly Williams of Milwaukee, began in the fall of 1990. Williams wanted to raise the educational standards of black students by providing vouchers for public school students for use at private schools in the inner city. Black Milwaukee students consistently score below their white counterparts on standard achievement examinations. A task force in Milwaukee found that in the system's public high schools, blacks were scoring an average of 24 on a reading test on which white students were averaging 58.[18]

To raise their achievement levels, Williams lobbied the state legislature to carry out a voucher system that would permit 500 low income students to attend private, non-sectarian schools with the state paying participating schools $2,500 per student, and transportation being provided by the city school system.[19] Since its establishment, the Wisconsin plan has survived several legal challenges. While courtroom battles continue, however, students have been taking advantage of the program. In September 1990, 341 participated; the following year enrollment rose to 562.[20] By 1996, the program was in its fifth year of existence.

At the national level, however, the Bush agenda of promoting Choice to solve the nation's education problems never received the necessary support from Congress. In fact, not a single piece of education reform legislation made it into law during Bush's four years in office. Lawmakers, both Democrats and some Republicans, stalled the president's education initiatives because they would provide support to children attending private and parochial as well as public schools.

Voucher proposals also collapsed at the state level when state legislators failed to reach a compromise or consensus on the reform. In the late 1980s, grass roots groups scattered across the country were working to promote educational Choice through the use of vouchers.[21] These coalitions were an amalgamation of interests and included representatives from business and government, as well as sectarian and non-sectarian private schools. TEACH (Toward Educational Accountability and Choice) in Michigan, TEACH America in Illinois and a business-led reform proposal in Indiana called COMMIT pursued voucher initiatives. These coalitions began with the express purpose of lobbying state legislatures to set up voucher programs in the public school system.

Although the voucher coalitions appeared well organized and well funded, their proposals lost support in state legislatures because they would provide funds for private schools. This was true in Pennsylvania, where a Choice package promoted by the REACH (Road to Education Accountability and Choice) Alliance never won approval from the state legislature. Although the bill passed the State Senate in December 1991, public opinion turned against the Choice initiative when a report by the House Education Committee called it unconstitutional and detrimental to public schools. The Choice proposal came to an end when the bill lost in the House by 13 votes.

A Politically Feasible Choice Model Emerges from the Education Reform Debate

As the 1980s came to a close, Choice no longer reflected the conventional liberal versus conservative alignments on social issues. Nowhere was this change more evident than during the 1992 presidential campaign. Although both the Republican and Democratic candidates supported an exit strategy as a way to improve the schools, incumbent President George Bush continued to include vouchers for private schools in his program whereas his opponent, William Clinton, eliminated the voucher issue when he would only support programs that confined parents to a choice among public schools.

Clinton's rise to national prominence was due, in part, to his education reform record in Arkansas. As governor, Clinton's push for educational change began in 1983 with a legislative program that established standards for teachers and students, mandated smaller classes and included the nation's first 8th grade test that students had to pass before beginning high school. Clinton's educational reform effort culminated in 1989, when at his urging the overwhelmingly Democratic Arkansas General Assembly enacted a Choice plan that would allow students to attend virtually any public school in the state.

With the passage of the Arkansas Open Enrollment plan, Clinton became part of a nationwide restructuring movement and enacted a reform that would gain him popularity with both conservative and moderate Republican voters. At the same time, however, Clinton was able to retain the political support of the traditional Democratic liberal constituency. For example, because Clinton's Choice proposals as governor of Arkansas and as a presidential candidate in 1992 only included public schools, he received the endorsement of the country's two major teacher unions, the National Education Association (NEA) and The American Federation of Teachers (AFT), both represent over two million teachers. The NEA, with 1.6 million members, is the largest union in the United States.[22]

Many other politicians began to support Choice because of its appeal to middle class constituencies. For example, former Alabama Democratic Governor Guy Hunt and Mississippi Republican Governor Kirk Fordice repeatedly introduced interdistrict and intradistrict Choice legislation even though Choice is not feasible in their states. In Alabama and Mississippi, middle class whites, who lived in predominantly black school districts, wanted to have the option of sending their children to schools in adjoining white school districts. But this type of interdistrict Choice, where students cross district boundaries, is not legally permissible because the school systems in both states operate under court-ordered desegregation plans. An interdistrict Choice plan would cause a change in racial balance and violate the court order to desegregate the schools. On the other hand, intradistrict Choice, where a student can choose a school within the district other than the assigned school, is not possible because most of the counties in Alabama and Mississippi have only one elementary school and one high school. Nonetheless, both governors included Choice in their education reform packages.

Politicians have also tried to win the support of the business community for their voucher and Choice proposals. In general, the notion of injecting competition into the public school system appeals to businessmen. Much of the support for the exit option comes from their belief in the free market.[23] Business leaders argue that the free market works for companies and their products. The free market principle, then, should work for the schools.[24] But full exit from public education is impossible for the business community. It remains a consumer of the product of the public schools because it is dependent on the schools to produce graduates to fulfill its work force needs.

Vouchers, however, make some form of exit possible. But much of the leadership for vouchers in the business community has come from individual businessmen rather than established business organizations. For example, although former Business Roundtable Chairman and Union Pacific Corporation Chief Executive Officer Drew Lewis is a staunch Choice proponent, the Business Roundtable did not put its considerable political clout behind efforts to enact the reform. Instead, the Roundtable supports Choice among public schools but acknowledges that it is "not a panacea nor a self-contained reform."[25] The Committee for Economic Development, as well as the National Alliance of Business, has a similar position. School Choice, they find, sparks such bitter debate that a consensus on the reform is not attainable within their organizations.[26]

In California, however, businessman Joseph Alibrandi formed the Excellence through Choice League (EXCEL). Alibrandi proposed The Parental Choice Initiative which sought to change the California state constitution so that students receive vouchers for $2,500 for use as private or public tuition.[27] The Excel group, however, failed to gather enough signatures to ensure the measure's inclusion on the California ballot in June 1992.[28] In 1993 it was on the ballot but lost by a 2:1 margin. In addition to supporting ballot initiatives, individual businesses have also invested in private school voucher programs with the purpose of demonstrating that competition will improve the schools and student performance. The nation's first privately funded program started in the fall of 1991 in Indianapolis, where businesses provided money that allowed 750 low-income children to attend private schools. When the Indiana General Assembly failed to enact a Choice program, insurance executive and chairman of the Golden Rule Insurance Company, J. Patrick Rooney started his own voucher program. The program, called the Choice Charitable Trust, is open to students who live in the Indianapolis Public School District, and pays half the tuition of a private school, up to $800. The only eligibility requirement is that the parents have an income level that qualifies them for participation in the federal lunch program.

The basis of the program is the notion that when underprivileged parents and children have a choice in the education of their child, the resulting of competition among schools will in turn result in an improved public school system. Choice proponents like Rooney say the issue is fairness, that the public school system is failing children from low-income areas because it need not compete for funding. Therefore the avowed goal of the voucher program is to enable low-income students to choose private schools, while forcing the public schools to improve.

The program sponsored 744 students in its first year. By 1992-1993, the Trust released $520,000 to students qualified for the program. In the following academic year, 1993-1994, 1,100 students enrolled in the program, with 400 on a waiting list.

The program's popularity, however, is not limited to Indianapolis. A second program, in San Antonio, Texas, began accepting applications in 1992. The Texas Public Policy Foundation (TPPF) is sponsoring the San Antonio program. The Foundation is a conservative think tank. Three other programs also began the following year in Detroit, Atlanta and Grand Rapids, Michigan.

The Golden Ring plan, however, forced the city's public schools to respond. As a result of the private sector initiative, the Indianapolis School Board placed Choice on their educational policymaking agenda. In fact, in February 1992, school board members approved a Public School Choice plan entitled "The Select Schools" program. The program allows parents to help choose which public school their child attends. For the 1993-1994 school year, 86 percent of parents participated in the Select Schools program, with almost three out of four getting their first choice.

Although voucher programs like the one sponsored in Indiana by the Golden Ring Insurance Company can enhance parental Choice, increase competition among different kinds of schools, and even serve as the impetus for intradistrict Public School Choice programs, they subordinate education's public ends to private market choices. For example, one student's withdrawal from the Indiana public schools, costs the system over $4,000 in badly needed state assistance. Because Indiana distributes educational funds on a per-student basis, the departure of 400 students to take part in the Golden Rule program has drained more than $1.6 million from the public schools. The local chapter of the National Association for the Advancement of Colored People as well as other organizations say that if Golden Rule wants to improve education, it should give its money directly to the public school system.[29] In general, opponents of such programs say that vouchers undermine the nation's system of public education; to improve American education, politicians, businesses and others should focus their efforts on schools that are open to all. They charge that vouchers are that first step toward abandonment of the system of universal public education.[30]

Other critics dismiss Choice on the ground that it widens race and class division in the public schools. Members of the education establishment argue that in addition to fostering educational inequity and racial segregation, free market principles will not eliminate underfinanced, inferior schools, and that those schools will simply become repositories for children who are poor or disabled, or whose parents may not be able to make informed choices. The need, opponents of Choice say, is to create an environment in which popular control of the school is encouraged within the community surrounding the individual school. School-Based Management is one way to do this. Although there has been considerable support for Choice at both the state and federal level, support for School-Based Management has come from the state and local level. A Florida Citizens' Committee on Education first recommended School-Based Management in 1971. This group, appointed by Governor Reuben Askew to make recommendations concerning the improvement of Florida's public schools, concluded that educational reform should begin where and when instruction occurs.[31]

The report by the Citizens' Committee on Education, while not necessarily having an immediate impact, set an important precedent. In 1973 the school system negotiated its first contract with the local teachers' union -- the United Teachers of Dade. During contract negotiations, the union set up a task force that included union members and representatives from the school administration. They met to reconcile differences not worked out at the bargaining table. From the work of these task forces, a new type of cooperation between the teachers' union and the school system's administration emerged.[32]

As the 1970s progressed, the popularity of School-Based Management rose when reformers began to realize that it was a means of offsetting the centralizing tendency that the push for equity in school finance had inspired.[33] In many states, lawsuits challenging inequities in the financing of public education were working their way through the courts. Increasingly, the courts had to rule whether a state's system of financing public education could be unconstitutional because of the spending disparities that resulted between rich and poor school districts.

The earliest challenge to state school spending inequities began in Texas during the 1960s. Like most states, the Texas system relies on a combination of state funding and local property taxes. The controversy surrounding equity in financing in Texas has continued for twenty-five years. By 1993 the Texas legislature overcame years of partisan debate and approved an amendment to the state constitution that would force wealthy school districts to transfer money to poor ones.[34] But in a subsequent referendum on the issue in the 1993 election, the voters rejected this equalization proposal.

Challenges of school financing formulas have mounted in a number of states. A June 1989 ruling by the Kentucky Supreme Court, however, went further than most recent rulings. In a five to two decision the Court found that not only spending disparities but the state's entire system of public education -- from the organization of the state bureaucracy to the selection of local school boards -- was responsible for the inequities of Kentucky's system for financing schools. As a result, legislation passed in the state in 1991 mandated a variety of reforms ranging from new management "Councils" in all schools to alternative certification for teachers -- as well as a new finance system.[35]

School-Based Management Enters the Reform Debate

Following subsequent rulings by the courts, which resulted in an increase in the state's authority over local school districts as a way to remedy the disparities in spending, proponents of School-Based Management began to argue that individual schools needed greater decision making powers to offset the expansion in state control.[36] Previous attempts to increase the authority of the individual school occurred during the decentralization efforts of the 1960s and 1970s which shifted decisions away from the central education bureaucracy and down to the schools themselves in an effort to give parents more political control of their neighborhood school. During the excellence movement and the subsequent efforts to restructure the nation's schools, management at the school building level acquired renewed interest in School-Based Management.

Business leaders in particular were interested in School-Based Management as an effective management strategy for the school system. The private sector interest in decentralizing school functions stems from its own successful experience with participatory decision making at the factory floor level.[37] For example, the Ford Motor Company, a company awakened by Japanese success in the automobile industry, now organizes workers into teams, giving them collective responsibility and rewarding them for new and better ideas. Public schools in the United States have traditionally modeled their management practices on prevailing fashions in industry. In the late 19th century, American corporations adopted the top-down organizational style advocated by managerial theorists like Frederick Taylor.[38] At that time, manufacturing formed the basis of the economic system. The Taylor model became a system in which legions of skilled managers and engineers directed line workers in the minute repetitive tasks assigned to them.

The Taylor model of scientific management inspired "the factory floor model of public schools." Authority rests with strong principals, the educational counterparts of factory foremen. Teachers have little say in decisions that effect their teaching and classroom practices. Students, on the other hand, are considered products moving along an assembly line.

The need, business leaders maintain, is to decentralize decision making and shift resources downward in the school system. The administration working in the central offices consumes resources needed to provide direct services to children and to pay for classroom supplies. Decentralization, they maintain, would more effectively distribute scarce resources.

Busines

The Business Community and School-Based Management

Recent developments in Boston provide one example of how the impetus for School-Based Management can come from the business community. Business involvement in the public schools began in 1982. At that time, area businesses started the Boston Compact, which promised 1,000 jobs a year to high school graduates and 3,000 summer jobs to high school students in Boston. The Compact, an agreement between the school system and some 400 corporations, links jobs to school performance and has been replicated in several other cities.

In 1988 when the Compact underwent renegotiation, there were many successes that participants could point to. For example, the business community had forged a strong alliance with the school system, set up a successful high school career service, and financed a $24 million endowment. The school system, on the other hand, made some headway toward school improvement, as evidenced by increases in average daily attendance and the introduction of reading and math standards. But it was clear that the Boston Compact was not succeeding in two of its principal aims -- improving test scores and a reduction in drop-out rates. In addition, participating businesses still reported dissatisfaction with the quality of the students they were getting from the public schools.

In 1988, the Boston Private Industry Council, which administers the employment division of the Compact, would not renew the agreement until the school district promised major reforms including decentralization. The business community wanted the schools to give some assurance that every high school would provide an improved education.[39] Coalition members negotiated new goals, and in March 1989, the Boston Compact steering committee agreed to adopt new measures that addressed key issues facing the education community, including site-based management, parental involvement, post-graduate assistance and improved academic performance. In 1989, School-Based Management began and the Boston Compact has since remained in effect.

Surprisingly, parents and other constituent groups of the Boston public school system did not question the business community involvement in the school nor its dictating reforms to a public agency. A MassInsight poll, for example, that was conducted by Opinion Dynamics Corporation, a Massachusetts public policy good government group, shows support for the business community's aggressive stance in education reform. In fact, the Compact would take power away from groups in the school system that Massachusetts residents perceived as having too much power -- administrators, teachers' unions, legislators, and the state Board of Education. Instead, the Compact would redistribute authority to groups perceived as having too little power -- parents, citizens in general, teachers and the business community.[40]

School-Based Management: Problems in Design

Despite the agreement in Boston, critics of School-Based Management remain skeptical about this reform proposal. They argue that School-Based Management provides a system of self-governance that simply moves political battles from the district and state level to the level of the individual school. Without external directives and restraints, they argue, the individual school will fall victim to incompetence and political conflict.

To support their criticisms, opponents of School-Based Management point to the failures of the decentralization movement of the 1960s. Like decentralization, say the critics, political conflict can easily side track School-Based Management.[41] In general, decentralization is prone to two types of political conflict. The first occurs within the public school system itself. In many instances, political struggles occur when school systems shift from a bureaucratic, top down system to a bottom up organization.[42] Conflict occurs between those at the top of the hierarchy, the central administration staff, and those at the bottom, the principals, teachers, and parents. The authority of administrators from the "top down" rests on very different assumptions from those underlying the power of teachers (collectively and individually) to influence school operations from the "bottom up." Those at the top of the hierarchical ladder stress control, regularity, standardization, and predictability, while those at the school level prefer a course of autonomy, local decision making, decentralization, and professional discretion, all in order to shift authority to the level closest to the classroom. Decentralization, however, forces top management to share power, and to restructure its own authority. At the same time, these programs require that school-site educators (teachers and principals) take more responsibility for designing, staffing, budgeting and setting the school program.[43]

The second form of political struggle associated with decentralization is the conflict between the educators and others that share an interest with the students. Since their founding, public schools in large United States cities have been neighborhood and community institutions. The units of city politics -- more generally ethnic groups from particular residence communities organized on a ward basis -- have also been the units of the school population and, at times, of school governance. Thus, from their founding, urban schools were potential objects of ethnic and territorial conflict.[44]

Previous attempts at decentralization came about as a means of improving the channels of communication between the clientele of the public school system and its management.[45] To buttress the argument for community control, proponents cite research linking educational achievement to the "extent to which an individual feels he has some control over his destiny." [46] The alternative to community control, decentralization proponents argue, is a ponderous, insulated, centralized school bureaucracy which is insensitive to the needs and aspirations of minority children.[47]

During the 1960s two models of school decentralization emerged from the education reform debate -- community control and administrative decentralization. Those participating in the restructuring process significantly shaped the type of school decentralization enacted in a given school district. Community control would occur when the decision to decentralize came from outsiders, mainly groups and individuals who were not part of the local school district organization.[48] Administrative decentralization, on the other hand, occurred when decentralization reflected an internal choice by school personnel and administrators.

The movement in favor of community control developed in the wake of the failure of racial integration in the large cities of the North. As municipal governments, often under court order, initiated a variety of plans to integrate urban schools, more whites took their children out of the public schools and enrolled them in private schools or fled to the suburbs. White resistance to forced integration triggered resentment among African-Americans toward the implicit premises of integration: namely that black children can achieve only if integrated with white children.[49] By the 1970s, racial integration as originally conceived was virtually impossible, since racial and ethnic minority children formed a majority of the nation's large-city school populations. Instead of busing minority students from predominantly black schools to white institutions outside their neighborhoods, decentralization, reformers hoped, would encourage parents to take an active and effective role in the education of their children. In the process, a decentralized system would also force the individual schools to become more responsive to the concerns of the communities they served.

In New York City, for example, a 1967 decentralization law divided the city's school system into 32 community districts. The authority to govern elementary and junior high schools with oversight provided by the central Board of Education shifted to elected neighborhood school boards.

But decentralization in New York City attempted to address the political demands of blacks and lower-middle-class whites and had little effect on educational outcomes.[50] In the process, the community school boards became another layer of bureaucracy that clouded accountability even further. Almost thirty years after it established the most comprehensive system of decentralization in the United States, New York City is now attempting to cope with the excesses, patronage, mismanagement and theft that ensued. Many parents maintain that they are still dealing with a faceless bureaucracy which is not accountable to the public, a problem decentralization advocates hoped the new structure would alleviate. Some critics, including many former central board members, have said that the decentralized system of education has created rich opportunities for corruption and encouraged the election of politicians to local school boards rather than people interested in education.[51]

Additionally, decentralization has failed to achieve the improvements sought in student performance. The exit of students from the public schools to the suburbs or to private schools added to the system's overall deterioration. As a result, student achievement levels declined. Today in New York City, two-thirds of the city's school children suffer from reading retardation, and the pace of reading decline has grown since the 1960s.

Along with parents, some educators also pushed for school decentralization. In cities like Chicago, the schools underwent decentralization in an effort to assign more administrative tasks to building level administrators. With increased authority and control, administrators in the schools could respond with more flexibility to their schools particular needs.[52] For the central education bureaucracy, the advantage of decentralization is that it tends to keep local controversies local, not that they do not distract central administrators from system wide planning and policymaking.[53]

But School-Based Management is different from past decentralization efforts because it changes the entire organization of the system and restructures most roles in the district. The purpose of School-Based Management is not simply to reorganize administrative or policymaking responsibilities, but to make changes in traditional structures of authority, with authority divided among teachers, administrators, students and parents.[54]

Educators Enter the Restructuring Debate

Much of the impetus for School-Based Management has come from the teachers themselves. Teachers came into the restructuring debate when influential education reform studies from 1986-1988 released by the National Governor's Association, the Committee for Economic Development and the Carnegie Corporation's 1986 report *A Nation Prepared: Teachers for the 21st Century,* strongly emphasized the value of allowing teachers to participate in expanded decision making at the school site by giving them more authority in their own classrooms and schools and compensating them according to their effectiveness.[55] The Carnegie Commission, for example, after noting that many school staff members view the bureaucratic structure where they work as rigid and the opportunities for exercising professional judgment quite limited, advocated "giving teachers a greater voice in the decisions that affect the school."[56]

The Carnegie Commission also proposed several changes to enhance the professional role of teachers. One recommendation entailed adding a new category of teachers called lead teachers. More experienced teachers, or lead teachers, would jointly manage with the principal both instructional leadership and business administration for the school. Other recommendations included establishing professional standards and training enforced by a new National Board of Professional Teaching Standards.[57]

These recommendations, the studies concluded, would enhance teaching as a profession. Enhancing teaching as a profession became a central feature of the restructuring movement in an effort to attract a better quality of teacher. Inadequate preparation at the higher education level and poor working conditions failed to attract talented college graduates to the profession.[58] Aspects of poor working conditions include administrative subservience and lack of control of the resources needed to teach effectively. As a result, some of the most dedicated teachers leave the profession early, while at the same time public school systems across the country are unable to attract a new generation of qualified young people into the profession.[59]

To attract a better quality of applicants to the profession, reformers paid considerable attention to upgrading teacher preparation, improving the conditions under which many public school teachers work and increasing the leadership potential of teachers.[60] The vision of operating the schools on a professional rather than bureaucratic model was a significant shift from earlier reforms, particularly those that followed in the immediate wake of the *Nation at Risk* report, which proposed top-down reforms that served to reinforce the existing bureaucratic model.[61] Routinely excluded from the design and implementation of school reforms were teachers. In an effort to increase the professional aspects of teaching, both the National Education Association (NEA) and the American Federation of Teachers (AFT) called for a greater voice in the educational system and policymaking arena.[62]

The demand of teachers for a real voice in policymaking is not a new phenomenon in American society. Its origins are found in the onset of collective bargaining in 1960 when New York City's United

Federation of Teachers (UFT) -- a local affiliate of the AFT -- conducted a successful one day strike for bargaining rights and changes in the salary schedule. Prior to this action, strikes had been considered unprofessional.[63] In addition, teachers' organizations affiliated with the NEA, while not identifying themselves as "unions," began in the late 1960s to act more like their union counterparts, using the same mechanisms of bargaining, contracts, and strikes to attain similar goals.[64]

The beginning of collective bargaining and teacher unionism in public education led to scores of divisive and often protracted strikes in the 1970s. As time went on, such teachers strikes became far more common as collective bargaining legislation, which mandated a negotiated contract between local school boards and public school teachers, sprang up in almost all fifty states. According to the Bureau of Labor Statistics, public school teachers struck 25 times between 1960 and 1965. Between 1975 and 1980, however, there were over a thousand strikes involving over a million teachers. In some school districts, it seemed, every time the school doors opened in September, the teachers were on strike. For example, when Philadelphia's 22,000 teachers manned picket lines for 50 days in 1981-82, it was the eighth time they had shut down the city's schools in 13 years.[65]

The growing advocacy of professional concerns by teachers today represents an expansion of the model of unionism. Like collective bargaining, School-Based Management represents a shift in power. Although the unions view School-Based Management as a way to move beyond traditional collective bargaining strategies to acquire professional status and autonomy, they are not abandoning the use of bilateral decision making like collective bargaining to achieve their goals.[66] The issue of School-Based Management itself has become an important element in contract negotiations between unions and school districts.

In an effort to further their members' interests, both the NEA and the AFT attempted to influence the direction of the restructuring debate. For the most part the NEA's involvement in school restructuring was a reaction rather than a stimulus to the nationwide reform movement. Almost two years after the teachers received recognition as essential to reform efforts, in a March 1988 news conference, NEA president Mary Futrell, announced that the organization was going to provide leadership in achieving restructuring. The NEA sponsored a series of pilot programs in

School-Based Management among its local affiliates. Union members in schools and school districts received funds and staff support from the NEA to undertake improvement projects that they selected themselves. The Learning Laboratory, Mastery in Learning (MIL), Operation Rescue and Team Approach to Better Schools (TABS) were projects sponsored by the NEA nationally that were designed to provide restructuring leadership in selected school districts.

In particular, Futrell called for the NEA and its affiliates and the other stakeholders in American education to create at least one district based Learning Laboratory in each state in the nation. Learning Laboratories, bargained for by local associations or in non-bargaining states, would start after an agreement between the local associations and management became finalized.[67] The Learning Laboratories, Futrell argued, would bring about systemic and fundamental changes in the school curriculum, the teaching and learning process, and the school environment by creating a process that would shift school governance to the classroom. Funding for this particular project, the NEA hoped, would come from the support and financing commitment of state and local public authorities, parents, business and civic leaders. But without much direction from the Association at the National level, the projects, executed over three to five years, received a lukewarm reception across the country. In 1989, only four Learning Laboratory projects began in the schools.

The Mastery in Learning program (MIL), on the other hand, was more popular and successful than the Learning Laboratories. MIL, conducted in 26 school sites, involved "mini-research studies" into such topics as increasing the involvement of parents in their children's learning. In contrast to the Learning Laboratories, the NEA selected the MIL program sites for the research-based school improvement project. With 26 sites being selected from across the country, the NEA attempted to have a test program that would be broadly representative of all schools in the country. The sites selected were geographically diverse and included students from all social, economic and racial groups.

Working with program staff and using planning instruments designed by the MIL, the faculty at each school identified improvement priorities, explored relevant research, and prepared a specific plan for the changes necessary for school improvement. Mastery in Learning, according to the NEA, had some success. Because of the experience gained in the MIL program, these 26 facilities have moved into comprehensive school renewal programs.

While the Mastery in Learning program focused on those in school, Operation Rescue focused on school dropouts. Through the National Foundation for the Improvement of Education, the NEA initiated community based, teacher-designed and implemented projects aimed at reducing the school dropout rate. Fifteen states received grants to set up 21 projects.

Finally, the Team Approach to Better Schools (TABS) project was the largest project run by the NEA with 1,200 participating schools. But some TABS projects were more comprehensive than others in their efforts to restructure the schools and the roles of teachers. For example, Memphis, Tennessee, is one of the 11 school districts in the nation that have experimented with School-Based Management with the help of the National Education Association through the TABS program. Elected local councils made up of three teachers, two parents, a principal and a community representative now run each school. Superintendent Willie W. Herenton with the cooperation of the Memphis Education Association developed the project and set it up in seven schools in 1989.

At the national level the AFT played a more prominent role in the restructuring movement than the NEA's piecemeal approach. As early as 1985, Albert Shanker, president of the AFT and the nation's most influential and militant teacher unionist, warned that in order to make teaching a more attractive career, the AFT had to go beyond the traditional fruits of collective bargaining -- shorter hours, guaranteed wage scale, classroom size -- to make teaching a more attractive profession. This was a dramatic change in focus for Shanker because he had led the campaign to unionize public school teaching two decades earlier.[68]

Since the onset of the excellence movement, the AFT has lessened the importance of adversarial collective bargaining and has pledged itself to taking a greater responsibility for the professional performance of teachers. The role of the union varies from place to place, but by the late 1980s a number of school districts reached settlements with their teachers' unions that created frameworks for education improvement as well as addressing union interests.

For example, in Miami, the United Teachers of Dade, an AFT affiliate, took their cues for several years from a union activist, Pat Tornillo, who pursued confrontational politics in behalf of improved teacher pay and working conditions. Tornillo led strikes and teacher work stoppages in the late 1970s and early 1980s. But by 1987, Tornillo had concluded that teachers could advance their interests more effectively in the context of school-site decisions than by contesting general labor contracts.[69] During negotiations with the school district, he agreed to relax some parts of the teacher contract in return for higher pay and more flexible use of resources by teachers in School-Based Management sites. By agreeing to School-Based Management, the unions not only advanced the local school improvement effort but also traditional AFT concerns -- hours, wages and working conditions.[70]

AFT affiliates effectively used contract negotiations for School-Based Management as a way to increase wages. In Rochester, for example, wages figured prominently in contract negotiations that centered on the implementation of School-Based Management. Rochester teachers received one of the highest paying contracts in the country in return for taking on more responsibilities.[71] In 1986, the district reached an agreement with the Rochester Federation of Teachers that gave teachers a pay increase of more than 40 percent over a three year period. This increase in wages raised the average teacher salary to $45,000, almost $15,000 more than the national average. Some veteran teachers' pay rose to nearly $70,000.[72]

In New York City, the interests of the United Federation of Teachers (UFT) figured prominently in the 1989 selection of School's Chancellor Joseph Fernandez. UFT President Sandra Feldman supported Fernandez's appointment because of his cooperative relationship with the teachers' union in Miami and his involvement with the representative of the United Teachers of Dade during contracts negotiations with the county that included School-Based Management. School-Based Management was attractive to New York education reformers largely because previous attempts at school decentralization had failed to produce any measure of accountability.[73] In addition to the union's support, Fernandez's appointment received the support of former Mayor David Dinkins and the business community.

Fernandez's supporters, however, abandoned their hand-picked leader when the office of the Chancellor began to take on a more controversial role. Following a tumultuous three-year tenure that centered on issues such as a school condom distribution program, AIDS education and homosexuality in the school curriculum, the Board of Education, after a number of confrontational hearings with parents, teachers and community leaders, decided not to renew Fernandez's contract in 1993.

Nonetheless, the influence of political leaders, the business community and the teachers' union in the selection process of Chancellor Joseph Fernandez is reflective of the most important spheres of influence in the reform debate and educational policymaking in general during the 1980s. With the entrance of business and political leaders into the education debate, a proliferation of interest groups now characterizes the educational politics of the excellence movement and the subsequent calls to restructure the nation's schools.[74]

Conclusion

During the 1980s, interest groups external to the educational system succeeded in advancing their agendas and made significant inroads into state and local educational policymaking arenas. Once they were involved in public policy formation, the notion of excellence in education became supplemented by the idea of restructuring as a way to improve the schools. In fact, restructuring the schools in an effort to improve students' performance has been an issue in American education for several decades. To a large degree, today's Choice and School-Based Management proposals received their genesis from earlier restructuring attempts. During the 1960s, in particular, education reformers advanced proposals such as vouchers and school decentralization in an effort to grant parents more opportunity to improve the education of their children. Reformers argued that vouchers would give parents the right to exit the public school system entirely, whereas school decentralization would provide parents with a voice in a child's education.

But despite a history of ineffective and misguided restructuring efforts based on the notions of exit and voice that included failed efforts like the Alum Rock voucher plan, numerous attempts by lawmakers at the national, state and local level to enact some form of a voucher program and school decentralization in New York City, education reformers continued to look to new ways to restructure the public schools based on the same premises. The efforts of reformers culminated in the 1980's with plans to carry out School Choice and School-Based Management programs in numerous school systems across the country.

This brings us to the case of Minnesota, where business leaders and politicians supported a Public School Choice program as a way to qualitatively improve the schools. Although much of the debate surrounding the use of the exit option began at the national level, it was the state of Minnesota that led the way in setting the national agenda for School Choice.

Notes

[1]   Albert O. Hirschmann, Exit, Voice and Loyalty: Responses to Decline in Forms, Organizations, and States. (Cambridge: Harvard University Press, 1970)

[2]   Leonard Ross & Richard Zeckhauser, "Education Vouchers" *Law and Contemporary Problems*, 48: 451.

[3]   David K. Cohen and Elizabeth Farrar, "Power to the Parents? - The Story of Education Vouchers" *The Public Interest.* 48: 81.

[4]   Cohen and Farrar, 82.

[5]   Cohen and Farrar, 83.

[6]   Myron Liebermann, *Beyond Public Education.* (New York: Praeger, 1986), 184.

[7]   Jencks, 1966, Sizer and Whitten 1968. See G.R. La Noue, *Educational Vouchers: Concepts and Controversies.* (New York: Teachers College Press, 1972).

[8]   M.W. Kirst, "The Crash of The First Wave." ed. S.B. Bacharach, *Education Reform: Making Sense of It All.* (Boston: Allyn & Bacon, 1990), 21.

[9]   Kirst, 21.

[10]   *Green v. New Kent County*, 391 U.S. 430.

[11]   C.H. Rossell & C.L. Glenn. "The Cambridge Controlled Choice Plan," *Urban Review*, 20, (1988): 77.

[12]   Rossell and Glenn, 78.

[13]   Anthony J. Lukas, *Common Ground: A Turbulent Decade in the Lives of Three American Families*, (New York: Alfred A. Knopf, 1985), 603.

[14]   Rossell and Glenn, 76.

[15]   William P. McKenzie, "Is George Bush A Progressive Republican?" *Ripon Forum*, September 1991, 13.

[16]   The White House Office of the Press Secretary. Remarks by the President to Distinguished School Principals. Room 450. Old Executive Building. October 18, 1989. 10:20 A.M. EDT.: 2

[17]   Director of Public Relations, Colorado Education Association, Deborah Fallin, interview by Author, 19 August 1992, tape recording.

[18]   James Traub, "Separate and Equal," *The Atlantic*, September, 1991, 24.

[19] The plan was challenged by the Wisconsin Department of Public Instruction on constitutional grounds. The Wisconsin Supreme Court, however, upheld the program and overturned a 1990 state appellate court ruling that the state legislature had improperly enacted the plan.

[20] Jeffrey R. Henig, *Rethinking School Choice: Limits of the Market Metaphor.* (Princeton: Princeton University Press, 1994), 114.

[21] According to the Education Commission of the States and The United States Center for Choice, there were 12 groups by 1991.

[22] Former Senior Assistant for Education to Governor William Clinton, Kathy Van Laningham, 24 August 1992, tape recording.

[23] Former Executive Director, Education Project, The Business Roundtable. Member, Maryland State Board of Education, Christopher Cross, interview by Author. February 26, 1992, Washington. Tape Recording.

[24] Vice President, Education Initiative for International Business Machine, Chairman, Education Task Force, the Business Roundtable, 1987-1990, John Anderson, interview by Author, 6 March 1992, tape recording.

[25] Internal memo, Michael A. DiConti. Executive Assistant to the President. The Business Roundtable. New York, New York. No Date.

[26] John Anderson, interview by Author.

[27] Tim W. Ferguson "Executive Make School Choice a Yes-or-No Proposition." *Wall Street Journal* 27 August 1991, 13(A).

[28] "California Voucher System: Falls Short of Ballot." *Daily Report Card,* 2, 26 June 1992, 6.

[29] Steve Kaelble "Enough Talk." *Indiana Business Magazine.* November 1991, 12.

[30] Hilary Stout "Business Funds Programs in Indianapolis Letting Poor Children Flee Public Schools." *Wall Street Journal* 27 February 1992, 1(B).

[31] Provenzo, Eugene F. "School-Based Management and Shared Decision Making in the Dade County Public Schools." in *Allies in Education Reform*: 146.

[32] Provenzo, 148.

[33] John E. Chubb and Terry Moe, *Politics, Markets and America's Schools.* (Washington, D.C.: Brookings Institution, 1990), 208.

[34] Sam Howe Verhovek "Legislature in Texas Sends School-Aid Plan to Voters." *The New York Times*, 12(A).

[35] Thomas Toch, "Plugging the School Tax Gap: Education: Courts Nationwide are Challenging Funding Inequities," *U.S. News & World Report* 25 June 1990, 59.

[36] Chubb and Moe, 208.

[37] The Business Roundtable, *The Business Roundtable Participation Guide: A Primer for Business on Education.* Developed by the National Alliance of Business. (New York: The Business Roundtable), 31.

[38]   See Raymond Callahan. *Education and the Cult of Efficiency* (Chicago: University of Chicago Press, 1962.)

[39]   The Business Roundtable, 10.

[40]   Opinion Dynamics Corporation, "Public Attitudes Toward Education Issues," *MassInsight Survey* Study Number 3271, Cambridge: Opinion Dynamics Corporation, October 1990.

[41]   Chubb and Moe, 109.

[42]   Bruce C. Cooper "Bottom-Up Authority in School Organization: Implications for the School Administrator," *Education and Urban Society* 21, 4 (August 1989).

[43]   Cooper, 383.

[44]   Katznelson, 12.

[45]   Hirschmann, 17.

[46]   James S. Coleman et al. *Equality of Educational Opportunity* (Washington, D.C. U.S. Office of Education, 1966.

[47]   Schiff, "The Educational Failure of Community Control in Inner-City New York. " *Phi Delta Kappan*, February 1976, 375-378.

[48]   Priscilla Wohlstetter and Karen McCurdy "The Link Between School Decentralization and School Politics." *Urban Education* 25 (January 1991): 391-414.

[49]   Schiff, 375.

[50]   See Herbert Kaufman. "Administrative Decentralization and Political Power," *Public Administrative Review* (Jan/Feb. 1969), 8, and D. Rogers, *110 Livingston Street* (New York: Vintage Books, 1969), 96.

[51]   J. Traub, "Fernandez Takes Charge," *The New York Times Magazine*, 17 June 1990, 23.

[52]   William L. Boyd, David W. O'Shea. "Theoretical Perspectives on School District Decentralization." *Education and Urban Society* 7 (August 1975): 357.   Paul E. Peterson. "Afterward, The Politics of School Decentralization." *Education And Urban Society* 7 (August 1975), 476. Peterson uses Chicago as one example.   He writes, "Without changing the formal governing structure, the school boards, by creating new offices and allowing citizens groups to participate in the selection of principals, increased substantially the number of blacks serving in administrative positions."

[53]   Peterson, 476.

[54]   Paula A. White, "An Overview of School-Based Management: What Does the Research Say?" *NAASP BULLETIN* (September 1989), 2.

[55]   The National Governors Association, *Time For Results*, (Washington, D.C.: The National Governor's Association, 1986).   The Committee for Economic Development, *Investing in our Children*, (New York: Committee for Economic Development, 1985) and *Children in Need*, (New York: Committee

For Economic Development, 1990). The Carnegie Corporation 1986 Task force report *A Nation Prepared: Teachers for the 21st Century.*

[56] See Conley, 366 and *A Nation Prepared.*

[57] See *A Nation Prepared.*

[58] The Carnegie Corporation 1986 Task force report *A Nation Prepared: Teachers for the 21st Century.* The National Education Association/National Association of Secondary School Principals (1986), the Holmes Group (1986), a task force of education school deans.

[59] The Carnegie Foundation for the Advancement of Teaching, *Teacher Involvement in Decision Making: A State-by-State Profile.* New York: September 1988.

[60] Sharon C. Conley "Who's on First?" School Reform, Teacher Participation, and the Decision Making Process." *Education and Urban Society* 21, 4 (August 1989): 366-379.

[61] Carnegie Task Force on Teaching as a Profession, 55.

[62] National Education Association. "Final Report of the National Education Special Committee on Restructuring Schools: Toward Restructured Public Schools" *Restructuring Issues* 6 (Washington, D.C.: National Education Association, December 1988).

[63] Alan Rosenthal. "New Voices in Public Education." *Teachers College Record,* 68, (1966): 13-14.

[64] Dorothy K. Jessup, *Teachers, Unions and Change: A Comparative Study* (Greenwood: Praeger, 1985), 10.

[65] Toch, Thomas. *In the Name of Excellence: The Struggle to Reform the Nation's Schools, Why its Failing and What Should be Done.* (New York: Oxford University Press 1991), 5.

[66] Paula A. White, "An Overview of School-Based Management: What Does the Research say?" *Bulletin* (September 1989): 5.

[67] National Education Association. "Final Report of the National Education Special Committee on Restructuring Schools: Toward Restructured Public Schools" *Restructuring Issues* 6 (Washington, D.C.: National Education Association, December 1988).

[68] Toch, 134.

[69] Paul T. Hill, A.E. Wise, and L. Shapiro, 33.

[70] Hill, et al., 34.

[71] Carol Ascher, "Urban School-Community Alliance, *Trend and Issues* 10, (December 1988).

[72] Carol Innerst, "Teachers' Pact Says Parents Must Pitch In." *Washington Times.* 21 January 1991.

[73] Peter J. Cistone, Joseph A. Fernandez, Pat L. Tornillo, Jr., "School Based Management/Shared Decision Making in Dade County (Miami)." *Education and Urban Society,* 21 (August 1989): 397.

[74]   Thomas Timar, "The Politics of School Restructuring." *The Education Digest*, (May 1990), 7.

Chapter Three

Public School Choice Emerges in the Reform Debate: The Case of Minnesota

During the 1980s the movement to restructure the nation's schools focused attention on several educational policies that would provide students with alternatives to their neighborhood or assigned school. Proponents of the "exit option" in particular supported a welter of policies that would bring dramatic changes to the delivery system for public education. Such changes, proponents hoped, would range from magnet schools to broader applications of the exit option through voucher plans or tuition tax credits.

But as the decade progressed and student achievement levels remained stagnant, many exit option proponents began to shift their focus away from vouchers and tuition tax credits, which generally addressed particular needs for a particular student. An entirely new structure for public education in the United States began to emerge in the reform debate -- a market system of education. In a market system, all schools, public and private, receive charters from the state. The government's per pupil expenditure follows each individual student with the schools competing for dollars in the marketplace of primary and secondary education. Students are then free to "shop" for a school of their choice. In turn the competition for students, reformers argued, would stimulate reform by allowing good schools to thrive and bad schools to close.[1]

Although the market system of public education brought new life to an old debate, lawmakers consistently rejected this version of the exit option. They hesitated to enact into law new measures that would fund private elementary and secondary as well as public schools. They feared that non-public, and particularly religious schools, would be able to promote their own private agendas with the support of state dollars. In addition, the market system of education would result in a new set of expenditures of public funds without any new educational results, largely because parents already sending children to private or parochial schools would receive a payment from the government to support the same education that their children were already receiving.

At the same time the market system started to emerge in education reform debates, lawmakers in many states across the country were enacting into law yet another version of the exit option. Formally called Open Enrollment the reform became widely known as Public School Choice. The idea first emerged in 1985 when the state of Minnesota drew a distinction between Public School Choice and private school vouchers. The distinction was significant. It successfully removed the most contentious issue -- the flow of public dollars to sectarian as well as other types of private schools -- from the exit option debate. The Minnesota School Choice proposal would allow students to move freely within the public school system.

Education in Minnesota

Traditionally, Minnesota has been a strong supporter of its schools, and education policy issues have always comprised a substantial segment of the legislative agenda. This legislative support, in turn, has made the state a leader in educational spending. The dollar amount that the state contributes to the cost of each student's educational expenditure per year, has consistently been far greater than the national average. During the 1970s, Minnesota ranked fourth among the states in the proportion of personal income devoted to state and local funding for public schools; it ranked fifth in per capita state government expenditures for all education.[2] Since 1983 the operating expenditures per student have consistently been above the national average and third among the 12 Midwestern states in public-school expenditures.[3]

In addition to high levels of spending, equity in the provision of educational resources has received far greater attention in Minnesota over the past several decades than in other states. In the early 1970s, when school finance issues began to emerge in many states, the Minnesota legislature enacted equalizing legislation, without the stimulus of a school finance lawsuit, in an effort to increase aid to local school districts while compensating for differences in local property tax bases.

The reforms of 1971 and 1973 became widely known as the Minnesota Miracle because of their dramatic restructuring of state and local responsibilities for education funding. Before the new financing formula began, the public schools themselves, as well as local governments, generated revenue through the local taxation of property, supplemented by revenues from the state sales tax. But under the new financing scheme, a statewide income tax would redistribute revenues to local governments and school districts permitting them to reduce their reliance on local property taxes. Local governments with poor property tax bases would receive more aid per pupil, while those with strong tax bases would receive less. In the process, the state began to assume a bigger percentage -- about 66 percent -- of the total cost of local education in an attempt to lessen disparities between districts.[4]

In addition to high levels of spending and equity in the provision of educational resources, Minnesota has also been progressive in the way it spends money on education. For example, the Transportation of School Children Act passed in 1969 required that all children on an equal basis receive bus transportation whether they attended public or private schools. The 1969 legislation directed public school districts that provide bus transportation for students who live a certain distance from school to provide similar service to students who attend non-public schools the same distance from their homes.[5]

Other special services are equally available to students in public and private schools. In 1976 the state legislature passed the Non-public School Aid Bill which allows loans of non-religious books, materials, and equipment to non-public schools and their students. The 1976 legislation also provides the services of public school counselors, compensatory special education, psychologists, speech teachers, remedial instructors and other "auxiliary service" providers to non-public school students.[6]

In other areas of educational policymaking, Minnesota has pursued innovative education policies that would provide students with alternatives to their assigned schools and increase the choices of students and parents. But the policies did not produce divisive debates in the legislature that were so common when lawmakers in other states introduced vouchers or tuition tax credits.

Lawmakers could avoid controversy largely because the policies had little to do with educational substance or quality. For example, in 1955 the state enacted legislation that would allow public and private school parents to deduct up to $200 in tuition and other school expenses from their gross income for state income tax computations. Under this program parents received a reimbursement for educational expenses at both public and private schools.

Because lawmakers were making significant education policy as an element of tax policy, there was very little debate on the educational merits of the program. The absence of debate is also due to the fact that the new policy proposals went to the legislature's tax committees rather than education committees. Many legislators supported these new tax measures without assessing their impact on educational policy. At the end of the legislative session, the deduction provision passed unanimously as part of a routine, noncontroversial income tax bill.[7]

When the state legislators enacted policies that would specifically provide assistance to students attending non-public institutions, rather than taxpayers in general, controversy erupted almost immediately. In 1971, for example, the state legislature adopted a non-public school cost tax credit. For the first two years of the program, the tax credit could not exceed $100 per pupil and then continue at a certain percentage of the average per pupil foundation aid payment for public school students thereafter.

But the Minnesota Supreme Court in 1974 declared the tax credit statute unconstitutional in response to a legal challenge supported by the state's two teachers' unions, the Minnesota Education Association and the Minnesota Federation of Teachers. Despite the controversy surrounding the tax credit policy, however, lawmakers successfully continued to expand the tuition tax deduction program. In 1976, the legislature responded to the loss of the tax credit by increasing the 1955 deduction allowance to $500 and $700 for grades K-6 and 7-12 respectively, and by extending the statute to cover textbook as well as tuition and transportation expenditures.[8]   Then in 1984, the state legislature raised the deduction ceilings to $650 and $1000 for elementary and secondary school students respectively to reflect the increase in non-public school costs since 1976.

Although these deduction ceilings have been increasing for almost thirty years, the changes in tax law did not have much effect on private school enrollment. In fact, private school enrollment declined from a peak of 18.7 percent of all students in 1959-60 to 9.1 percent in 1974-75, while both the tuition tax deduction and the short-lived tuition tax credit were in effect. But after the 1984 increase, enrollment began rebounding and leveling off at 11.1 percent in 1984-85. Since then it has slipped to 10.4 percent, a proportion lower than the national average of 12 percent. Minnesota's enrollment rate for non-public schools is only slightly lower than in neighboring states like Nebraska (13 percent), but sharply lower than in Eastern states. In New York State, for example, 20 percent of all school age children are in non-public schools.[9] In all likelihood, the declines in private school enrollment minimized the level of controversy about educational deductions in the Minnesota state legislature.[10]

There was also little controversy surrounding the enactment of the 1979 Transfer Agreement Law even though the law clearly provided students with alternatives to their assigned schools. The state legislature, however, enacted the law with the intention of codifying an existing practice rather than expanding the choices of students. For several decades prior to the passage of the 1979 law, a number of Minnesota students were already moving freely from one public school district to another. The majority of students were transferring for convenience -- many students lived closer to a school in the adjacent district rather than to the one assigned to them in their own school district. Roughly 500 students a year were then participating in the Non-resident Transfer Agreement Program, out of 707,000 public school students in the entire state.[11]

Although the transfer of a student from one school district to another was a simple procedure, the transfer of the student's state per pupil expenditure remained a complicated matter. Across the state, school districts were following different procedures to ensure that state money would follow the transferring student to the new district. In response to a State Department of Education request to formalize the transfer procedure, the legislature passed the 1979 Transfer Agreement Law. The new law established the use of a single form for transfer requests to assure that state aid and students transferred together.

Even though the Transfer Agreement Law permitted students to choose schools other than their assigned schools, legislators and members of the education community viewed the measure as a housekeeping matter that would guarantee the smooth administration of state education funds, rather than permitting students greater freedom to choose their schools. What is more important, however, is that although the law was a policy mandated by the state, it did not intrude upon the local control of public schools. Under the prevailing principle of local control, the transfer of a student is considered a matter for the school district superintendent and school board to decide, not the State Department of Education. Because there was an approval process at the school district level, the practice of allowing public school students to cross district lines continued without controversy.[12]

Minnesota Educational Policymaking Enters a Controversial Stage

By 1980, however, policymaking became significantly more controversial when lawmakers began to make changes in school policies that had the clear intention of expanding educational offerings to high school students. In 1980 the Minnesota legislature brought a new twist to the restructuring debate in general and the exit option in particular with the enactment of the Levi law. The new legislation permitted public school students to make a choice between taking high school classes or taking advanced course work at nearby colleges, in addition to the opportunity they already had to transfer among secondary schools.

The idea of allowing students to make a choice between high school and college came from the frustration experienced by one state legislator, Conni Levi. Levi sought to expand the educational offerings available to her daughter, a senior in a small school district in suburban St. Paul. In 1980 Levi, a freshman Independent Republican from Northern Washington County, requested the local school board to release her daughter from study hall at her high school so that she could take advanced courses at a nearby community college that were not available at the high school she attended. Levi's request to have her daughter released from study hall was not unusual. In many high schools, students could leave study hall in order to participate in athletic activities or to work at part-time jobs.

The Ottameada school board, however, rejected Levi's request. School board members argued that district policy prohibited students from leaving their school during class hours for academic reasons. The prohibition stemmed from a financial concern. When a student left their high school to attend another institution, even on a part-time basis, the school district would then lose some of the state aid received for that student.   In essence, the Ottameada school district, as well as the other 435 school districts in the state, enforced school policies that blocked use of the exit option for academic reasons.

In an effort to change the policy, Levi succeeded in enacting a 1980 law which granted school districts the authority to establish programs permitting high school students to enroll in courses at post-secondary institutions.   Levi reasoned before her colleagues on the House Education Committee that if students could get out of school for work or for athletic activities, then the same rule should apply to a student who wanted to pursue education at institutions other than their own schools.[13]

Levi's impetus for increasing the options of students and giving them more choices in their education stemmed from a need to create opportunities for all students including the "at risk," gifted and talented, and any other student whose requirements the traditional educational delivery system failed to meet.   But representatives from the state's major educational lobbying groups, consisting of the Minnesota Federation of Teachers (MFT), the Minnesota Education Association (MEA), the Minnesota School Boards' Association (MSBA), the Minnesota Association of School Administrators (MASA), the Minnesota Association of Secondary School Principals (MASSP) and the Minnesota Elementary Principals' Association (MEPA) wanted to offer the program only to the gifted and talented, thereby limiting potential students that might opt out of the school district's control. Levi, however, convinced her colleagues that the program should include every student.   Any limitations placed on the program, she argued before her colleagues, might be difficult to reverse in subsequent legislative sessions.

Levi was able to gather support in the legislature principally for two reasons.   The first was that it represented a relatively small change in existing school policy that did not effect the entire kindergarten through 12th grade system.   Secondly, it did not require new expenditures for transportation.   Legislators sitting on the school aids division -- the finance division of the full Education Committee -- approved Levi's proposal.   But once enacted, the Levi law met resistance from the two teacher unions and the various education associations.   High school principals in particular were reluctant to allow students to enroll in the program, arguing that it would encourage the best students to leave their schools.   District superintendents were also reluctant to allow students to participate. In order to discourage students from enrolling in nearby colleges, many school districts would not allow high school students to count college credits toward their high school graduation requirements.

Because principals and superintendents were making it difficult for students to participate in the program, Levi requested that the legislature consider removing all decision making authority in the program from the local school boards and district personnel. But the MEA, the MFT and the state's education associations refused to give up their authority over the schools. Instead they launched a fierce lobbying campaign when Levi introduced her new bill in the state legislature.

The legislature enacted a compromise measure. It created a process for students that permitted them to appeal to the state board of education if disputes arose when high school students sought to earn credits at colleges under the Levi law. Although the 1984 legislation permitted students to circumvent the authority of their principals and their local school boards, the appeal process remained under the jurisdiction of the state's educational apparatus. This compromise smoothed the way for the bill's passage.

Despite the efforts within the education lobbying groups to limit the new program, the Levi law signaled a significant change in Minnesota's education policymaking system. Although final decision making authority remained with the state school board, the Levi law broadened the opportunities available to students and their parents to make choices about education. According to Levi, "it produced a little bit of market in the educational system."[14]

Equally important, however, the Levi law began to question the delivery system in educational institutions and its impact on student achievement. The new law effectively pushed the education debate to questions of authority, legitimacy and quality. It focused attention on the schools and their curricula, and it suggested that the education system did not meet the needs of all Minnesota's students, particularly the gifted and talented students. The Levi law became the forerunner of all Choice programs in Minnesota that policymakers hoped would raise student achievement levels in general and serve the special needs of students in particular.

The Status of Education in Minnesota

Questioning the quality of education was something new in Minnesota. Minnesota is an education minded state with a high level of educational attainment. During the 1970s, 91.5 percent of Minnesota students graduated from high school -- the highest percentage in the nation.[15] Other indicators of student performance reflect high levels of educational achievement. During the 1970s, the percentage of Minnesota students taking the American College Test (ACT), the primary college entrance test in 28 states, remained well above the national average. In addition, Minnesota students consistently scored above the national average of 18.5 on this test with 21.4 out of a perfect score of 36.[16] On the Scholastic Aptitude Test (SAT), Minnesota's national rankings consistently hovered around 5th in Verbal (506) and 3rd in Math (552).[17]

But at the start of the 1980's, Minnesota students began a slow decline in educational achievement that mirrored national trends. Like overall education levels in the United States, the downward shift in Minnesota was consistent and long term. For over twenty years, student test scores were in decline. In fact, from 1969 to 1989, Minnesota scores began to drop more than the national average. From 1971-72 to 1978-79, Minnesota students' average score on the ACT, the test taken by the majority of Minnesota students who are planning to attend college, declined from 21.4 to 20.5 while the national average declined from 19.1 to 18.6. The state decline occurred at a faster rate than was true nationally.[18] By 1980, SAT scores slipped by almost 30 points, and by 1985, a 10 year decline in the SAT stood at 36 points.[19]

At the same time post-secondary schools in the state reported a sharp expansion in remedial course work for incoming freshman.[20]

The percentage of dropouts also increased. Relative to other states, Minnesota does not have a high dropout rate. Only 2.1 percent of the seventh to twelfth grade enrollment did not finish high school in 1982-1983. But more troublesome is the concentration of high school dropouts. The dropout rates are highest in the larger cities where nearly 46 percent of all the state's public school students attend school.[21] During the late 1970s and early 1980s, the drop out rate in the Twin Cities of Minneapolis and St. Paul steadily began to increase, reaching 11 percent in 1983.

While the number of dropouts increased, the minority populations in the Twin Cities school system also expanded.[22] Although Minnesota ranks 43rd in the nation in the relative size of minority student population, the percentage of minorities in the Minneapolis public schools increased from 14.4 percent in 1971 to 26.1 percent in 1978, while in St. Paul, the percentage of minority group students in the public schools increased from 11.2 percent in 1971 to 19.9 percent in 1978.[23] Despite gains in recent years, African-Americans and Native Americans, the state's two largest minority groups, continued to lag far behind whites in overall scores on school district tests. In Minneapolis, for example, four of the seven high schools, those with the highest percentage of minorities, ranked among the lowest in the state on college entrance exams in the 1980s.[24]

In addition, the central city schools enrolled an increasing number of disadvantaged students eligible for free or reduced-price lunches (one measure of students' economic background). Nearly one-third of Minneapolis' total student enrollment received some form of government assistance.[25] Even worse, 1 of 28 female students in grades 7 through 12 was pregnant in 1984-85, compared with 1 of 49 in 1974-75.[26]

Restructuring Enters the Education Reform Debate

These declines were coming at a time when support for the schools was waning. For example, although Minnesota has always been a strong supporter of its schools, the Minnesota state legislature raised the basic aid formula from the 1980-81 level of $1,265 per pupil unit to $1,318 in 1981-82 school year and $1,475 in 1982-83. These represent the lowest biennial percentage increases since the current school finance system began in 1971.[27]

In addition, total state appropriations declined from 54 percent of state appropriations in 1971-1973 to 41 percent of state appropriations during the 1979-1981 biennium. Competition for funding began to occur within the public education system as well. Over the course of the decade, within the appropriations for all publicly supported education, proportionately fewer dollars went to elementary and secondary education while proportionately more dollars went to higher education and other types of education (i.e., post-secondary, vocational, and community as well as adult education). Elementary and secondary education accounted for almost 78 percent of all education appropriations in 1971-1973, but represented 72 percent in 1979-81. On the other hand, state appropriations for higher education increased from 20 percent to 22 percent of all education appropriations during that same period.[28] A decline in federal spending further exacerbated the school funding issue when federal spending also declined from almost 10 percent of school funding in school year 1979-1980 to 6 percent in 1989-1990.[29]

Nevertheless, educational expenditures continued to be Minnesota's single largest area of public expenditures. In an age of scarce public resources and diverse needs, however, education remained in a vulnerable position. One sign of decline in public support was the fact that the number of taxpayers with children in the schools decreased. During the 1970's, the state's school aged population decreased by 17 percent. At the same time, the number of persons over the age of 65 continued to increase. According to the U.S. Census Bureau figures, the number of Minnesotans over 65 increased by 17 percent during the last decade.[30]

By 1985, however, the drops in student achievement in the cities and the rest of the state produced a demand for change in Minnesota from non-educators. More than a dozen reports and studies were released highlighting the deteriorating conditions in the public schools. In numerous school reform discussions the notion of restructuring the school system began to gain widespread popularity. Restructuring, reformers argued, would raise student achievement levels, and in the process, the schools themselves would improve.

School Choice was at the center of the school restructuring debate. The following case study is a careful examination of the Minnesota educational reform movement which reveals that the rationale for School Choice reflected a broad shift in the general climate for policymaking that sought new ways for the government to distribute scarce resources effectively. The support for School Choice emerged from a conservative fiscal agenda and significantly affected the reform debate. Minnesota's fiscal circumstances, not the condition of its public schools, were responsible for stimulating an interest in government reform in general and School Choice in particular among groups outside of the traditional educational policymaking arena that promoted reform. In addition to Governor Rudy Perpich, two organizations, the Minnesota Business Partnership, which represents 75 of the state's largest companies, and the Twin Cities Citizens League, a Minneapolis based good government group, launched the government reform debate and advanced the ideas that would eventually drive and shape the education policymaking system. Their efforts pushed Minnesota steadily toward providing students and parents with more options. But for many school observers of the Minnesota experience,

School Choice did not evolve naturally out of the preexisting educational policymaking domain. They point to the non-incremental intervention of Governor Rudy Perpich, a new participant in that domain, to remove policymaking from its otherwise normal course of incremental adjustment. Thus, they argue, School Choice is a fundamental, structural change rather than an incremental one.[31]

But these early observations of the Minnesota experience are misleading and fail to recognize that School Choice has evolved through many stages. In fact, School Choice in Minnesota was in the making for more than a decade.[32] The process extended from the 1980 Levi law, the first step toward Choice in the restructuring debate, to the 1991 Charter School Law.   During each stage, the desires of the reformers prevailed over the best interest of the students. Policymakers outside the educational arena successfully met their political needs in education reform, and the result, not surprisingly, was very little improvement in the quality of education.

Education Reform Reaches the Top of the State's Agenda

Like the rest of the nation, Minnesota began to experience a deep recession in the late 1970s and early 1980s. Structural changes in the economy that reduced employment in mining, construction, and durable goods manufacturing exacerbated the recession. Between 1979 and 1982, employment in mining declined by 62 percent. Construction jobs in the state declined by 26 percent, and 17 percent of durable goods manufacturing jobs were lost. Even wholesale and retail jobs declined. The Soviet grain embargo, declared by President Carter, precipitated a recession in the agricultural sector of the Minnesota economy, which had become heavily dependent on the export market.[33]

For the business community, Minnesota's growth in existing and new markets stagnated during the recession. The state's high tax rates also began to have a detrimental effect on the Minnesota economy.[34]
In the late 1970s and early 1980s, the Minnesota Business Partnership sought to improve the business climate by examining the state's tax structure. Compared to other states, Minnesota has a relatively high corporate tax rate and a high sales tax rate of 5.5 percent.

The high tax rates are necessary to support a wide range of government services. A consensus produced by the state's two major political parties, the Democratic Farm Labor (DFL) and the

Independent Republicans (IR), has led the state legislature to perform an active and innovative role in the provision of public services. Both political parties have generally been responsive to demands for high quality roads, health services and social welfare programs. While the state climbed from 14th to 6th highest in public expenditures per capita, it also had the distinction of having the highest nominal income tax rate in the country.

Reasoning that high taxes were the result of legislative spending decisions, the Minnesota Business Partnership decided to examine the state budget to see if a change in spending priorities would produce a more cost-effective use of public funds. Since education accounts for over half of the state's budget, the Minnesota Business Partnership concluded that it should focus on K-12 education issues.[35]

While the Business Partnership began to examine the education portion of the state budget, the business community itself was beginning to focus on the problems presented by the declining quality of education in the state. In general, members of the Partnership reported a growing employer dissatisfaction with the skills and work attitudes of new employees. High school graduates, companies reported, were unable to keep pace with the rapidly increasing need for students to learn more. Minnesota graduates began to show a difficulty in reasoning, critical thinking and problem solving. Students must acquire these skills, often called "higher-order skills," in order to perform such tasks as making simple calculations about mortgage rates, writing a clear business letter or understanding written directions.[36]

Concluding that the ultimate fate of their businesses rested upon the quality of public education, the Education Task Force of the Minnesota Business Partnership hired Berman Weiler Associates, a California consulting group, to conduct an analysis of the status of the state's education system. The two year, $250,000 study, the Business Partnership hoped, would help them establish and develop an education agenda designed to meet their dual objectives of containing educational costs and stimulating improvement in the schools.[37]

Shortly before the state legislature convened in 1984, the Business Partnership issued its report. It recommended sweeping changes in secondary education, including the expansion of opportunities for high school students to exercise free choice in attending any public school in the state, with the state per-pupil subsidy to school districts following the student rather than staying in the home district. The Minnesota Business Partnership wanted to restructure the incentives for school districts in such a way as to encourage improvements in educational quality without increasing across-the-board school expenditures. For the Minnesota Business Partnership, School Choice became part of a strategy to examine and question the highest expenditures in the state budget.

The concept of Free Choice within the public school system received warm endorsements from other business and civic groups, particularly the Twin Cities Citizens League. The Citizens League is a good government group based in Minneapolis that was formed in 1952 as an independent, nonpartisan, nonprofit, educational corporation. Volunteer research committees of the Citizens League discuss and then develop recommendations for solutions after months of intensive work.

Support for the League comes from membership dues of individual members and membership contributions from businesses, foundations and other organizations throughout the metropolitan area. A great deal of their committee work centered on improving the schools. In fact, the Citizens League had long been an advocate of some form of School Choice in the public schools. Its interest in expanding the enrollment options of public school students, however, began as a way of addressing the issue of equal opportunity for minority students in the Twin Cities.

Minneapolis and St. Paul were not unique in their concern about minority students. Many large urban school systems during the 1970s had to confront the issue of equal opportunity following court orders to desegregate. The Twin Cities, however, aggressively pursued several mechanisms in an effort to desegregate following a 1972 District Court order. Both districts modified or enriched the curriculum in certain schools. They also offered different types of learning environments, such as open schools. In both districts, a pupil could transfer to any school building elsewhere in the district, provided that the transfer would improve the racial balance in both the sending and receiving schools.[38]

Despite the efforts of the school system, the Citizens League concluded that little progress toward genuine racial integration or excellence in learning occurred. A low-income voucher program, League members argued, would meet these two objectives by permitting students, particularly those from poor and minority sectors of the cities, to buy a better education. Under their voucher proposal, low-income families would use state funds to send their children to public schools outside their residential areas or to a state approved independent school. Advocates of the plan argued that in addition to expanding the opportunities for students from low-income families, a voucher system would enhance equity in education by giving families the same choice as middle and upper level income families had under the Minnesota tax deduction plan. In general, the poor did not benefit from the tax deduction for educational expenses because most families did not earn enough to pay state income taxes or send their children to non-public schools.[39]

By 1984 the Citizens League, along with a coalition of liberal and conservative Minnesota legislators that called themselves Citizens for Educational Freedom, proposed a low-income voucher program to the state legislature. The voucher bill, however, died in the Education Committee and the League subsequently abandoned its efforts to enact a voucher program, reasoning that it would be difficult to get support for a program that would redirect state funds to private schools in a state where more than one-fourth of the state legislators were former or current educators, mostly from public institutions.[40]

In addition to the problems it experienced in the state legislature, the Citizens League also encountered resistance to the voucher program within its own ranks. Several members took the unusual step of submitting dissenting opinions along with the League's report calling for vouchers. The voucher program, these League members argued, threatened the existence of the public school. Those against the measure feared that it would have a detrimental effect on the public schools because it would allow state dollars and students to leave the system entirely rather than addressing the problems of the public schools. Many League members feared that a voucher system would permit the most talented and successful students to exit their assigned public schools, leaving the least talented and resourceful behind.[41]

A New Strategy for Government Reform: The Exit Option

Despite the controversy surrounding vouchers, in general the League continued to support a new strategy for government reform based on the proposition that the delivery of public services would improve if citizens could employ the exit option and take their business to the private sector or to a different provider in the public sector. The new approach reflected the promotion of "Public Service Options," which would shift the League's method of public action from a traditional reliance on the institutions of "voice" toward increasing reliance on a strategy of "exit."[42]   The exit strategy, the League argued, would help solve problems of bureaucratic response by addressing the inherent conflict of interest found in a bureaucratic government -- the conflict that arises when an agency tries to represent faithfully both the consumers and producers of public services.   When a government agency creates a bureaucratic work force, it also brings into being an interest group that will resist change, accountability, and demands for greater productivity or reduced expenditures.[43]

The rise of oil prices and the deeper recession in 1981 and 1982 to a great extent drove the idea for service options.   In the short term, it became evident to many Citizens League members that there would be less resources and more demand for services.   At that time the Citizens League Executive Director, Ted Kolderie, was a long term advocate of market driven public services.   Kolderie orchestrated a League study entitled *Issues of the 80s: Enlarging Our Capacity to Adapt.*   The report explored alternative ways to change and improve the major community service systems in the Twin Cities and the rest of Minnesota.   That report set the tone for further Citizens League studies in the 1980s, the majority of which would concentrate on service delivery.[44]

Following the release of *Issues of the '80s*, the League began to advance the idea of using market mechanisms as a way to make public agencies more responsive to consumers' needs and to improve the quality of government services.   The Minnesota Business Partnership proposal for Public School Choice was one example of the League's idea for market-driven public services.   Citizens League members who supported some form of School Choice argued that this type of policy would bring about three significant structural changes in the schools. The first was financial.   The Minnesota public sector was facing revenue shortages which were severe and likely to persist throughout the 1980s.   A School Choice program would not require any new expenditures.

Second, structural change would strengthen incentives to deliver quality education.   The incentive structure in the present educational system, League members argued, was so weak that it could not encourage the adoption of programs proven successful at one school among other schools and promising alternatives in the system as a whole.   The existing incentives were also insufficient as a way to induce administrators to seek out modes of service-delivery that saved money.[45]

Finally, structural change would introduce flexibility into the K-12 educational system and create a climate of innovation and responsiveness. Such an environment would presumably result if decisions about where to go for educational services shifted to the family. Public educators would no longer possess a monopoly on students. Permitting students to walk away from one school to another they liked better would presumably make schools and teachers more responsive to the needs of students and parents. Unresponsive schools would not survive.

Governor Perpich Enters the Education Reform Debate

The Citizens League was not alone in its support for the Business Partnership's Choice program. Governor Rudy Perpich was also receptive to the idea. The governor perceived an improvement in the schools as one way to address the needs of the faltering Minnesota economy.[46] During the 1982 gubernatorial campaign, for example, Perpich repeatedly said that a strong education system had been an important element in the state's past economic success. Minnesota did in fact rank seventh in the nation in the number of high technology manufacturing and corporate headquarters located in the state.[47] But in order to retain existing business, as well as attract new investment, Perpich argued, the state needed to produce a well-trained and well-educated work force.[48]

The notion of linking education to economic development did not originate in Minnesota. Difficult fiscal conditions across the country prompted elected officials to make education and economic development their highest priorities. Intense international and interstate economic competition for high-growth, high technology industry made it increasingly clear that the nature of state policymaking in economic development, employment, and education needed to change. Economic development no longer meant simply tax abatements to lure industry, for that strategy attracted businesses with little long-term commitment, which were easily lured away by more generous tax benefits or cost savings in other states and nations. Frequently, investment in human capital and its cultivation became the focus of both economic development and employment policies.[49]

The governor had a strong interest in Public School Choice as the way to address the problems in Minnesota's schools. Unlike most reformers, however, the governor's interest in School Choice did not begin in the early 1980s. Perpich had been thinking about expanding the enrollment options of students for quite some time. In 1962 when Perpich moved his family to St. Paul after being elected to the State House of Representatives, his two children transferred to a district in the Twin Cities. The children reported that their classes were little more than a review of what they had learned in their old school.[50] Like Conni Levi, Perpich wanted to expand the enrollment options of his children because their school did not offer them a challenging academic program.

When he was elected governor, Perpich renewed his interest in School Choice. Representatives from the Minnesota Business Partnership met with the governor's chief policy advisor, Lani Kawimura, and finance commissioner Gordon Dunhowe shortly before the Partnership released its report. It was not unusual for the finance commissioner to attend a policy meeting. Perpich enlarged the responsibility of the Department of Finance following a state budget crisis in 1982. Other state agencies had to consider the department's revenue projections, cost data, and budget control mechanisms.[51]

The Minnesota Business Partnership and the governor easily reached an agreement on the new policy initiative, largely because they both had the same objectives: to keep taxes down while at the same time stimulating school improvement.[52] Public School Choice was a comprehensive reform, which the governor and Minnesota Business Partnership hoped, would bring about fundamental change without requiring a large increase in public expenditures. Instead, they would use the same level of appropriations but attempt to do things differently in public education.[53]

Before Choice, or Open Enrollment, could successfully pass the scrutiny of the state legislature, Perpich had to win support from two key institutions -- the State Board of Education and the state legislature.

In order to win the support of the state's education policymaking apparatus, however, the governor first needed to restructure the state's education bureaucracy. To begin with, the mode of appointing the state's Commissioner of Education reduced the authority of the Governor and weakened lines of accountability in educational policymaking. At that time in Minnesota, the governor did not appoint the Education Commissioner directly. The governor appoints the members of the state Board of Education, and the members in turn appoint the commissioner.

The fact that the commissioner's term in office does not coincide with the governor's further dilutes the governor's authority and control. A new governor, therefore, works with a commissioner appointed by the previous administration until the commissioner's six year term has expired. Because the Governor has little or no control over the state commissioner of education, the governor and the commissioner would seldom work on joint policy initiatives.

Given the weakness of gubernatorial leadership in education policy, the state Department of Education was more dependent that it might otherwise have been on its own constituency -- the educators of Minnesota. The education community, however, began to fragment and weakened by the emergence of collective bargaining in 1973 from which the teachers' unions emerged as an independent force in the politics of education.[54] There were also numerous education associations, such as the Minnesota School Boards Association, for example, and separate associations for elementary and secondary principals. As a result of these many and separate political interests, there was little capacity among the k-12 groups to collaborate with the Department of Education -- or with one another - in promoting new legislation. Instead, the Department of Education became the object of cross pressures from the various groups. A restructured Department of Education and state Board of Education, Perpich hoped, would allow the Governor's office to have more control over the department and bring more coherence to the state's educational policy making.[55]

Minnesota was not the only state to structurally change the education bureaucracy. Signs of a growing dissatisfaction with state boards of education were evident since the reform movement began in the early 1980s. Chief among these signs has been changes made in governance structures in a number of other states as well. For example, Texas, Tennessee and Mississippi created new state boards of education as part of their reform legislation, abolishing existing structures in the process. In Mississippi and Louisiana, a state superintendent appointed state board replaced an elected one. In Iowa the governor, rather than the state board, now appoints the school chief; and in Massachusetts, the legislature took authority to select the chairman of the state board away from the board and gave it to the Governor.

In 1983 Perpich successfully pressed legislative leaders to grant him sole authority to appoint the Commissioner of Education. As a result, the direction of the Minnesota Department of Education changed significantly. By May Perpich selected Ruth Randall, the Rosemount School District superintendent, as his new commissioner. Randall had a statewide reputation as an education reformer and a staunch proponent of restructuring programs that would shift decision making down the hierarchical ladder to the consumers of education themselves. She supported School Choice in particular.

Perpich needed to gain support from the legislature to overcome the potentially detrimental lobbying efforts of the state education groups. From a political perspective, Choice was an anomaly in Minnesota at best, because Perpich was a Democrat and Choice was most often identified with voucher programs -- a conservative Republican policy. In the state legislature, bi-partisan support, Perpich hoped, would ensure the enactment of School Choice.

In the House, Perpich required the backing of the majority party, the Independent Republicans, to pass his legislation. The Independent Republicans had come to power following the 1984 mid-term elections.

At that time the balance of power in the State House of Representatives shifted away from the Democrats, thus ending more than a decade of smooth cooperation between the two houses of the legislature.[56]

Governor Perpich sent Commissioner Ruth Randall to meet with House Republican Majority Leader Conni Levi to find out if he could count on the support of the Independent Republicans. Levi's support for the governor's package, however, did not entirely stem from a desire to keep spending levels down. Instead, Levi traded her support for Choice for the governor's support of improvements in the Levi law.

Levi told Randall that the only circumstance under which she would support the governor's legislative package would be if an expansion of the Levi law became part of his plan.[57] Levi wanted to remove all controls of the program away from the individual districts and place them in the province of the state. For her part, Levi realized that any effort to shift control in the program away from the district to the state level would need the strong support of the governor in order to overcome the opposition from the state's education lobbying groups.[58]

In the Minnesota House, Conni Levi became the driving force behind Perpich's Open Enrollment plan. In the Senate, the governor had been meeting with Democratic Senator Tom Nelson. Perpich began talking with the state senator in 1983, when Nelson was chairman of the Education Funding Division of the Senate Education Committee.[59] Perpich convinced Nelson that Open Enrollment was a good idea for the Minnesota Public Schools. As an educator, Nelson was interested in new ideas for the schools. As a legislator, School Choice was particularly appealing to Nelson because of the minimal cost involved.

Nelson took the lead in putting together a proposal in 1984 that would introduce Open Enrollment to the Democratic Senate. Nelson and Sue Hanaker, the administrator for the Senate Education Committee, gathered national reports and state studies and looked at programs that the committee members might want to support. From those deliberations, Open Enrollment emerged.[60]

With his own commissioner in place, bipartisan support in the legislature growing, and the backing of the business and civic communities, Perpich began to formulate a school improvement plan. The governor asked Lani Kawimura and Ruth Randall to start gathering material for a speech he was preparing to deliver in January 1985, shortly before the first meeting of the state legislature, to reveal his education reform initiative. Randall spoke with members of the House and Senate, including Levi and Nelson, and also to members of the Citizens League. Both Verne Johnson and the current executive director, Curt Johnson, indicated support for the program, but wanted to extend it to private schools. The same was true for Ted Kolderie, who left the League following the publication of *Issue's of the '80s* to become a senior associate at the Hubert Humphrey Institute on the Minneapolis campus of the University of Minnesota. According to Kolderie, a voucher program would be a further refinement of public service options for students.[61]

Finally, Kawimura and Randall consulted with Joe Nathan. Nathan, a principal and teacher, had earned a reputation as a staunch Choice proponent. As director of People for Better Schools, Nathan cultivated grass roots support for Choice in Minnesota.

School Choice in the Education Reform Debate

In his January 1985 speech to a breakfast gathering of the Citizens League, Governor Perpich unveiled his school reform package for grades kindergarten to 12. The governor's proposal, named "Access to Excellence," had several components.

To begin with, Perpich wanted to change the focus of the Department of Education from a regulatory institution to a support mechanism for the schools. A central purpose of Perpich's "Access to

Excellence" was to provide assistance to districts that were losing students by giving them the resources needed to improve their programs. The department would assist school districts unable to meet state standards. Each school would be encouraged to create its own distinctive environment in order to attract and retain students.[62]

These proposals outlined in "Access," however, did not get much attention because they simply refined an existing program called the Instructional Effectiveness Program, which under Perpich's leadership became the Minnesota Educational Effectiveness Program (MEEP) in 1983. That program began in 1970 when the State Department of Education had an instructional improvement committee whose members met with principals to discuss the possibility of instituting new programs in the schools. The legislature codified the state's support for School-Based Management in 1983.[63] MEEP expanded, without controversy, from 26 pilot school sites in 1984 to 593 (244 districts) in the 1991-92 school year.[64]

The state's six major educational groups, the Minnesota Federation of Teachers, the Minnesota Education Association, the Minnesota Elementary Principals' Association, the Minnesota Association of Secondary School Principals, the Minnesota Administrators and Supervisors' Association, and the Minnesota School Boards' Association all supported MEEP because it was a pilot program that would shift more control from the state to the local school district and the schools themselves. A shift in authority would augment local control of the schools rather than diminish it. As a result of the state's incremental approach to School-Based Management, groups external to the system did not coalesce around this one program to support or oppose it.

In addition, "Access" outlined a Choice initiative in the public school system that became the most controversial aspect of the governor's plan. The attention of reformers, educators and policymakers focused on this aspect of the governor's program largely because Public School Choice would shift authority and control away from the local school districts to the students themselves. Under the Perpich proposal, students between the ages of 5 and 18 could attend public school in other districts, as long as the receiving district had room.

The Open Enrollment program, Perpich argued, would allow market forces to work on Minnesota's educational system by giving families the power to select schools. Through competition each school would be forced to create its own distinctive environment -- a kind of product differentiation -- in order to attract and retain students. If parents could select their child's school, they would become more involved in the schools, and demand a better quality of education.

Members of the governor's staff, however, were naively optimistic about the reception of Perpich's plan in the state legislature largely because they avoided two potential confrontations with state lawmakers. The first controversy would have centered on appropriations for the program. The new program would cost virtually nothing. Perpich requested state lawmakers to appropriate $50,000 for the transportation of low-income children during each biennium.

Secondly, Perpich did not adopt the Minnesota Business Partnership and Citizens League recommendation to include both public and private schools in his Choice plan. Perpich confined School Choice to the public schools. Because of this provision, the governor's proposal evaded a head-on confrontation on the public/private issue that had stymied so many voucher plans at the federal and other state levels.

Despite the ability of the governor to sidestep these potentially explosive issues, the ensuing debate on School Choice divided and enraged education groups. The Minnesota Association of Secondary School Principals (MASSP) publicly lined up with supporters of the plan. When the MASSP Board of Directors decided to support Open Enrollment, several members quit the organization in protest. Despite the dissension within their organization, MASSP elected not to join the other education associations in resisting the legislation largely because they wanted to change the public's perception that they would be an education group unwilling to consider changes that might be initiated outside the education community.[65]

The same was true for the other principals union, The Minnesota Elementary School Principals' Association (MESPA). The Association did not support Perpich's plan outright. Instead, to minimize the amount of dissent within their own organization, the Board of Directors gave Open Enrollment its tacit approval by not opposing it in 1985.

Open Enrollment had initially been a concern in the cities of Minneapolis, St. Paul and Duluth when the Education Committees of both the House and Senate were debating the legislation. But the issue of desegregation quieted almost all of the opposition from those locations. Larry Harris, the director of legislation and community relations for the Minneapolis Public School system, raised the issue of desegregation in the cities with Representative Ken Nelson. Nelson, a member of the Minneapolis delegation to the state legislature, worked with Harris and other representatives from the various city school systems to make sure there was a clause in the bill that would keep intact desegregation plans.

By 1985 and after 12 years of court-ordered desegregation, the school systems in all three cities remained under a system of state monitoring. For his efforts to protect desegregation, numerous Choice proponents who perceived any limit on the proposal as interfering with the intent of the policy criticized Harris. According to Harris, some people perceived the city delegation "as . . . opposed to Open Enrollment. In reality, we were much more worried about survival than Open Enrollment."[66] The desegregation amendment would limit the transfer of students of color into the city and white students out of the cities' schools. The inclusion of this amendment in the Open Enrollment bill made School Choice a non-issue to the school systems of Minneapolis, St. Paul and Duluth.

Because of the desegregation provision, the Minnesota Federation of Teachers did not strongly oppose Open Enrollment. For this teachers' union, Choice would have a minimal impact because most of their members taught in the Twin Cities.[67] The MFT is the exclusive bargaining agent in 60 school districts, mostly in the large cities and the metropolitan area surrounding the cities. Although the MFT joined the MEA in its initial resistance to the legislation, its leaders subsequently offered to endorse a pilot testing of the Choice idea in a few districts.[68]

Other education organizations located in the cities took positions on School Choice similar to that of the MFT. The Minneapolis Citizens Committee on Public Education and the Association of Metropolitan School Districts, two organizations that normally address issues facing the city schools, did not take positions on School Choice. Although the Minnesota Association of School Administrators (MASA) objected to the plan, the strongest opposition came from the Minnesota Education Association (MEA), which represents more than 80 percent of the state's teachers, most of them in suburban and rural districts, and the Minnesota School Boards Association (MSBA).[69] Teachers feared that Public School Choice would mean a loss of jobs for MEA members. School board members, on the other hand, viewed Open Enrollment as an unnecessary and unwarranted erosion of local control. Local control stems from each school district governed by a six or seven member school board. Each member is elected to three year terms.[70]

Moreover, both associations saw open enrollment as a threat to small, especially rural, school districts. Teachers as well as local school board members feared that Public School Choice would force these districts to combine with others -- or consolidate -- in order to remain competitive under the Open Enrollment program.[71]

Consolidation was not a new issue. For many years, the state legislature debated the criteria which would yield an optimum number of school districts. Minnesota has an unusually large number of school districts. In 1985, there were 435. The school districts vary in size from 89 to 38,742 students.[72] The smallest of them are generally the most expensive to run, and despite their high costs, they are sometimes unable to offer courses that students must take to enter the University of Minnesota. But school consolidation plans caused furors during the 1960s and 1970s, as small towns vehemently protested the proposed death of their local institutions, fearing that when their school closed down, their town would die.[73]

For these reasons, the 1985 Choice proposal caused a falling out between the governor and two groups he normally considered allies, the School Boards' Association and the teachers' unions. Perpich won strong support during the 1982 election from both education organizations. Responding to the opposition of the MEA and other education organizations that lobbied against Open Enrollment, the governor announced that he would not seek or accept their endorsements when he expected to run for re-election in 1986.

The 1985 Legislative Session

To overcome the opposition of his former allies, Perpich and Education Commissioner Ruth Randall attempted to mobilize grass-roots support for School Choice after the proposal went to the state legislature in 1985. Together they traveled to school districts in different parts of the state over a four-month period to speak about Choice at school assemblies and citizen meetings. At each speaking engagement, the local print and broadcast media interviewed the governor.[74] In addition, Perpich wrote a letter to 160 superintendents in the state identified as running superior school districts. The governor challenged them to join the Choice program. He argued that if their districts were indeed superior and meeting the needs of students, then there was little chance students would choose other schools in other districts.[75]

In response to Perpich and Randall's statewide campaign, the MEA began their own crusade to defeat School Choice. The MEA Executive Director, Marty Zims, called Open Enrollment a way to cut costs and argued that Perpich and Randall were attacking the public school system in America.[76] Zims contended that a public school system should offer everything to everyone in every school district.[77] To counter Perpich's statewide campaign for Open Enrollment, Zims had the MEA produce a six-minute videotape attacking the idea and distributed copies of it to 40 television stations in Minnesota and surrounding states. The MEA videotape called the idea "ridiculous. . unworkable" and predicted that it "would create chaos in the schools."[78] The tape voiced the MEA concerns that Choice would benefit rich children and fail to address the needs of the disabled. It also charged that school systems would engage in a variety of educationally irrelevant tactics to entice students to enroll in their schools such as using pretty cheerleaders as recruitment attractions.[79]

The Minnesota Education Association largely succeeded in its effort to defeat Public School Choice. When "Access" went to the state legislature in 1985, House Majority Leader Conni Levi delivered the support of her Republican colleagues, but State Senator Tom Nelson was unable to deliver the support of the Democrats. Although Nelson, a respected Minnesota Education Association member, supported the governor's initiatives, the education community's opposition to the Perpich proposal remained insurmountable in the Senate. Despite an emotional speech by Nelson in support of School Choice, the education lobbying groups succeeded in removing Open Enrollment from the Perpich bill in conference committee by one vote, fourteen to thirteen, on a motion proposed by Representative Leonard Price, a social studies teacher and a member of the MEA's board of directors.[80]

Post-secondary Options, however, was the one Choice element of the Perpich package that survived the 1985 legislative battle. Post-secondary Options was an expansion of the 1980 Levi law. Perpich renamed the program and wanted it to continue as a state-mandated plan instead of a district by district program. In addition, Post-secondary Options would allow juniors and seniors to attend colleges and vocational schools, with state funds going toward their college courses and paying for tuition, lab and book fees.

Post-secondary Options survived the legislative battle for two reasons. First, the program was simply a refinement of an established policy, the Levi law. Second, Post-secondary Options escaped scrutiny in the legislative battle because most of the public's attention focused on the Open Enrollment provision of Governor Perpich's plan. For example, although the Minnesota Education Association opposed Post-secondary Options, its defeat was less important to the organization than the rejection of Choice.[81] According to Levi, "Frankly I think that the major lobbying organizations were so intent on [defeating] the rest of the Choice legislation, that they did not realize the significance of the Post-secondary Options."[82]

In retrospect, it is remarkable that the state teachers' unions opposed an Open Enrollment plan that limited transfers to public schools, while simultaneously accepting legislation that allows state aid for public schools for use at private as well as public institutions of higher education -- a significant use of the voucher principle.[83] Once the program passed in the January 1985 session of the legislature, it was in operation by May 1985.

The Governor's Discussion Group

Following the acrimonious 1985 legislative session, Perpich invited Choice adversaries to join a new committee, the Governor's Discussion Group. The idea for the group came from Lani Kawimura, who Perpich promoted to Commissioner of State Planning in the beginning of that year. According to Kawimura, the purpose of the group was to put together a Choice proposal that would be acceptable to everyone, including Choice proponents and opponents.[84]

The Discussion Group would be a mechanism for reaching consensus on School Choice in Minnesota and help smooth out differences that might present threats to Perpich's proposals when he presented them again to the state legislature. The governor felt that Open Enrollment initially failed, in part, because it was not presented to the legislature with supporters as a united front. In fact, there were not many supporters who testified for Choice before the legislature. Barbara Zohn, the former resolutions chair for the Minnesota State Parent Teacher Association, represented the only education organization with an affirmative written position on Open Enrollment. There were, however, a lot of detractors, principally from the education establishment.

The Governor's Discussion Group began its deliberations with the governor's policy agenda, not a blank slate. Not only did it allow Perpich to define the issues for the group to address, but the Group's existence also tended to distract interest groups from lobbying the state legislature. The existence of the Discussion Group also allowed Perpich to defer commenting on controversial issues until the Group forwarded its recommendations.[85] In his instructions to the group, Perpich said he would propose to the legislature whatever the Governor's Discussion Group came up with but "there would be no end runs."[86] In other words, the governor would review proposals that had won the collective support of the Discussion Group. According to Kawimura, because Perpich would not meet with individual interest groups to discuss their position, the Group's participants were forced to hold serious deliberations about School Choice.[87]

The Group met for over 80 hours from August 1985 to December 1986 in order to prepare legislation for the January 1987 session. Commissioner Randall chaired the Group and ruled it by consensus, not majority rule, largely because it would have been unfair to give the same weight to the votes of individuals as to organizations that represented thousands of people. In many instances, consensus seemed an elusive goal that would not be easily attainable, but according to Commissioner Randall, "the longevity of the group helped bring about consensus."[88]

The group meetings became an open arena of policymaking accessible to anyone concerned about education or the School Choice issue. But Randall never publicly announced the creation of the Governor's Discussion Group and did not receive any press coverage. As a result, only the people and organizations initially involved in the 1985 legislative session knew about the Group's deliberations.

The Group included representatives from the governor's office such as Dan Loritz, Perpich's chief lobbyist, as well as numerous organizations concerned about the public schools. The Group, however, divided into two factions: a cross-section of community representatives who became restructuring proponents and members of the education associations who were against School Choice.

Restructuring advocates in the Discussion Group included the League of Women Voters and the Minnesota Parent Teacher Association. Most notable, however, were restructuring advocates such as Ted Kolderie from the Humphrey Institute. Kolderie, the former Citizens League director who began the organization's campaign for

Public Service Options, continued to support the idea of market competition for improving public services -- particularly the schools. Verne Johnson, a former Citizens League director and vice president at General Mills, along with the League's director, Curt Johnson, supported Kolderie's work in the Group. In addition, parents, students, superintendents, principals, counselors, teachers, and citizens supporting Choice came together in the organization, People for Better Schools, headed by a former teacher and analyst at the Humphrey Institute, Joe Nathan.

Kolderie, Verne Johnson, Curt Johnson and Nathan pushed hardest for Choice in the Discussion Group. Joining them in their support for Choice was the Brainpower Compact, a temporary alliance of organizations and individuals created to support the governor's initiatives. The organization had two primary purposes. The first was to make a case for the need for educational improvement in Minnesota in the Governor's Discussion Group. The second was to create a public relations program in concert with the Minnesota Business Partnership that would bring about a change in public attitudes toward Choice in the public schools.

In the meetings, former Republican Governor Al Quie generally spoke for the Brainpower Compact.[89]   Quie and Perpich had a begrudging respect for one another.   In the 1978 election, Quie defeated Perpich in the governor's race. By 1982, however, Quie had decided not to run again for the governor's office largely because the state was in a recession and re-election seemed improbable. Nevertheless, Quie came out in support of Perpich's Open Enrollment plan. Before he was Governor, Quie had been a congressman for 22 years and worked on a great deal of legislation in the area of special education. A capable politician, Quie became influential in the group's deliberations.   He took an active part in his former opponent's legislative agenda, because, as he told Perpich, he wanted to break any party line opposition to the legislation.[90]

Choice opponents also tried to band together into one organization. Despite being at odds on major policy questions, reflecting primarily the labor-management cleavage, leaders of education organizations met separately as the "6-M coalition," consisting of the Minnesota Federation of Teachers, the Minnesota Education Association, the Minnesota School Boards' Association, the Minnesota Association of School Administrators, the Minnesota Association of Secondary

School Principals, and the Minnesota Elementary School Principals' Association.

Between the fall of 1985 and the fall of 1987, the debate in the Governor's Discussion Group centered on what some observers and participants perceived as two competing approaches.[91] One approach, most explicitly advanced by the Minnesota School Boards' Association and the Minnesota Education Association as an alternative to Choice, would establish and enforce performance requirements for all Minnesota districts. Schools that performed poorly and could not meet these mandates would, as a last resort, be closed. This was the "standards and mandates approach."[92]

Restructuring advocates dismissed the standards and mandates approach and argued that it would only set minimums but not instill excellence. Those in support of Choice argued for an "opportunist" approach which would stress expanded autonomy for individual schools and professional teachers to generate educational improvements, with the loss of students being the consequence for schools and districts that did not improve.[93]

The 6-M coalition, however, was never united and never developed their own agenda to deflect the Choice initiative. The division among the education groups on the governor's panel helped the rest of the members of the Governor Discussion Group come up with a feasible Choice proposal. Quie and other proponents of Choice would meet privately with those representatives in order to build support for Choice which would eventually lead to a consensus in the group. Choice opponents were basically forced to switch tactics. Instead of trying to block the Choice proposal, they sought to place limitations or restrictions on the plan.

One restriction had to do with school athletic programs. Discussion Group members feared that non-academic athletic and performing arts programs might figure in the student choice of schools. It would be unlikely, Discussion Group members argued, that top performing athletes, for example, would choose to move from their schools. On the other hand, students who were unlikely to become members of a varsity team, might choose to move to another school where they had better prospects of making the varsity squad.

To combat the problem of recruiting athletes, Discussion Group members agreed to prohibit a student from playing competitive sports for a full academic year after transferring to a new school. In this way,

Choice proponents and opponents hoped to reduce the role of non-academic considerations in the transfer decisions of students.

But Choice purists, like Kolderie, argued that any limitation on the student's right to choose would limit the effectiveness of the reform. The idea was to expand the autonomy of Minnesota's schools to develop innovative and distinctive programs that would encourage parents and their children to exercise the Choice option that they had under the Open Enrollment program.

Kolderie also tried to fight against political compromises from changing the basis of a free Public School Choice system. The athletic provision, for example, had nothing to do with educational substance. Instead, it was a political compromise necessary so that the education establishment, in particular the Minnesota School Boards Association and the Minnesota Education Association, would not oppose statewide open enrollment or lobby legislators to stop a comprehensive system of Choice from being carried out in Minnesota. Despite the divisive and sometimes bitter debate in the Governor's Discussion Group, by the fall of 1987, two more political compromises that had little to do with educational improvement or the substance of the Choice program smoothed the way for the bill's passage in the state legislature. Both compromises placed restrictions on the Choice initiative.

The first made the participation of school districts voluntary for the first year of operation under the "K-12 Enrollment Options Program," thus winning the acquiescence of the School Boards' Association because it left school board members in control.[94] Local school boards would retain the right to decide whether or not their district would participate in the new program. Nearly one-third of the public school districts in the state enrolled in the first year of the program.[95]

The second compromise occurred when the bill reached the state senate. In conference committee the Senators held firm against the opposition from education lobbying groups, particularly the MEA, but agreed to delay implementation for schools below a certain size and provided small school districts -- those with less than one thousand students -- a second year's delay before participation in the Choice program became mandatory. The additional year, educators believed, would give teachers more time to create distinctive programs and academic offerings in the hope of holding on to their students and surviving competition with larger districts.

By 1990, the governor's Open Enrollment program became mandatory for all school districts. As a result of the state mandated plan, school districts would have the legal authority to transport students who lived in neighboring districts, even if those districts objected. Before 1990, students who switched schools had to provide their own transportation to the district's borders.

After the Group reached compromises on the Choice initiatives, the Governor's Discussion Group continued to meet to discuss educational improvement in Minnesota. But once the state legislature passed the Open Enrollment law, many of the major players, like Ruth Randall, Al Quie and representatives from the teachers' unions, left the group. The Brainpower Compact also folded. As a result, the Governor's Discussion Group gradually dissolved.

The Minnesota Open Enrollment Program Begins: An Evaluation of School Choice

Once enacted, the Open Enrollment programs did not have much effect on school enrollment or educational performance. The massive movements of students that the teachers and school board members feared did not in fact materialize. Fewer than one half of 1 percent of all students in the state changed districts under the Open Enrollment option in the 1989-1990 school year. That is a total of roughly 5,800 students out of a possible 690,000 students that could participate in the program.[96] As more school districts joined the choice program, many legislators and members of the education lobbying groups who initially opposed Choice became convinced that some of the problems initially envisioned would not arise.[97]

Participation in the Post-secondary Options program was also sparse. For example, out of a possible 107,000 juniors and seniors enrolled in high schools, only 6,500 participated in the 1990 school year. However, participation in the Post-secondary Options program increased from 7 percent in 1991-1992 school year to 10 percent by 1993-1994.[98] Even though an increasing number of students enrolled in the program, overall participation in the program is meager at best, because Post-secondary Options had been in existence in one form or another for almost 15 years.

As a result of the sparse participation in the both programs, the schools were not forced to produce a diversity in learning environments in order to attract and retain their market shares.

Therefore, the claim that Open Enrollment stimulates schools and school districts to change or improve their programming to meet the demands of consumers remains in question. To begin with, after the first year of Open Enrollment, most district personnel viewed the program as having no impact on variables that might be associated with school improvement or educational reform initiatives, even in districts that gained or lost the most students. Administrators in those districts tended to comment that little had changed as a result; some added a course or two, but none had restructured their educational programs.[99]

Some evidence suggests that the program may motivate administrators of districts that lose students to strive to improve their school program. Other evidence, however, suggests that Open Enrollment is not the causative factor in program improvement, at least in the view of the administrators surveyed by a Department of Education study in 1992 and 1993.[100] Moreover, it is difficult to say with certainty if Open Enrollment stimulated any improvement largely because data collection has been difficult. Many districts are either unwilling or unable (due to record keeping practices) to provide information on Open Enrollment participants. Even worse, the state Department of Education does not track the progress of the programs, does not issue reports, nor does it publish numbers concerning the movement of students. According to Barbara Zohn at the state department of education Office of Alternative Programs "We believe that numbers do not tell the whole story."[101]

Second, most student transfers continued to occur for reasons of convenience -- the same reason for which they had taken place under the 1979 Transfer Agreement.[102] In general, although academic considerations dominated the selection of a particular school, the school's proximity to the student's home was a major factor for transferring.[103] In particular, suburban parents and low-income parents in all types of communities cited proximity to home as the most important factor in their decision.[104]

Third, school improvement has not come about as a result of increased involvement on the part of parents. Advocates of Open Enrollment argued that when parents can choose a school for their children, they are more likely to become involved in their child's education. This was not the case in Minnesota. The majority of school administrators surveyed did not observe any impact on levels of parent participation as a result of Open Enrollment.[105]

Finally, in some districts where Open Enrollment should, in theory, stimulate improvement, because of the loss of students, it forced actions such as staff layoffs and the cancellation of programs or services. In a few cases, administrators said Open Enrollment caused or hastened the district's closing.[106] For example, although the rapid consolidation of districts did not occur, as originally feared by teachers and school board members, there was some consolidation of school districts as the program continued. By 1994, there were 420 operating school districts, as opposed to 438 ten years earlier.[107]

A Further Refinement of the Exit Option:
The Introduction of Charter Schools in the Reform Debate

Open Enrollment was a structural reform that the Minnesota Business Partnership, the Citizens League, Governor Perpich and other participants in the education reform debate hoped would bring about fundamental change at minimal cost. When it failed to produce the improvements anticipated by its supporters, the attention of reformers shifted from Open Enrollment to the substance of school programs.

Charter Schools were one way to do address the substance of school programs.[108] They entered Minnesota's reform debate when Albert Shanker, president of the American Federation of Teachers, gave a speech in April 1988 at the National Press Club in Washington, D.C. Shanker warned that education reform was not moving "fast enough." Teachers, Shanker argued, should create distinctive programs from which families could choose as a way to stimulate improvement in the education system.

The notion of giving teachers more authority to create distinctive programs was not new. In New York City's School District Four, a group of teachers in East Harlem has been creating new programs since the start of the 1980s. Prior to the teachers expanded involvement in the schools, many problems plagued the district during the mid-1970s, including poor attendance, a high dropout rate and low levels of student achievement. The predominantly Hispanic and African-American district ranked 32nd out of the city's 32 districts on standardized reading and mathematics tests.[109]

Student achievement levels, however, began to rise when a group of teachers, along with local leaders, started to channel their efforts to improve the schools. To begin with, alternative schools opened in the District. The first three schools opened in 1974; three more were added in 1975, two in 1976; and two in 1978. Among the options available to the district's students are the Isaac Newton School for Science and Mathematics, the Jose Feliciano Performing Arts School, and the East Harlem Maritime School.[110]

Secondly, teachers also began a program that would give them the authority to set up small schools-within-schools where they would have more control over the curriculum and teaching techniques. Although the schools remained under the district's supervision, the teachers were free to begin new schools, which would, for example, take up only a single floor of a traditional school building. In this new environment for learning, students, parents and teachers become well acquainted with one another. By 1985 the district had 23 programs.

Under the direction of Sy Fliegel, the district's former deputy superintendent, the poverty-ridden district rose to 15th on standardized tests in the city, competing with richer, predominantly white districts. By the late 1980s close to 90 percent of the district's students finished high school.

The Charter Schools proposal shared several characteristics with the school reforms in East Harlem -- notably enhanced autonomy and distinctive programs. But a theoretical connection between the East Harlem program and Charter Schools did not enter the reform debate in Minnesota largely because policy analysts identified the East Harlem effort as a School Choice program, calling it "the most celebrated example of choice in the country."[111] East Harlem parents could select which school their child would attend. Charter Schools, on the other hand, started in Minnesota primarily as a means for giving teachers greater control and authority, not parents.

Following the Shanker speech, the idea of the Charter School became immensely appealing to a number of Minnesota education reformers, particularly Ted Kolderie and Joe Nathan. The Citizens League, however, used Shanker's recommendations as the basis for its Charter School report. Charter Schools, the Citizens League argued, would provide teachers with the necessary mechanism to develop better ways of teaching, better programs, and in the long run, provide high quality learning opportunities for more students.[112] Specifically, the League called for the establishment of joint committees of teachers, administrators, and community members to govern and plan the Charter Schools system of governance. The teachers' unions would appoint the teacher members, the school boards would have the authority to appoint the management representatives, and parent/community organizations would appoint the community representatives.[113]

Teachers' unions were receptive to the League's recommendation for Charter Schools. The Minnesota Education Association, which had initially opposed Governor Perpich's Open Enrollment proposals, saw the Charter School as a vehicle for achieving "teacher empowerment," one of its long-standing objectives. In 1989 the vice president of the Minnesota Education Association and the president of the Minneapolis Federation of Teachers wrote a report supporting the Charter School proposal. Charter Schools, the unions argued, would finally provide two essential ingredients needed to stimulate educational improvement -- adequate resources and local autonomy.

On June 4, 1991, a new Minnesota governor, Arne Carlson, signed a law allowing school boards to sponsor Charter Schools, with no more than two in any one district and a limit of eight in the entire state. The Charter Schools legislation allows groups of teachers to set up "totally autonomous" schools of Choice within existing school buildings with the right to decide on the curriculum, the allocation of funds, and the hiring and retention of staff. Minnesota's charter schools must be nonprofit and nonsectarian.

Charter School purists such as Kolderie and Nathan, however, quarreled with two of the requirements in the new law: (1) there is no way for teachers to appeal if school boards reject their charter school application, and (2) only licensed teachers, not parents or community members, can start a school. These provisions, however, were compromises needed to build a majority in the state legislature for the Charter Schools bill. The original Minnesota bill would have enabled the state Board of Education to grant charters directly to schools, circumventing school districts. But strong opposition from the two state teachers' unions and the Minnesota State School Boards, eliminated that provision.

Some educators, however, opposed the Charter School law even with its compromises. They argued that it was a back-door means to introduce private school vouchers. Charter School legislation did in fact make it possible for previously private schools to gain access to public funds. The Bluffview Montessori School in Winona, Minnesota, provides one example. The school's principal, Michael Dorer, proposed that the Montessori be available to any community child, even if the family could not afford the $1,600 tuition. Almost 1,200 Winona residents agreed with Dorer. They signed a petition supporting the private school's proposal to stop charging tuition and become a public school under the law. In November 1992, the Winona School Board voted to support that change, making Bluffview the nation's first Charter School.[114]

Minnesota's Charter Schools, such as the Bluffview Montessori School, may be free to break new educational ground, but their independence also means several problems for the new schools. Schools that have opened have met with poor funding levels, bitter relations with school board members, and transportation problems. These problems have occurred because Charter Schools require extensive planning in both education and operation. While teachers tended to concentrate on curriculum and other educational aspects of planning, opening a school has all the funding, maintenance and administrative needs of a business. For example, the absence of start-up funding makes the establishment of Charter Schools difficult and low appropriations have all but halted the growth of Charter Schools across the state.[115] The original charter bill authorized the creation of eight schools. By 1993, the legislature approved 20. By 1994, however, there were only 14 Charter Schools operating. Although the new schools receive state per-pupil aid just like other schools, they receive no additional money to open, rent or maintain buildings. Because of funding problems, some schools paid their teachers $20,000 a year to start, regardless of experience. Even worse, several schools opened with a shortage of desks, chairs and books.[116]

The teachers have also had little support for their efforts in educational innovation, particularly from the local school boards where relations with members continue to be a problem. Many school board members remain concerned that the new schools would take away pupils and, therefore, funding from their school districts. Additionally, while they had few concerns about the educational aspects of the new schools, they worried that the schools might create liability problems for districts or skim off the best students. Such concerns are one reason school boards refused to sponsor 7 of the 21 charter school proposals presented to them.[117]

School boards have, however, approved proposals that target specific populations, particularly populations that include at-risk pupils, special education pupils or drop-outs. In fact, half the schools served special populations. These are students that districts often find difficult or expensive to educate.[118]

Finally, the transportation arrangement has caused some frustration for both the Charter Schools and the districts responsible for transportation. Current law requires that the school districts that have Charter Schools provide transportation for students who live in the district and attend the school. The district of residence then receives transportation revenue for the resident Charter School pupils. With this arrangement, the Charter Schools are often forced to coordinate their calendars and starting times to fit the district's transportation schedule, making it difficult to structure anything but a traditional school day and year.

Although fourteen schools make little difference in a state with more than 700,000 students, the popularity of Charter Schools has led to the adoption of legislation similar to Minnesota's in 18 other states. Some, like Iowa and Arkansas, where Public School Choice was already operating, have adopted Charter Schools. Other states with Charter Schools include Alaska, Arizona, California, Colorado, Delaware, Florida, Georgia, Hawaii, Kansas, Louisiana, Massachusetts, Michigan, New Hampshire, New Mexico, Rhode Island, Texas, Wisconsin and Wyoming. A 1995 survey, conducted by the Education Commission of the States in Colorado and the Center for School Change at the University of Minnesota, counted 200 Charter Schools nationwide.[119]

The acceptance of Charter Schools may stem, in part, because the schools illustrate a central component of the exit option as a recovery mechanism for an organization that is in a state of decline. Mechanisms for recovery, exit and voice, are not mutually exclusive, and in fact, the two mechanisms can strengthen one another, particularly in the case of the public schools. The public schools can perfect the exit option while at the same time working to improve the voice option. As principals and teachers make decisions over what happens in their schools, the more the public expresses interest in having a choice over which school their child might attend. Hence, the two principles have become increasingly interrelated.

In the case of the public schools, many would argue that there can be no meaningful School Choice programs unless School-Based Management is in place. Without a voice mechanism inside an institution, exit is ineffective in accomplishing change. The reverse may also be true. The system could benefit from an increase in the use of exit, as a way of making voice more effective.

Conclusion: The Future of Choice

The schools respond to political demands and the main benefit of Open Enrollment was that it allowed politicians to present themselves as reformers without the need for a new set of appropriations for public education. In fact, in the areas with the highest levels of academic decline and disadvantaged students, the Twin Cities of St. Paul and Minneapolis, where the need for reform was the greatest, the School Choice program was not available to the majority of students because the movement of students would adversely affect desegregation efforts. In general, education for the disadvantaged is extremely expensive and the fraction of children that were educationally disadvantaged increased in the 1980s. The increasing number and proportion of disadvantaged students have a significant effect on school budgets, because educating these students costs more than educating students in regular programs -- on an average 2.3 times what was spent for regular students in the 1985-1986 school year.[120]

In the rest of the state, Public School Choice is not likely to become a significant engine for improving school quality. Less than 2 percent of the state's school population took advantage of the program in 1993-1994 school year. Even worse, students continued to participate in the program for reasons of convenience, not education.

Public School Choice has had an impact on education because it represents a fundamental change in the definition of public education in America. The School Choice initiatives in Minnesota attempted to set up schools that were autonomous and distinctive and in many cases served non-academic interests. Expanded autonomy, reformers hoped, would encourage the schools to develop distinctive programs -- to discover their niches in the education market -- in order to attract students. Choice, which sought to create different educational experiences, brought a new question of product differentiation into the reform debate: that of the needs of students, i.e., better education, stronger curriculum, versus their less academic desires, i.e., better varsity teams, going to school with friends, certain music or art programs. Opponents of the plan argued that such a system of public education might not necessarily further the quality of education by expanding opportunities in education. Although Public School Choice programs have yet to threaten the hegemony of the public schools, based on Minnesota's experience reform efforts in the future will continue to rely on the further definitions of the exit option in the hope of achieving inexpensive and systemic reform.

Notes

[1]   Chubb and Moe.

[2]   See Linda Darling-Hammond, and Shelia Nataraj Kirby *Tuition Tax Deductions and Parent School Choice*, 22.

[3]   Paul Berman, *The Minnesota Plan: The Design of a New Education System* One (November 1984) (Berkeley: Berman Weiler and Associates). See also Henig, 161.

[4]   Royce Hanson, *Tribune of the People*. (Minneapolis: University of Minnesota Press, 1989), 1989.

[5]   Darling-Hammond and Kirby, 24.

[6]   All of these services are made available under the "child benefit" theory found by the courts as a means of aiding non-public schools, Darling Hammond and Kirby, 24.

[7]   Betty Malen, "Enacting Tuition Tax Credit Deduction Statutes in Minnesota" *Journal of Education Finance*, 11, (Summer 1985): 13.

[8]   Minnesota's tax deduction policy, upheld by the U.S. Supreme Court in *Muller v. Allen*, was the first state policy subsidizing private school tuition costs to pass judicial review through all levels of the court system. In a 5-4 decision the Court upheld the tax deductions for parents of public as well as private (including denominational) schools, a critical element of its constitutionality.

[9]   "Table 58. - Enrollment, Teachers, and High School Graduates in Private and Elementary and Secondary Schools, by State: Fall 1980 and 1979-1980." *Education Digest*, 69. "Table 41-Enrollment in Public Elementary and Secondary Schools by Grade and State: Fall 1988." *Education Digest*, 54. "Table 39 - Enrollment in Public Elementary and Secondary Schools, by Level and State: Fall 1980 to Fall 1990."

[10]   About 95 percent of those children were in religious schools, mostly Catholic and Lutheran. See Betty Malen, 13.

[11]   Director for Open Enrollment, Minneapolis Public Schools, Richard Sandhofer, interview by Author, 4 September 1992, tape recording.

[12]   Minnesota was not the only state that permitted transfers between public school districts. For example, Utah has had a general statute statement since 1946 that permits students to go from one district to another as long as the student had consent from both districts. New Mexico and Idaho have also permitted students to transfer to neighboring districts.

[13] Former Republican Majority Leader, Minnesota House of Representatives, Conni Levi, 1979-1986, interview by Author, 14 September 1992, tape recording.

[14] ibid.

[15] National Center for Education Statistics, "Table 128. -Profile of Scholastic Aptitude Test Takers: 1989-1990." *Digest of Education Statistics 1991,* (Washington: Government Printing Office, 1991), 126.

[16] National Center for Education Statistics, "Table 129. American College Testing Score Average, by sex: 1969-70 to 1988-89." *Digest of Education Statistics 1991,* (Washington: Government Printing Office, 1991), 127.

[17] National Center for Education Statistics, "Table 128. -Profile of Scholastic Aptitude Test Takers: 1989-1990." *Digest of Education Statistics 1991,* (Washington: Government Printing Office, 1991), 126.

[18] *Education Digest,* 127.

[19] *Education Digest,* 126.

[20] The Minnesota Business Partnership, *An Education Agenda for Minnesota: The Challenge to our Communities and Schools.* (Minneapolis: The Minnesota Business Partnership, 1991), 5.

[21] The Citizens League. *Linking A Commitment to Desegregation with Choices for Quality Schools.* (Minneapolis: The Citizens League, 1979), 1.

[22] See Janie E. Funkhouser & K.W. Colopy, *Minnesota's Open Enrollment Option: Impacts on School Districts,* (Washington: U.S. Department of Education, 1994): 5-13.

[23] In real numbers, the school age population decreased from 63,761 to 45,610. See *Education Digest,* 126.

[24] Minority encompasses much more in Minnesota than persons identified as African-American. In the suburbs, Asians are the dominant minority. Native Americans are the second largest minority group in the state of Minnesota. Statewide only a plurality, not a majority of minority pupils in public schools, is black. In the central cities, however, blacks make up a majority of minorities. See "Enrollment in Public Elementary and Secondary Schools, by Race or Ethnicity and State: Fall 1986 and fall 1989" *Education Digest,* 58.

[25] The Citizens League. *Chartered Schools=Choices for Educators + Quality for All Students.* (Minneapolis: The Citizens League, 1988), 3.

[26] Pat Doyle, 1.

[27] The Citizens League. *Rebuilding Education To Make it Work.* Minneapolis: The Citizens League, 1978, 32.

[28] The Citizens League, 32.

[29] The Congressional Budget Office, Congressional Budget Office Study, *The Federal Role in Improving Elementary and Secondary Education.* (Washington, D.C.: Government Printing Office, 1983) xiv.

[30] The Citizens League, 32.

[31] Mazzoni, and Roberts, N.C., and King, P.J. "The Process of Public Policy Innovation." Eds. A.H. Van de Ven, H.L. Angle & M.S. Poole, *Research on the Management of Innovation.* (New York: Harper and Row), 303.

[32] Mazzoni, Tim. L. "Bureaucratic Influence in the Formation of State School Policy." 16, *Planning and Changing* (Summer 1985): 77-78.

[33] Hanson, 200.

[34] Paul Berman, Rick Clugston, "A Tale of Two States, the Business Community and Education Reform in California and Minnesota" in *American Business and the Public Schools* 121-149.

[35] Berman and Clugston, 133.

[36] Berman, *The Minnesota Plan: The Design of a New Education System.*

[37] Sandra Peddie and Aaron Kahn "Minnesota Gets Fired Up For the Task." *St. Paul Pioneer Press* 3 March 1985, 1.

[38] The Citizens League, *Linking A Commitment to Desegregation with Choices for Quality Schools.* (Minneapolis: The Citizens League, 1979) 3.

[39] ibid.

[40] Darling-Hammond and Kirby, 22.

[41] The Citizens League, 47.

[42] The Citizens League, *Issues of the 80's: Enlarging Our Capacity to Adapt* (Minneapolis: The Citizen League, 1980).

[43] See Matthew Crenson, "Urban Bureaucracy in Urban Politics: Notes Toward A Development Theory."

[44] Program Officer, The McKnight Foundation, Marina Lyon, Former Citizen League Member 1984-1990, interview by Author, 11 September 1992, tape recording. Finance Director, The Citizens League, Phil Jenni, interview by Author, 24 August 1992, tape recording.

[45] Citizens League, 16.

[46] Former Commissioner of Minnesota State Planning Agency, Lani Kawimura, interview by Author, 9 September 1992. tape recording.

[47] Berman and Clugston, 132.

[48] Bruce Benidt "Much of Minnesota's Brainpower is Being Exercised Elsewhere." *Minneapolis Star and Tribune*, 19 July 1987.

[49] Susan McManus, "Linking State Employment and Training and Economic Development Programs: A 20 State Analysis," *Public Administration Review.* (November/December 1986), 21.

[50] Michele Cook, "At Hometown School, Perpich OK's Open Plan." *St. Paul Pioneer Press-Dispatch*, 7 May 1988.

[51] Tim Mazzoni, 77-78.

[52] Lani Kawimura, interview by Author.

[53] Former Minnesota State Commissioner of Education, Ruth Randall, interview by Author, 15 September 1992, tape recording.

[54] Tim L. Mazzoni "Bureaucratic Influence in the Formation of State School Policy." *Planning and Changing* 16, (Summer 1985): 71.

[55] C.M. Achilles, W.H. Payne and Z. Lansford. "Strong State-Level Leadership for Education Reform: Tennessee's Example. *Peabody Journal of Education*: 28.

[56] Hanson, 157.

[57] Conni Levi, interview by Author.

[58] ibid.

[59] Perpich subsequently appointed Nelson Commissioner of Education in 1989.

[60] Minnesota Senate Education Committee, Administrator, Sue Hanaker, interview by Author, 18 September 1992, tape recording.

[61] Ted Kolderie, interview by Author.

[62] Ruth Randall and Keith Geiger, *School Choice: Issues and Answers*. (Bloomington: National Education Service, 1991), 154.

[63] A 1991 Amendment expanded MEEP to include Early Childhood Family Education Programs (ECFE) and post secondary teacher preparation.

[64] Barry Sullivan "Draft: Selected Education Reforms and Policy Trends Since 1983." (Minneapolis: Minnesota Government Relations Office, 1992).

[65] Executive Director Minnesota Association of Secondary School Principals (MASSP), Robert St. Clair, interview by Author, September 3, 1992, tape recording.

[66] Former Director of Legislation and Community Affairs 1967-1988, Minneapolis Public Schools, Larry Harris, interview by Author, 8 September 1992, tape recording.

[67] National Education Association. Internal Document. "Listing of AFT Local Affiliates Where they Represent Employees in Bargaining." September 17, 1992: 19.

[68] Tim L. Mazzoni. "State Policymaking and Public School Choice in Minnesota, from Confrontation to Compromise." *Journal of Education* 63, (1986): 48.

[69] "Minnesota's Experiment with Choice Could Be a Wave of the Future." *National Journal* 19 October 1985: 2370-2371.

[70] Director of Legislative Services, Minnesota School Boards Association Carl Johnson, interview by Author, 3 September 1992, tape recording.

[71] Nathan, 304.

[72] Over 70 percent of students are educated in only 20 percent of the school districts.

[73] Bruce Orwall "Plan Would Merge 185 Minnesota School Districts." *St. Paul Pioneer Press-Dispatch* February 8, 1991.

[74]   Randall and Geiger, 42.

[75]   Randall and Geiger, 54.

[76]   The Humphrey Institute, University of Minnesota, Education Consultant, Joe Nathan, interview by Author, 10 September 1992, tape Recording.

[77]   Toch, 251.

[78]   Joe Nathan, "State's Attitudes Changing Over School Choice." *Saint Paul Pioneer Press* August 24, 1992.

[79]   Toch, 251.

[80]   See Toch, 251. Price subsequently became a Minnesota State Senator in 1990.

[81]   Former Minnesota Commissioner of Education Eugene Mammingay, 1990-1993, Minnesota Education Association Director of Governmental Relations, 1987-1990, Chief Lobbyist, Minnesota Education Association, 1974-1984, interview by Author, 30 September 1992, tape recording.

[82]   Conni Levi, interview by Author.

[83]   See also Lieberman, 191. In 1986 the Minnesota Federation of Teachers filed suit challenging the legality of the Post Secondary Options based on the legal principal of separation of church and state (See *Minnesota Federation of Teachers v. Department of Education, State of Minnesota 1986.*) Following several legal challenges, in which the state continued to prevail, the Minnesota State Supreme Court refused to hear an appeal filed by the Teachers Union following a Circuit Court decision which found that based on the Minnesota Constitution, the Post-Secondary Options program was constitutional.

[84]   Lani Kawimura, interview by Author.

[85]   Mazzoni, *Confrontation to Compromise*, 54.

[86]   Lani Kawimura, interview by Author.

[87]   ibid.

[88]   Ruth Randall, interview by Author.

[89]   Former Minnesota Governor, 1978-1982, Former Minnesota Congressman, 1956-1978, Speaker and Consultant, Al Quie, interview by Author, 15 September 1992, tape recording.

[90]   ibid.

[91]   Mazzoni, 55.

[92]   Mazzoni, 79.

[93]   Mazzoni, *Confrontation to Compromise*, 44.

[94]   Director of Legislative Services, Minnesota School Boards' Association, Carl Johnson, interview by Author, 3 September 1992, tape recording.

[95]   More precisely, 95 of the state's 433 districts agreed to participate in the 1987-88 school year. See Joe Nathan and Wayne Jennings, *Access to*

Opportunity: Experiences of Minnesota Students in 4 Statewide School Choice Programs, 1989-1990. (Minneapolis: Center for School Change: Hubert H. Humphrey Institute of Public Affairs: University of Minnesota, 1990).

[96]   Minnesota State Department of Education. Unpublished figures.

[97]   Minnesota State Senator Ember Reichgott, interview by Author, 7 September 1992, tape recording.

[98]   In the 1991-1992 school year, a total of 7,467 juniors and seniors participated in the program, out of a possible 104,830. In the following school year, a total of 13,313 juniors and seniors participated in post-secondary enrollment options, out of a possible 107,047 students, roughly 8 percent. By school year 1993-1994, 15,400 students participated out of a possible 110,601. Minnesota State Department of Education. Unpublished figures.

[99]   Rubenstein, Hamar & Adelman used survey data collected from a census of Minnesota school districts, participating parents, and participating secondary school students during school year 1989-1990 to study the early effects of the program. *Minnesota's Open Enrollment* Prepared Under Contract by: Policy Students Associates, Inc. Washington, D.C. U.S. Department of Education. Office of Policy and Planning. 1992.

[100]   Kelly W. Colopy, H.C. Tarr, *Minnesota's Public School Choice Options* (Washington: U.S. Department of Education, 1994), 45.

[101]   Program Specialist, Alternative School Programs, Minnesota State Department of Education, Barbara Zohn, telephone conversation with Author, 17 February, 1995.

[102]   Nathan and Jennings. See also Clewell and Joy (1990), Maddus, (1990) and Bridge and Blackman (1978) provide evidence to support this argument. See Bridge, R.G. & Blackman, J. *A Study of Alternatives in American Education Volume IV: Family Choice in Schooling.* Santa Monica: The Rand Corporation: 1978. Clewell, B.C. & Joy, M.F. *Choice in Montclair New Jersey.* Princeton: Educational Testing Service Policy Information Center: January 1990. Maddus, J. "Parental choice of School: What parents think and do." *Review of Research in Education*, 16, 1990: 267-295.

[103]   Michael C. Rubenstein, R. Hamar & N. Adelman. *Minnesota's Open Enrollment Option*, (Washington: U.S. Department of Education, 1992), iv.

[104]   In 1990 and 1991, only 1 percent of Open enrollment use occurred in urban areas compared to 48 percent in suburban districts and 51 in rural districts. The racial/ethnic background of students applying to use the Open Enrollment Option generally reflects their statewide representation in the school-age population. In 1989-90, approximately 94 percent of students who applied to transfer under Open Enrollment reported their race/ethnicity as White, and the remaining 6 percent reported their race/ethnicity as African-American (1 percent), Hispanic (1 percent), Native American (2 percent) and Asian (2 percent). There was a slight migration of students from urban areas

into the suburban districts. Urban districts experienced a net loss of 250 students (roughly 7 percent of students using Open Enrollment), with students leaving St. Paul accounting for most of this loss. As a group, suburban districts experienced a net gain of 202 students. See Kelly W. Colopy & H.C. Tarr *Minnesota's Public School Choice Options*, (Washington: Department of Education, 1994).

[105]   Rubenstein, et. al., 52.

[106]   The findings of the Impact study were based on mail surveys of all the state's school districts and of families who submitted applications to have their children change districts beginning in September 1989. Impact. The results reported represent only the districts sampled -- districts experiencing more than the average amount of student movement as a result of Open Enrollment, rather than Minnesota school districts as a whole. See Janie E. Funkhouser & K.W. Colopy. *Minnesota's Open Enrollment Option: Impacts on School Districts.* (Washington: U.S. Department of Education, 1994), 56.

[107]   Colopy, et al., 23.

[108]   The idea first gained currency when a Massachusetts education consultant, Ray Budde, published a slim volume in 1988 entitled, *Education by Charter*.

[109]   Thomas McArdie "The Harlem School Revolution Parental Choice is Key to District's Turnaround." *Investor's Business Daily* (April 15, 1992), 18-19.

[110]   Henig, 111.

[111]   Jeffrey R. Henig, *Rethinking School Choice: Limits of the Market Metaphor.* (Princeton: Princeton University Press, 1994), 112.

[112]   The Citizens League, *Chartered Schools=Choice for Educators+Quality for All Students* (Minneapolis: The Citizens League, 1988), 21.

[113]   Citizens League, 21.

[114]   Quarterly Review of State Choice legislation, Washington, D.C.: Center for Choice in Education, U.S. Department of Education, February 1992.

[115]   Minnesota House of Representatives, House Research Department. *Minnesota Charter Schools: A Research Report*, (Minneapolis: December 1994).

[116]   Mary Jane Smetanka "Liberated Learning: Minnesota is First to Give Teachers, Parents the Right to Open Schools." *Minneapolis Star and Tribune* 26 May 1991.

[117]   Minnesota House of Representatives, House Research Department. *Minnesota Charter Schools: A Research Report*, (Minneapolis: December 1994).

[118]   Other general characteristics of charter schools that were operating by 1994 included three of the charters served elementary/middle school students,

two served grades K-12, one served secondary students. The schools had very small class sizes with student:teacher ratios ranging from 4:1 to 20:1. The schools received varying amounts of grant funding, ranging from none to $300,000.

[119] DeNeen L. Brown, "Plotting A New Course for Education." *The Washington Post,* 21 August 1995, 1(B).

[120] These characteristics include membership in some minority racial or ethnic group, a family whose income falls below the poverty line, limited proficiency in English, a learning disability, and a single-parent family. Each of these attributes is related to relatively poor performance in school -- lower test scores and higher dropout rates -- although the cause of the association is not always clear. See, *Federal Role in Improving Elementary and Secondary Education,* 22.

Chapter Four

School-Based Management Emerges in the Reform Debate: The Case of Baltimore City

While the Minnesota public school system suffered from a decline in quality, the Baltimore City Public Schools, on the other hand, suffered from genuine crisis. Like Minnesota, questions of accountability and effectiveness surrounded the day to day operations of Baltimore's public school system.

Although public policymaking in Minnesota started in the state house and in Baltimore at the municipal level, in both cases, restructuring proceeded from a political agenda, rather than an educational one. In Baltimore, restructuring took on a more political role when School Superintendent Alice G. Pinderhughes and the business community introduced the notion of moving the Baltimore City public schools from a centralized system to School-Based Management as a way to diminish the role of the central administration in educational policymaking. Other city organizations, like the Baltimore Teachers' Union eventually joined the restructuring effort. What follows is an examination of the crisis in the Baltimore City Public Schools and the emergence of School-Based Management in that city's education reform debate.

A Crisis in Education: The Baltimore City Public Schools

At the start of the 1980s, the Baltimore City public school system was widely reported as ineffective, undisciplined and dangerous.[1] Their reputation was not undeserved. National rankings help to underline the seriousness of Baltimore's school problems. For example, in 1983, Baltimore ranked next to last among the nation's 15 largest cities in the proportion of people in the 20-24 year old age category who had completed four years of high school.[2] The same was true as the decade progressed. By 1987, one-third of the city's population did not have a high school diploma.[3] The National Coalition of Advocates for Students found that of the nation's 100 largest school districts, Baltimore ranked ninth in suspensions, with an annual rate of close to 13 percent.[4]

Even worse, the U.S. Department of Education's Office of Civil Rights reported that of the nation's 100 largest school districts, Baltimore City ranked first in the percentage of students classified as learning disabled and first in the number of African-American students labeled as such.[5] By 1990, each day, over 17 percent of all of Baltimore's students that went to school were in special education classes.[6]

Two factors contributed to the crisis in the schools and helped speed the downward trend in student achievement. The first was a change in the city's spending priorities. The shift came in 1971 when the citizens of Baltimore elected a new Democratic mayor, William Donald Schaefer. Unlike Minnesota's Governor Rudy Perpich, Schaefer did not view education as an effective public policy instrument of economic development. Instead, from the start of his first administration, Schaefer moved the focus of city government away from providing services to residents. During his 17 years at City Hall, Schaefer concentrated his economic development efforts on the revitalization of the city's central business district and creating new attractions for tourists along with the hotels to house them and the restaurants to feed them.[7] By 1977, the Federal Urban Development Action Grant program delivered a total of more than $90 million to encourage the building of projects such as the Hyatt Regency Hotel and various downtown developments. By 1986, the downtown Inner Harbor, surrounded by office buildings, a National Aquarium, a World Trade Center, and luxury hotels, could boast of more tourists than Florida's Walt Disney World.[8]

City agencies, however, bore the burdens created by Schaefer's economic development strategy.   In order to finance city projects and maintain a good rating on the bond market, all city agencies received reduced budgets during the Schaefer administration.   While real expenditures on economic development rose 400 percent between 1974 and 1984, total municipal spending decreased by 20 percent.[9]

The Department of Education was one of the agencies whose budget contracted, even though the City Charter placed limits on the mayor's control over the appointment and budgetary processes in the field of education.   In an effort to insulate the school's budget from the political process, the City Charter gives a Board of School Commissioners the responsibility for overseeing the Baltimore City Public Schools.   The mayor selects the school board members and the City Council then confirms the appointment of the new members.   The nine-member Board then selects the Superintendent of Public Instruction to run the schools.   The superintendent is legally responsible only to the school board, and submits the annual budget to the commissioners, thereby limiting the mayor's control over the city's public education system.

Baltimore's mayors, however, have been able to influence the schools to a significant degree.   To begin with, Mayor Schaefer followed the practice of choosing school board members who were either lawyers or businessmen with little or no experience in education, but with established loyalty to the mayor.[10]   As a result the board appointed superintendents who would respect the mayor's budget demands.   One Superintendent in particular, Alice G. Pinderhughes, who presided over the schools from 1982-1987, never submitted a budget request to the board without first consulting Schaefer.[11]

Secondly, the mayor is able to move money around in the school budget.   The mayor has the authority to do this because the City Charter stipulates that the Board of School Commissioners must submit the school budget to the Board of Estimates which the mayor effectively controls.   The City Charter allows the mayor, who sits on the five member board, to make two appointments, giving him the majority support needed in the budgetary process.   Once the school commissioners submitted the budget to the board, the board determines final appropriations across four categories: (1) educational supplies (2) maintenance (3) administrative expenses, (4) miscellaneous.   The final disbursements can differ significantly from the appropriations requested by the superintendent and school commissioners once the mayor and his allies on the Board of Estimates have reviewed the budget submitted to them.[12]

The mayor's influence on the school budget had a significant impact on the city's expenditures for education. By the start of the 1980s low spending levels on the schools were seriously affecting educational quality. Significantly, with the highest local tax rate in all of the state's 24 subdivisions, Baltimore ranked 19th in expenditure per student. In the 1984 school year, Baltimore's spending level was $3,100 per student, far behind the state average of $3,670.[13] As a result of low spending levels, the city schools operated with a shortage of books, a shortage of teachers and low staffing levels in libraries and counseling offices. Eliminated from the school budget were enrichment programs, such as art and music.

Inadequate spending on the city's public schools also had a significant effect on the quality of instruction. The average salary in October of 1984 for all school-based instructional staff in the city was $27,202, while the average in surrounding Baltimore county was $32,923, over $5,700 more.[14] The gap in salaries hindered the Baltimore City Public School system's effort to recruit high quality teachers and also resulted in the growing loss of seasoned teachers to nearby counties where salaries were higher and working conditions were considered safer and more desirable. Although Baltimore City teachers have shorter work days and work years, which in some ways compensate for reduced pay, these reductions also adversely affect a predominantly disadvantaged student population which might benefit from more instruction.[15]

To a large degree, Schaefer was able to deflect much of the criticism for low levels of spending on the Baltimore City Public Schools. Schaefer argued that the problems of low spending levels resulted from inadequate state support. In 1971 during his first campaign for mayor, Schaefer called for greater state funding of schools leading "ultimately" to 100 percent of state financing for operating costs. In 1980, the city filed a lawsuit along with other poor Maryland subdivisions seeking to require equal expenditures per pupil across the state.

The Maryland Court of Appeals denied the existence of a constitutional principle requiring equal expenditure. Subsequently, Governor Harry R. Hughes appointed a commission under Benjamin Civiletti to look into the matter of state financing for public schools. The Civiletti Commission recommended increased state financing for education distributed so as to reduce inequalities among the state's 24 subdivisions. The commission's recommendation 1A, its most popular recommendation in an array of alternative proposals, mandated a formula by which the state would assume just under 40 percent of local school costs. Throughout his years as mayor, Schaefer's concentration on state funding arrangements allowed him to sidestep responsibility for under funding of the city's schools.

While the mayor pursued the city's lawsuit, the quality of the Baltimore Schools continued to deteriorate. Meanwhile the ongoing flight of the middle class from the city continued -- and further weakened both the city and its school system. This increase occurred even though Schaefer's economic development strategy for Baltimore included several programs to keep the middle class from fleeing the city. A comprehensive venture to attract and retain middle-class taxpayers began in the late 1970s with an urban homesteading program offering dilapidated homes for a dollar to people committed to renovating them. In addition, the city spent money to promote cultural attractions such as the Mechanic Theater, the Meyerhoff Symphony Hall and the Lyric Opera House. Despite efforts to keep the middle class from fleeing to nearby counties, the population of the city continued to decline. In 1960, the city's population was 939,000. In 1970, only 786,000 residents remained. In 1990, Baltimore had less than 749,000 residents.[16]

The residents who left the city were disproportionately white and affluent, and they moved to suburbs where property taxes were half as high as the city, and the schools were considered safer and better. In 1960 whites made up 65 percent of Baltimore's population. By 1985 whites comprised 39 percent of the city's population.[17] African-Americans, on the other hand, comprised 82 percent of the schools population.[18]

As the city's population contracted, it also became increasingly impoverished. In 1970 almost 43 percent of Baltimore's households fell into the "middle income" category of $15,000-$30,000 annually. That proportion fell to 29.4 percent in 1980. The city's median annual household income in 1985 was $16,700.[19] In contrast, the median income in the same year for the surrounding five counties exceeded $31,000, almost twice as high.[20] Despite the urban renewal efforts, Baltimore had become home to a large and growing segment of the region's dependent population. By 1987, more than 40,000 families were receiving welfare, the same as there were in 1971 before the city's renaissance, even though the population had fallen. Over 70 percent of the school system's students received some form of government aid.[21] The percentage of teenage pregnancies is the highest of any of the largest cities in the country.[22]   Baltimore had become one of the country's ten poorest cities.

Urban renewal in Baltimore also resulted in a massive structural change in the city's economy. As professional services expanded in the downtown area, manufacturing, retail, wholesale and civil service employment opportunities contracted. In the manufacturing sector, the steel industry declined. The Sparrows Point plant of Bethlehem steel, whose smokestacks had dominated the city's harbor for the first sixty years of this century, laid off thousands of employees. In 1950, 44 percent of Baltimore's jobs were in manufacturing. In the Baltimore region today, only 11 percent of the jobs in the city are in manufacturing.[23]

Other low skill jobs in the Baltimore area also contracted. Between 1970 and 1985 the wholesale and retail industries lost 17,000 and 12,000 jobs respectively. Although the number of jobs provided by state and city government grew by more than 20,000 during the 1970s, from 1980 to 1985, they decreased by more than 15,000.[24]

Despite the loss of jobs in several employment areas, total city employment remained virtually unchanged.[25]   Thousands of the jobs created in the white collar and service industries offset the decline in manufacturing, retail, wholesale and government employment. Medical, legal, consulting and architectural services expanded in the city, along with employment opportunities in finance, insurance and real estate industries.[26]

Although downtown economic development projects created employment opportunities between 1960 and 1980, the number of Baltimore City residents commuting to Baltimore City jobs actually dropped by 23 percent.[27]   By 1984, the Baltimore city unemployment stood at 7.6 percent, the highest unemployment rate in the state.[28]   In 1985, the labor force participation rate, or the proportion of persons 18 to 65 gainfully employed, was 57.8 percent for Baltimore City. The rate for the rest of the region was 67 percent.[29]

While unemployment in the city remained high by comparison to the surrounding suburban counties, the state and even the nation, more workers were commuting into Baltimore for employment then were commuting out. In particular, suburban to city commuting rates for residents of surrounding Anne Arundel and Baltimore counties increased rapidly. In 1960, only 25 percent of the county residents held jobs in Baltimore City. By 1980 the suburban to city commuters increased to 41 percent.[30]

For city officials and the business community, one of the greatest concerns was that Baltimore was losing business and potential growth to nearby counties. Computer-related and data processing jobs declined by more than a quarter in the city between 1977 and 1982. Business and financial institutions began to move data processing operations to less expensive sites in the suburbs and out of the state. Over a twenty year period ending in 1990, job creation was most significant in Baltimore (127,000), Anne Arundel (91,500) and Howard (57,100) counties. Baltimore City, on the other hand, lost more than 43,000 jobs during this period.[31] For the majority of residents in the greater Baltimore area, the surrounding suburbs have become increasingly attractive places to live and work. Between 1960 and 1980, the number of workers commuting from suburban homes to suburban jobs increased by more than 145 percent -- from 189,000 to 465,000.[32]

The low employment rates for city residents and the increase in commuting rates for non-city residents led the Greater Baltimore Committee, which represents the views of over 1,000 area business firms on economic development and public policy issues, to the conclusion that many city residents were without work because their skills were not as attractive to employers as those of residents in surrounding counties.[33]

The Impact of Interest Groups on Educational Policymaking

To advance their economic development objectives, the Greater Baltimore Committee turned its attention to the public schools. The declines in student achievement were beginning to have a profound effect on the city's economic well-being. Along with poorly trained workers, local companies started to encounter employee shortages. It became increasingly evident to local businesses that the city's public schools were inadequately preparing graduates to fill the jobs created by economic development policies. For example, on any given school day in Baltimore, at least 20 percent of the students are absent from school. Of those who managed to graduate from high school, fewer than a quarter went on to college.[34]

The reform movement gathered momentum when an alliance occurred between the Greater Baltimore Committee and Baltimoreans United in Leadership Development (BUILD), a predominantly African-American church-based organization. Many young African-Americans, BUILD leaders argued, were missing the benefits of economic development because they could not qualify for the new jobs created in Baltimore's growing service industry. For example, while the drop-out rate soared to 50 percent in 1983, between 1970 and 1984, the number of jobs in the Baltimore area requiring less than a high school degree declined by 46 percent. At the same time, jobs requiring at least two years of college increased by 56 percent.[35]

Collectively the Greater Baltimore Committee and BUILD would work to solve essentially the same problem: an inadequately prepared labor force that could not fill the jobs being created by economic development. The Greater Baltimore Committee wanted the public school system to graduate students that could participate in and help create a productive labor force. BUILD, on the other hand, wanted a guarantee that Baltimore's minorities would not miss the promising employment opportunities created by economic development.

The Greater Baltimore Committee and BUILD pushed education reform to the top of the city's agenda and set the direction of reform. For almost a decade, beginning in 1982, the Greater Baltimore Committee and BUILD pursued an anti-bureaucratic strategy in educational policymaking as a way to develop and strengthen the mechanisms of private sector voice in running the public schools. Eventually these two organizations would work together with Superintendent Alice G. Pinderhughes. The triparae arrangement would focus on decentralizing school programs. This strategy in turn would set the stage for the introduction of School-Based Management.

But Pinderhughes' successor, Superintendent Dr. Richard Hunter, would work to obstruct their efforts. Although private sector involvement in school policy increased as the decade progressed, it was the Baltimore Teachers' Union, an affiliate of the American Federation of Teachers, which successfully institutionalized the mechanism of voice in the city's troubled schools. During the 1980s in general, Baltimore teachers remained on the periphery of the reform movement and got much of the blame for poor pupil performance. Most of the programs proposed by private-sector groups ignored teachers' interests.

Irene Dandridge, at the time president of the Baltimore Teachers' Union for more than fifteen years, saw the direction that reform was taking in the city schools. Dandridge knew that the interest groups pressing their ideas on the superintendent would be receptive to a School-Based Management proposal because this reform would shift decisions away from the central office bureaucrats and down to the schools themselves. This downward shift in authority would in turn increase the role of teachers, parents and school-based staff by diminishing the role of the central education administrators. School-Based Management might also further the teachers collective interests.

By 1989, the Baltimore Teachers' Union succeeded in capturing the city's School-Based Management movement when they negotiated a contract provision that called for a joint committee of administrators and teachers to work out a restructuring plan for the schools. In preparing subsequent drafts of the plan, representatives from Baltimore's civic, parent and business organizations joined the restructuring committee.

The Reform Effort Begins:
The Greater Baltimore Committee and Schools

To members of the business community, low spending levels and middle class flight from the city to the surrounding suburbs were significant problems for the city's schools. From the business community's perspective, Mayor Schaefer was aggravating the city's education problems by his disengagement from the school system.

It was not until his fourth and final campaign for City Hall, however, that Schaefer was forced to address the problems in the city's schools. During his 1983 reelection campaign, Schaefer's Democratic opponent William H. Murphy, Jr., a former circuit court judge, began his quest to unseat Baltimore's popular mayor. Murphy, a member of the prominent Baltimore family which owns the *Afro-American* newspaper, forced the mayor to address one of the city's worst problems, the public schools. While campaigning, Murphy attacked Schaefer for the city's low spending levels on the schools. In addition to low spending levels, Murphy also attacked Schaefer for the conditions of Baltimore's public schools which, he asserted, were atrocious.[36]

On the campaign trail, Schaefer usually ignored Murphy's charges. While Murphy's campaign concentrated on the city's problems,

Schaefer's re-election strategy naturally highlighted his accomplishments. Schaefer cited the renovation of City Hall, the building of a convention center and Harborplace, and the $600 million federally funded Baltimore subway system as his administration's achievements.

Murphy's election strategy did not help him get elected to office. The citizens of Baltimore rejected Murphy's contentions and returned Schaefer to office in November of 1983. Although Murphy attempted to divide the electorate along racial lines, Schaefer succeeded in retaining majorities in both African-American and white precincts. The mayor also received majorities in rich, middle-income, and poor precincts.[37]

Significantly, Murphy failed to receive support from the African-American community. Minorities compromise more than 60 percent of Baltimore's population. Their support is necessary for a city-wide candidate to be elected. Schaefer received the endorsement of black ministers, civil rights leaders such as Clarence Mitchell, and elected African-American officials such as City Councilman Clarence "Du" Burns.

Schaefer won the support of the African-American community because neighborhood leaders could easily point to the projects the mayor delivered to their communities and constituents. They cited neighborhood projects such as recreation centers, new low-income housing and health clinics as accomplishments of the Schaefer administration which helped their constituents in particular. As a result of their support, Schaefer became the first four-term mayor in Baltimore.

With Schaefer's victory over Murphy, however, came some concessions to Baltimore's minority leaders. Although Clarence Mitchell's sons, State Senator Clarence Mitchell III and City Councilman Michael Mitchell, endorsed Schaefer, they withheld their support until they received commitments from the mayor on better schools, more jobs and increased minority development.[38] In exchange for their endorsement, the mayor promised to address the problems in the city's public schools.

Almost immediately following his victory in the general election, the mayor turned his attention to the schools. "Some people have accused me of being a cheerleader for our city," the Mayor remarked in his inaugural address, "I think it's time to be a cheerleader for the school system."[39] He urged Baltimoreans to join him. Citing the city's urban renewal as a measure of success, the Mayor said renewal had worked because Baltimore had begun to believe itself. The next step for the people and the mayor "was to believe in our school system."[40] Yet none of the proposals Mr. Schaefer announced during his inaugural speech included a budget increase for the city's education department or any dramatic proposals to address the problems of low student achievement. Instead, the Mayor asked business and community groups to contribute to solving the problems of the schools. He said he would push city business to contribute to a new fund, the Fund for Educational Excellence, which would finance special school projects that were eliminated from the city budget, such as teachers' workshops and extra field trips for students.

Perhaps the most significant aspect of The Fund for Educational Excellence was that it followed two key strategies which Schaefer employed in the policymaking arena. First, the Fund allowed Schaefer to point to his administration's accomplishments immediately. When he first took the oath of office in 1971, the Mayor embarked on a campaign of unwavering boosterism that contrasted sharply with the city's historically low sense of self-esteem. Schaefer's popularity began to build as he capitalized on the announcement of federal grants during numerous ground breaking and ribbon cutting ceremonies. Privately, Schaefer's critics maintained that the Mayor did not have an interest in improving the schools because the schools frustrated him. The problems of poor attendance, high drop rates, and low test scores were too complex to respond to Schaefer's directives which called for immediate results. One example of Schaefer's impatience with the school system was the Westside Skills Center, a new school that opened in 1982 at a cost of $19 million. The Skills Center, equipped with the latest technology, would provide a dramatic improvement in the city's vocational training. But the Westside Skills Center was a failure. Attendance was poor and student performance was low. The problems of poor student achievement were too complex to respond to Schaefer's "do it now" philosophy and a quick influx of cash and chic.

Apart from the Westside Skills Center, the mayor followed a general pattern of concentrating his school reform initiatives on small projects that would yield immediate results and achieve high levels of visibility. Other projects, such as the city-wide writing programs and clean-up projects in the schools allowed the mayor to hold ceremonies for winners at City Hall. The Fund for Educational Excellence also followed this pattern and lent itself to highly visible fundraising efforts, such as a gala celebration aboard a luxury liner. Proceeds from the $60 tickets and $20 raffle for a cruise went to the Fund.

The second key strategy of the mayor employed through the Fund for Educational Excellence was the creation of an autonomous institution to achieve consensus in the educational policymaking arena.

In the field of economic development, Mayor Schaefer sought to minimize bureaucratic resistance to his policies from municipal agencies and to reduce public scrutiny. For this purpose he created an autonomous institution called the "Trustees" known more popularly in Baltimore as the "Shadow Government," to circumvent the traditional bureaucratic and political channels for policymaking and economic development.[41]   Schaefer gave the Trustees, Charles L. Benton, Jr., the city's director of finance, and Lawrence B. Daley, the treasury manager, control over $100 million dollars in bond money.   The Trustees had the power to allocate federal dollars and direct loans and loan guarantees to local developers. Quasi-public corporations, such as the National Aquarium and the Baltimore Economic Development Corporation (BEDCO) were set up to move redevelopment to a fast track pro-business setting.

In the process, Schaefer successfully removed his redevelopment efforts from public scrutiny. But when the Baltimore *Sun* publicized abuses such as bad loans and irregularities in the operations of the Trustees, the City Council in particular attacked the mayor for his development procedures. One City Council member noted that the system had too few controls and left too many possibilities for corruption and abuse. A few years later Schaefer quietly discontinued the financial activities of the Trustees.[42]

In school policy as in economic development, Schaefer created separate entities outside the municipal bureaucracy to function free of administrative control and political oversight. In addition to the Fund for Educational Excellence, the mayor created programs such as Operation Fail and Harbor City Learning Center, both of which were alternatives to traditional schooling for students that were classified as at risk of dropping out. The pivotal feature of all of Schaefer's education programs, however, was that the mayor's Office of Manpower Resources (MOMR) administered them from City Hall. Schaefer appointed Marion Pines, a trusted and loyal aide and supporter, to manage MOMR.

The Mayor's Fund for Educational Excellence, however, received a lukewarm response in the business community and at the time was never was able to raise large amounts of money. The poor reception was largely a result of the aimlessness of the Fund's projects for the school system. The Greater Baltimore Committee felt that a more coherently designed reform effort would better address such problems as the growing absentee rate, the drop out rate, and the declining quality of teachers. From the business community's perspective, Schaefer was aggravating the city's education problems by his insistence on establishing a competing center of educational policymaking attached the mayor's office. More significantly, however, the business community's feeble response was due to the unhappy history of the Baltimore City public school system. For several years, questions of equity and redistribution caused trouble in the schools. In the early 1970s, issues of race and desegregation had become potent sources of conflict.

Racial Tensions Dominate the Schools Agenda

During Schaefer's first term in office, internal turmoil and racial conflict dominated school politics in Baltimore City. In particular, there was an extremely acrimonious battle to remove the superintendent, Roland Patterson. In 1971 Patterson was chosen to be Baltimore's first African-American superintendent. Racial tension, segregation, and a bitter teachers' strike clouded Patterson's tumultuous four year tenure. Patterson charged more than once that criticism of the schools was an expression of racism. While the city was approximately 50 percent white at that time, the school system's student population was 70 percent black.[43]

The race issue emerged in other areas as well during Patterson's tenure. In the fall of 1974, the Department of Health, Education and Welfare ordered the system to desegregate by the time the classroom doors opened in the fall of 1975 or face the possibility of losing $22 million in federal aid. At that time, federal aid represented one tenth of the city's school budget. Federal officials rejected the school board's initial plan and finally accepted a proposal submitted in November 1975.

The desegregation order was only one in a series of disruptions for the school system. In the fall of 1973, the system underwent a massive reorganization plan that crippled the normal classroom procedures. Then in April of 1974, a month-long teachers' strike effectively stopped the day-to-day operations of the schools. Although the schools were considered officially open, 85 percent of Baltimore parents kept their children home. Through both crises, Dr. Patterson maintained that he knew of only one teacher who was unhappy and that the schools were operating as usual.[44]

The turbulent character of the school system went well beyond Patterson's stormy tenure, and outside interests continued to shy away from school politics as a result. Their inaction in these circumstances was not unusual. In many cities, the cooperation between businessmen and city hall fell apart as conflicts over city jobs, race and neighborhood assertion took over.[45]

Ever since desegregation, school politics has been controversial in other cities such as Boston, New York and Chicago to name a few. In general, nationwide observers of city politics regard school politics as one step removed from the partnership and conflict of local politics. But in Baltimore, school policy tends to be more controversial than other issues facing the city because it introduces racial division into local policymaking because the business community is predominantly white and the schools are the largest municipal institution in the city under the direct administration of African-Americans. During the 1970s and 1980s, the Baltimore City Public Schools increasingly became a major source of income and upward mobility for many African-Americans. In fact, since the 1970s, all superintendents have been African-American. By the 1990's a majority of the top administrators in the central office and principals were black. Sixty-four percent of the superintendents -- deputies, associates, and assistants -- were African-American. At the school sites, 70 percent of the principals were black and almost 64 percent of the teachers are African-American. Blacks are also in lower-level positions -- janitors, secretaries, and teacher-aides.[46]

Although the schools were an area of conflict in the city, some Greater Baltimore Committee members were involved in the schools in a limited way because of their belief that the schools were in deep trouble and that private sector intervention in the classroom might help to improve the performance of students.

In the 1970s the Greater Baltimore Committee had begun its "Adopt-A-School" program which linked particular business firms with particular schools. But most partnerships were weak ones at best, largely because the partnerships did not have a clear definition or purpose. Jeff Valentine, at that time, the Greater Baltimore Committee's deputy director for public policy, said, "In retrospect, I think it was the business community saying we need to get involved in the schools, but they [did not] want to commit too much energy."[47] Without a clear purpose, many of the partnerships amounted to little more than a few factory tours for school children.

By 1981 the Greater Baltimore Committee was ready to increase their involvement in the schools in an effort to promote educational policies that would serve their developmental interests. But the business community anticipated resistance to their policymaking efforts from the school system's central education headquarters. For years, the central education bureaucracy has been nearly impervious to outside interests.   This is not a circumstance unique to Baltimore. Contemporary critics of the schools assert that urban educators are generally resistant to outside influences. Educational professionals in big city school systems have used their expertise in school matters such as curriculum and instruction to secure greater control of jobs and funds, and Baltimore City's central educational bureaucracy has reflected this trend.[48] In fact, Baltimore is quite typical: it has a top-down management structure and a traditional curriculum with teaching methods that have changed little over the years. One result of this management model is that the school system has become top-heavy. The curriculum management office, for example, employs 142 people, at a cost of $6.1 million. These are the people who write the curriculum and determine what the teachers will teach in the classrooms.[49]

Reinforcing bureaucratic insularity in Baltimore was a tightly knit group of administrators from the black middle class who hold memberships in two African-American fraternal groups, Kappa Alpha Psi, a male fraternity and the Alpha Kappa Alpha, a female sorority.[50] In addition to being members of the same organizations, the senior people in the central education office have been together most of their careers. They have a reputation for pursuing protectionist policies that buffer and resist outside influences.[51] Their commitment to the organization tends to obstruct new policies or alternate courses of action, which they label as political interference. As Baltimore's education professionals strengthened their base of power, they also extended their control over public educational policy and routinely excluded potential participants from policymaking. As one superintendent recalled, "You are talking about people who are very insecure about their own skills and their own self perceptions. There used to be a little joke that went around the school system: everybody was scared of everybody but the children."[52]

In an effort to gain support for their involvement in the schools, the Greater Baltimore Committee held a series of informal meetings to which it invited representatives of the local business community, members of the African-American community, and officials of the school system. Beginning in 1981, the informal meetings provided opportunities for the Greater Baltimore Committee to see who would be willing to support business initiatives in the schools. The Greater Baltimore Committee also used the meetings as a way to build support among different sectors of the city, particularly from the minority community, while at the same time isolating any potential opposition to their initiatives. Baltimore's business community hoped that their involvement in the schools would also win them respect for their public spiritedness and at the same time promote economic development objectives.

While the Greater Baltimore Committee continued to meet with interested parties, there was a change in the superintendent's office. The Board of School Commissioners appointed Alice G. Pinderhughes, previously the superintendent for elementary education, interim superintendent in December of 1982 to replace the retiring John L. Crew. The Board of School Commissioners considered the 62 year old Pinderhughes a safe choice to fill the position temporarily because of her imminent retirement and lack of a graduate degree. The state of Maryland requires all local superintendents to have masters degrees. But with the support of Mayor Schaefer, Pinderhughes successfully sidestepped these obstacles. Schaefer asked State Superintendent David Hornbeck to waive the graduate degree requirement for Pinderhughes. Shortly thereafter, Mayor Schaefer endorsed her for the superintendency, thus forcing out her principal rival in the national search, St. Louis area Superintendent Rufus Young.

Ms. Pinderhughes came to the superintendent's position after a 45-year career in the Baltimore public school system. Almost immediately after her appointment, she adopted an open style of management which contrasted sharply with that of her predecessor, John L. Crew. Crew, appointed to replace Patterson, ran the public school system in an authoritarian manner that discouraged debate and limited the influence of outside interest groups. Pinderhughes, on the other hand, welcomed the support from education interest groups such as the Greater Baltimore Committee.

Pinderhughes' interest in broadening the schools' constituency was not unique to her or to Baltimore but reflected a change in the status of big city superintendents. In general, the superintendent is usually the most important actor in the school-improvement process. In fact, it does not matter whether the superintendent is the initial architect or an indispensable member of a coalition of improvement-oriented groups. The problems presented to superintendents by reduced budgets, the inattention of mayors, and external demands on the schools now compels school professionals to adopt a political, rather than administrative, role in order to gain the resources necessary to run the schools.[53]

Pinderhughes assumed this political role in order to bring more resources to a deeply troubled and neglected public school system. During her tenure, she turned the Office of the Superintendent for Public Instruction into the essential link between the schools and the community. Even before Alice Pinderhughes assumed the superintendent's post, she had already forged an important alliance with the Greater Baltimore Committee. In the early 1970s, the Committee helped her to lobby state legislators for more funds for elementary education. In 1983 when the president of the Greater Baltimore Committee, Robert Keller, offered Pinderhughes their assistance again, the Superintendent Pinderhughes asked Keller to expand its Adopt-a-School program and increase the partnerships in the schools.

Although the program achieved a limited success, Pinderhughes wanted to expand it for two reasons. First, the program would increase the schools' constituency by involving local area businesses. Secondly, Pinderhughes intended to use the Adopt-a-School program to get more resources into the schools as well as public attention for a deeply troubled school system.[54]

In response to Pinderhughes' request, the Greater Baltimore Committee upgraded its Adopt-a-School effort and scrapped the title because it implied that the schools were friendless orphans. They renamed the venture "The Partnership Program." Next the Greater Baltimore Committee hired a full time partnership coordinator, Judy Wereley, to act as a marriage broker, who would recruit business firms and arrange suitable matches with the schools.

The Greater Baltimore Committee agreed to an expansion of the Partnership Program because it allowed businesses to interact with the schools at the building level, and, in the process, eliminated any need to work through the city's difficult and obstructive central education bureaucracy. Wereley communicated directly with principals and teachers to see what resources business could bring into the schools. The businesses that participated agreed to make commitments to provide materials, supplies, and computers to the schools they worked with. Participating companies also agreed to teach classes and provide mentor and scholarship programs along with field trips for students. Most important, however, the Partnership program began a movement toward providing school-based services in the city's schools rather than programs sponsored and overseen by the school system's central bureaucracy.

The Greater Baltimore Committee continued to expand on this model. In April 1983, the Committee released a report which considered the need to decentralize some functions of the central education bureaucracy. The report followed a year long study of the school system, which examined administrative and accountability problems in the central education administration. Both problems, the Greater Baltimore Committee found, stemmed from the school system's budgetary process. Accountability in the school system diminished significantly because the central staff set spending priorities for the entire system across nine broad categories. To improve the budgetary process, the Committee recommended that the schools adopt site-based budgeting. This system would permit principals, in consultation with teachers and community representatives, to allocate funds across a variety of budget categories according to priorities established at the school level. The Greater Baltimore Committee argued that school personnel were better able than central administrators to meet the needs of students by budgeting for instructional supplies and equipment designed for students' specific learning needs.[55]

Following the Greater Baltimore Committee's recommendations, Pinderhughes decided to begin a pilot program of site-based budgeting based on the business community's study. The superintendent selected schools to participate in the program based on two criteria. The first was that the principal had to be considered a strong leader in his school by the Superintendent. Second, the principal had to be willing to take on more responsibility and work with Greater Baltimore Committee members.

By 1985, Pinderhughes selected seven schools that started experimenting with site-based budgeting, but only on paper, because the program met with strong resistance from the staff at the school system headquarters. Members of the central education bureaucracy would not relinquish responsibilities or needed information to the schools participating in the program. Without the support of the central education administrators, the program faded away.

The program also deteriorated because the Greater Baltimore Committee did not back up its recommendations with political influence. In general, the Greater Baltimore Committee makes broad policy statements designed to improve the region's business climate. The Committee also lobbies on behalf of its recommendations and may work closely on certain proposals with public officials. But the predominantly white business leaders were reluctant to undertake political action that might bring them into conflict with a predominantly black school bureaucracy. Nonetheless, the Greater Baltimore Committee's failed school-based budgeting pilot program became significant in educational policymaking arena for two reasons.

First, it began a dialogue in Baltimore about decentralizing central administration functions as a way to improve the effectiveness of the city's education system. Second, the program began an incremental movement during the Pinderhughes administration that would change the direction of educational policymaking by shifting functions, resources and responsibilities away from the central headquarters to the individual schools themselves. This shift in authority accelerated with the creation of two projects, the Commonwealth program and Project CollegeBound.

Private Sector Programs:
The Movement Toward Decentralization

The superintendent continued to welcome ideas from outside the public school bureaucracy on how to improve the effectiveness of the schools. In addition to the Greater Baltimore Committee, Pinderhughes was also able to secure the support of BUILD (Baltimoreans United In Leadership Development), a church-based group that could have easily become an antagonist of the Superintendent. In fact, Pinderhughes became the first official from the Schaefer administration to recognize BUILD.[56]

BUILD began in Baltimore in 1977 under the leadership of Arnie Graf, a protege of the late Chicago community organizer Saul Alinsky. The organization had a long history of confrontation with city agencies and local business firms. From its inception, BUILD became an agent for change in Baltimore's minority neighborhoods. Its efforts included a campaign against redlining in poor neighborhoods which led to negotiated agreements to end the practice with area banks and savings and loan institutions. BUILD also registered voters in the minority community. As the organization grew, it became a political force in the city that counted 46 inner-city predominantly African-American churches as member organizations.

In general BUILD had a poor relationship with city officials, but in particular with Mayor Schaefer.[57] That relationship worsened in early 1983 when BUILD conducted a series of meetings with public officials in a West Baltimore church. During his first meeting with BUILD, Mayor Schaefer arrived at the church just as Kwisi Mfume, now President of the National Association for the Advancement of Colored People (NAACP) and a former Democratic Congressman representing most of Baltimore, was about to speak to the BUILD audience. Mfume, at the time a Baltimore City Council member, was well liked in the BUILD organization. When he stepped up to the podium, he received an enthusiastic reception from the audience. Following Mfume's address, the mayor's reception was so lukewarm by contrast that he walked off the stage shortly after his introduction. In the back of the church, an angry mayor told BUILD officials that he was being set up to look bad. They denied that there was a set up, the BUILD officials told the Mayor that it was merely that Mfume was so popular.[58]

Superintendent Alice Pinderhughes was also on stage. The superintendent remained at the church and spoke after Schaefer's abrupt and disruptive departure. Pinderhughes told BUILD members gathered at the church that she wanted to work with them toward a solution for the schools. "This was significant," said Reckling, "because up until this time we had been considered confrontational with city agencies."

Following the incident at the church, in 1984, BUILD organizer Arnie Graf spoke to Pinderhughes about bringing a version of the Boston Compact to Baltimore. Under the Compact, local business firms guarantee hiring preference to high school graduates meeting a set standards agreed upon between business and the school system. A compact formula, however, would need the support of the business community.

At the same time the relationship with Pinderhughes was beginning, BUILD went through a year of confrontations with the Greater Baltimore Committee in an effort to get the members to agree to talk to them. In particular, BUILD wanted to discuss the generally dismal employment situations of African-Americans in the city. First, there was the problem of youth unemployment among African-Americans. BUILD evidence showed that young people who were graduating from Baltimore High Schools were unable to get jobs. Allegedly, there was a preference of hiring graduates from the county as opposed to hiring graduates from the city. Carol Reckling, a senior BUILD officer and member of the organization's education team   recanted that people were saying "in quiet corners that if a company had a choice and had to recruit for entry level positions that they might not even look to [the city's] high school graduates because there was an expectation that the county graduates would be better prepared," explained Reckling. This information, however, was all anecdotal. The school system did not document whether graduating students were going on to employment, college, or the military after high school.

The second issue was underemployment of African-Americans in the private sector and the third was unemployment in general. Because of her friendly relationship with the Greater Baltimore Committee, the Committee members were willing to meet with Pinderhughes and BUILD to discuss a problem that affected both organizations, youth preparedness for employment. Finally, in 1984 Robert Keller of the Greater Baltimore Committee agreed to talk to BUILD about youth unemployment in general and to negotiate an agreement similar to Boston's for the Baltimore City Public Schools in particular.

The Greater Baltimore Committee was receptive to the Compact formula for three reasons. First, it offered a program that would operate outside the central bureaucracy of the Baltimore City Public school system. The business community would negotiate with individual schools and their students concerning program benefits. These organizational arrangements would allow the private sector to avoid any administrative battles with the central administration staff, which generally resisted the introduction of new programs. Second, the business community believed that Schaefer's successor as Mayor would most probably be African-American and that it was time to build bridges to the minority community. Finally, the Greater Baltimore Committee needed support from BUILD and the rest of Baltimore's African-American community for its education initiatives. BUILD, for its part, saw the chance to gain a powerful and prestigious ally.[59]

The most important aspect of the program, however, was that it unified the predominantly white business community with a mostly

African-American organization in support of school reform. According to Reckling, BUILD and the Greater Baltimore Committee began their relationship by setting up "an agreement to agree to work together." As for Schaefer, Reckling said, "We did get him to agree not to try to stop us from organizing Commonwealth." But, Reckling added, that Schaefer was hostile to the Commonwealth and did not participate because it was out of City Hall's control.[60]

**Private Sector Programs for The Public Schools:
Commonwealth and CollegeBound**

By January 1985, the Greater Baltimore Committee and BUILD announced the beginning of a program designed to give every high school graduate a chance at a job. The "Commonwealth Agreement" would give high school students who met certain requirements a "passport" at graduation. To earn a passport, students would need to maintain a 95 percent attendance rate in their junior and senior years and an overall 80 percent grade average. Students who met these standards received a guarantee of preferential hiring at more than 110 Baltimore firms in banking, insurance services, and heavy industry. In addition, BUILD established advisory committees of parents to work with the school system to address the needs of children in particular schools. Each high school would also have a Commonwealth Committee that would include teachers, school officials and BUILD members who were parents of students.

But for its first two years, the Commonwealth effort achieved only limited success. Of the approximately 5,500 1985 and 1986 graduating classes, only 469 seniors had become eligible for the program's benefits by the spring of 1986. By 1988, only 625 graduating seniors met the Commonwealth grade average of 80 and the attendance record of 95 percent necessary to qualify for assistance after graduation.[61]

In 1988, the Commonwealth Agreement partners expanded and renamed the Baltimore Commonwealth. The expansion, reformers hoped, would enable it to reach more students. The new Commonwealth became a compact between the city's Office of Employment Development, the public schools, the Greater Baltimore Committee and BUILD. Both the mayor and the superintendent would hold *ex officio* positions on the board of the Commonwealth Agreement as assurance of the city's cooperation. Like the old Commonwealth program, the new Baltimore Commonwealth plan guaranteed job interviews for qualified high school graduates who did not plan to attend college and assured them of priority hiring in 157 Baltimore firms.

But the new program also turned its attention to providing more employment services at the school site. The private sector hired Commonwealth counselors, and assigned them to the schools where they provided training and counseling to students. The counselors also taught classes that were designed to help students learn how to write resumes and conduct themselves during job interviews. If an interview did not yield a job, the city's Office of Employment Training would evaluate the skills of the job candidate and provide additional academic or job training to improve the candidate's employability. In the public schools themselves, the Office of Employment Development sponsored jobs and career clubs. Finally, through elective courses offered during school hours, three areas of employment training received particular attention -- job readiness, communication, and social skills.

The Greater Baltimore Committee and BUILD also participated in the creation of a second program designed to address the shortcomings of the public schools, Project CollegeBound. The CollegeBound foundation's creation followed the release of a report sponsored by the Morris Goldseker Foundation, *Baltimore 2,000*, which warned of economic and social decline in the city unless the work force could take advantage of the employment opportunities created by economic development. Over the course of a year, the report's author, Peter Szanton, consulted with approximately fifty local civic leaders. His report relied heavily on their views. The report's conclusions held that the flashy downtown improvements in the Schaefer era masked "a rot beneath the glitter."[62] Baltimore's economic performance lagged far behind that of other comparable cities, and without innovative strategies, Baltimore would face an economic future of shrinking high-wage employment and increasing neighborhood distress. Recognizing that the school system would provide an essential ingredient in the future of a successful city, the report recommended improvement in the preparation of students for work. Without a skilled and educated work force, the report argued, Baltimore would miss the most promising growth trends in technical fields and knowledge-based industries.

By April 1988, Robert Embry, the president of Baltimore City's Abell Foundation announced the establishment of the CollegeBound Foundation. Embry, a former city housing commissioner and a former Secretary of the U.S. Department of Housing and Urban Development, had also served five years as a member of the school board and president. He worked closely with Pinderhughes, the Greater Baltimore Committee, the Community Foundation and BUILD to design the project.

Project CollegeBound began in the non-selective comprehensive high schools of the city and served students who did not normally think about going to college because such ambitions were rarely encouraged or even discussed at home or because the costs of a college education seemed prohibitive. The Foundation assisted students in applying for college and provided financial aid to those accepted. The CollegeBound Foundation planned to raise $25 million by soliciting $10 million from corporate contributions, another $10 million in endowments from Abell and other foundations, and the remaining $5 million from federal grants. The Abell Foundation committed $4 million dollars to the endowment. Interest income generated by the endowment fund would then pay for tuition grants, fees for college entrance exams, application expenses, preparation costs, and dormitory reservation fees. CollegeBound also provided "last dollar" grants that covered the shortfall remaining when students' family contributions and their financial aid packages totaled less than the cost of attending college.[63] By 1991 CollegeBound awarded $72,000 in last dollar grants to 59 college freshmen and more than $100,000 to 120 college sophomores and juniors.[64]

Both programs, however, achieved only limited success. By 1992 Project CollegeBound had raised only half of its original goal of $25 million. Even worse, very few students qualified for the Baltimore Commonwealth program. After the expansion of the Commonwealth program in 1988, which dropped the 80 percent grade average requirement, only 1,400 students out of the 4,800 who were graduating in 1989 qualified for its benefits. In both years, most of the qualifying students came from Baltimore's most selective high schools such as City College or Baltimore's Polytechnic Institute. These schools produce students who would encounter very little trouble getting jobs after graduation or going onto college, even without the assistance of Commonwealth programs.

The fact that both programs encountered stiff opposition in the educational bureaucracy was perhaps the most distressing element to the businesses involved in Commonwealth and CollegeBound. Despite the efforts of the private sector to bring some form of decentralization to the school system by not operating programs through central headquarters, administrators nevertheless managed to obstruct private sector efforts. For example, conflicts often arose between the city's school counselors and the CollegeBound advisers. Sarah Grey, the Director of City Counselors, according to Jeff Valentine of the Greater Baltimore Committee, was "the single most obstructionist force in the CollegeBound program."[65] The CollegeBound staff, which included four full-time and three part-time advisers, performed one task already assigned to city counselors -- getting scholarships for children. This angered many counselors who perceived the activities of the advisers as an infringement of their jurisdiction. The counselors refused to cooperate with CollegeBound advisors. The advisors perhaps also implied a judgment by those outside the school system that the counselors were not functioning adequately in their jobs.

The Commonwealth program also provided tickets to economically disadvantaged students to go on field trips to the city's cultural and entertainment institutions, such as museums, the National Aquarium, the Meyerhoff Symphony Hall, as well as Orioles baseball games. Under the Commonwealth Agreement, the superintendent's office had the responsibility of distributing the tickets to the schools participating in the program. Instead, administrators in the Office of the Superintendent distributed the tickets to teachers and other central staff personnel.[66]

A Lack of Leadership Impedes Decentralization Efforts

Pinderhughes had an interest in moving the Baltimore City Public Schools to a School-Based Management educational system. She welcomed decentralizing programs and private sector help in moving decisions closer to the schools and students themselves. According to Valentine, Pinderhughes appeared committed to School-Based Management, but the problem, he added, was that "Pinderhughes did not know how to dismantle the road blocks that would prevent it from moving forward." "In her case," Valentine said, "it was far less an issue of a commitment than how do you control this bureaucracy." The bureaucratic resistance to private sector programs highlighted a central problem of the Pinderhughes administration. She could not control the 700 person bureaucracy that reported to her.

As superintendent, Pinderhughes was considered a lax administrator. Even her allies in the local business community were critical of the superintendent's management of the school system. To assist Pinderhughes, the Greater Baltimore Committee and its members provided pro bono management services. They sent in teams of volunteer experts beginning in 1983 to work in areas such as budget management, data processing, personnel management, marketing and communications. But despite their repeated requests, Pinderhughes refused to appoint a chief executive officer to direct the day to day operations of the school system. She maintained that a chief executive officer would be more in charge of the schools than she was.[67]

In addition, the superintendent never provided a comprehensive and consistent plan outlining the objectives of the school system, weighing priorities and telling the system's administrators where to direct its attention. Most of the plans that Pinderhughes formulated were responses to emergencies, and their reactive nature often precluded a full consideration. In 1986, for example, Pinderhughes tried to address the school system's chronic textbook crisis. Teachers regarded the textbook inventory as out of date. Furthermore, neither teachers nor principals, nor central administration staff members could locate books or find who was responsible for them. To help save this inventory problem, Pinderhughes had a centralized computer system installed. The new system gave control over the textbooks to the central office rather than the schools and by centralizing the textbook inventory, sent a contradictory message throughout the system. The new textbook procedure left less authority to principals at a time when Pinderhughes had promised them more authority in running their own schools. Even worse, the procedure standardized the usage of texts at a time when the superintendent had begun to discuss with school personnel the need to meet a variety of individual student needs.[68]

Finally, fault was placed on Pinderhughes for not taking on a more assertive leadership role. The school system needed strong leadership to overcome bureaucratic resistance, to provide direction for the entire system, but also to reach agreements with members of the school board. While Pinderhughes opened the schools to the business community, the mayor attempted to tighten control over the Board of School Commissioners. The mayor's efforts included the appointment of Robert Embry, in August of 1985, to be school board president. Embry, a loyal and trusted Schaefer aide had been a school board member for two and a half years.

Pinderhughes was often forced to take a back seat to Embry, who envisioned grand and controversial plans to combat the schools problems. Embry received most of the attention when he announced, without prior warning, off-the-cuff proposals for dealing with the problems of the school system, many of them destined to provoke arguments during school board meetings. Embry was particularly interested in using the schools to solve many of the city's social problems. He wanted the school day extended to 5:30 P.M., for example, to combat the ills of disadvantaged homes which he maintained held back the school performance of Baltimore City students. He envisioned dividing the extended school day between academic and recreational activities. Another of his suggestions was to withhold Aid to Families with Dependent Children payments to mothers of truants. Such a policy, Embry maintained, would force parents to take a more responsible role in their children's education.[69]

School-Based Management Begins in Baltimore

During her fifth year as superintendent, Pinderhughes finally attempted to move the school system toward School-Based Management. But her plan was once again reactive. In January of 1987, William Donald Schaefer left his city hall office for the State House in Annapolis. Mayor Clarence "Du" Burns, the City Council President, assumed the post of interim mayor.

Once he became governor, Schaefer tried to contest the autonomy of the Baltimore City Public Schools. In April of 1987, Governor Schaefer released a controversial plan written by State Superintendent of Schools David Hornbeck recommending that state school officials with the assistance of outside experts study and evaluate Baltimore's troubled schools.[70]

Publicly, Pinderhughes along with Robert Keller, the executive director of the Greater Baltimore Committee, wondered why Schaefer bothered introducing a plan at all. Previous Maryland governors had regarded the city's school system as an autonomous municipal institution in which the state rarely intervened. Moreover, when Schaefer was mayor, he never demonstrated any interest in the schools: and his criticism of the system had always been extremely limited. Periodically, he would descend on a school and berate the principal for broken windows or graffiti. Although he called many of the internal management operations atrocious, he always maintained that he was pleased with the efforts of Alice Pinderhughes to control the system.[71]

The governor's recommendations forced Pinderhughes to develop an agenda for a school system she had tried to lead and manage for five years in order to upstage Schaefer's proposal. The Superintendent's staff took the lead in assembling a grand strategy for the schools, but Pinderhughes also asked the help of many outside groups and individuals, including for example, Jeff Valentine at the Greater Baltimore Committee and JoAnn Robinson, who was head of the League of Women Voters Education Committee at the time. Both Valentine and Robinson were advocates of School-Based Management and Pinderhughes wanted their advice for some type of decentralization plan for the city's schools.

Exactly, ten days after Schaefer's announcement, Pinderhughes released her own program for the public schools. Entitled "Focus for Individual Success," it called for long-term changes in the basic structure of the school system. School-Based Management was a central feature of the plan. Pinderhughes envisioned teachers and principals running their own schools, making decisions about how to spend money and what to teach, and developing distinctive academic plans for each school.

Following the release of her Focus report, Pinderhughes appointed JoAnn Robinson and Charlene Griffin, a staff member in the superintendent's Office, to co-chair a School-Based Management committee. Pinderhughes told them to explore further the concept of School-Based Management and develop a restructuring plan for the entire school system in consultation with members of the community.

Pinderhughes, however, never met with the committee, nor with the co-chairs. According to Robinson, "she was not 100 percent committed." That was evident from the way in which the Superintendent appointed the task force co-chairs. In fact, Pinderhughes did not tell Robinson or Griffin that they were going to be the chairs until five minutes before the task force met. That evening, Pinderhughes asked Robinson and Griffin to join her in the hallway. Once outside of the room Pinderhughes said she was going to announce to the crowd that Robinson and Griffin were going to be the co-chairs of this task force. "Charlene grimaced, and I was so shocked I [did not] say anything," said Robinson.[72]

But a few days prior to the appointment of Robinson and Griffin, there was another change at City Hall. Following a closely contested primary campaign, with Interim Mayor Du Burns, a veteran of a long-established East Baltimore political organization, Kurt L. Schmoke, the city state's attorney, became Baltimore's first elected African-American mayor in November of 1987. Schmoke, a graduate of Yale and Harvard Law School campaigned as the "Education Mayor" and staked the success of his administration on reversing the downward slide of the Baltimore City public school system. One month after his election victory Schmoke took action to fulfill his campaign pledge. He asked Superintendent Pinderhughes to resign. While the school board conducted a nationwide search to replace Pinderhughes, Robinson's committee, composed of representatives from the Public School Administrators and Supervisors Association (PSASA) -- an association of the principals and central office administrators -- parents and central education staff, continued to meet weekly to formulate a School-Based Management proposal even though the superintendent who had appointed the committee and formulated its charge was on her way out.

Teachers Enter the School-Based Management Debate

At the request of Pinderhughes, representatives from PSASA and the Baltimore Teachers' Union attended the weekly School-Based Management meetings. For the most part, Arnett Brown, president of PSASA was very hostile in the meetings. He argued that, like all the initiatives of the past, the new plan would give principals more to do, without making any substantial change.[73] Once he made his concerns known, Brown's attendance at the meetings became infrequent.

Reuben Ash, a representative from the Baltimore Teachers' Union, attended the committee's meetings regularly, but his organization attached little importance to its deliberations. The history of the city's school system did not give teachers and union officials much hope that Pinderhughes' successor would seriously consider the recommendations of a committee created under a previous superintendent.

In Baltimore, the average tenure for the superintendent's office over the past 30 years has been 4.3 years. Although Baltimore's average is significantly better than the national average of two years for large city school superintendents, the frequent turnover rate presents two problems for the city's school system. The first is that the strategy for the schools changes each time the school board makes a new appointment. The administration of George B. Brain illustrates this point. In 1960, Brain arrived from Bellevue, Washington, to become the city's 12th superintendent since 1866. During Brain's administration, a 25-member body the Citizen Advisory Committee, worked for two years and produced a report recommending over 300 changes in the schools and the central organization in order to improve student performance. For example, it called for greater administrative flexibility in the schools, for the establishment of an advanced technical institute, for greater emphasis on "team teaching," for a longer school day, and for one or more schools for "chronic troublemakers."[74]

Brain's recommendations stirred some controversy in Baltimore. For the most part, however, politicians and some members of the education and civic communities welcomed his ideas for reforming a school system that was no longer meeting the need for a well-educated citizenry. Following the release of his report in 1964, Brain retired from public life. His recommendations for the schools were left to his successor, Lawrence Paquin, to carry out. Paquin, however, had his own plan for reforming the schools and Brain's plans for the city schools never took effect. Paquin's proposals for reforming the high schools, known as the Paquin Plan, died because Paquin himself died. The next superintendent would undertake his own reform agenda.

The high turnover rate in the superintendent's office contributes to a second problem for the schools. New superintendents have taken a particular interest in reorganizing the central education bureaucracy as a way to improve the performance of the schools. In fact, the central office has undergone eleven massive reorganizations since the early 1970's. Some reorganizations have centralized control at the educational administration, then dispersed authority and control to regional units set up in the 1970's. Another reorganization moved the school system from regional control and divided the central education bureaucracy into two departments, one for elementary education and one department for secondary education. A more recent reorganization abolished these divisions and consolidated responsibility for elementary and secondary schooling.

Despite the history of reform, Robinson and the School-Based Management Task Force continued to meet. Although Reuben Ash was not an active participant in the committee's deliberations, the Baltimore Teachers' Union did, however, have a general interest in joining Baltimore's education reform movement. Since 1967, when the teachers staged a walkout designed to force the city to bargain collectively, the Baltimore Teachers' Union, which now represents over 6,700 teachers and 91 percent of the city's teaching force, has centered its demands on issues of salary and working conditions.[75] But the fruits of collective bargaining -- shorter hours, due process protection, a guaranteed wage scale -- did not provide teachers with a voice in school policy.[76] "Teachers had control over almost nothing," said Dandridge, "and the only control they had was when they went into the classroom and closed the door. In most instances nobody bothered them as long as they kept the kids quiet."[77]

By 1986, however, the teachers' union began to look to ways of developing opportunities for their members to have a voice in educational policymaking. An improved role in the policymaking arena, Dandridge argued, would also give teachers a say in the distribution of government resources. As a way to increase their presence in the policymaking arena, Dandridge met with Arnie Graf and Gerald Taylor of the BUILD organization in the early 1980's. The teachers' union joined BUILD, because, according to Dandridge, "We wanted to align ourselves with a group that had some power. It was that simple."

At that time, BUILD began to focus on the disparities in spending between the schools in the city and the wealthier subdivisions of the state. In fact, the Public School Administrators and Supervisors Association (PSASA) joined the BUILD organization as a way of making an issue of how much money the city and the state allocated to education. The distribution of city resources had been at the center of the BUILD's concerns for quite some time.

When the Baltimore Teachers' Union and PSASA joined BUILD, all three organizations concentrated on lobbying state legislators for more for Baltimore schools as a way of reducing the disparities in spending between school districts across the state. The efforts of the group, however, met with resistance from state lawmakers. Legislators hesitated to appropriate more money to a poorly managed local school system. They pointed to Chapter One Funds, which they argued, the city had spent inefficiently. Over two decades old, Chapter One is a federal program, known by its title in federal law, which distributes over $30 million dollars per year to all of the city's 122 elementary schools. The money goes to schools where academic performance is low and where at least one-quarter of the students come from families poor enough to qualify for free lunches. Chapter One pays for extra teachers, counselors, materials, and programs designed to improve the performance of low achieving students.[78]

The Baltimore City Public Schools, however, failed to meet the minimum standards city school officials set in their own school improvement plans submitted to the state. Schools must design a school improvement plan or guidelines when they apply for Chapter One aid.[79] In Maryland, the focus was on reading and math scores in particular. But one federal official found that the standards set by the city were too low to make a difference in children's academic performance.[80]

Without much hope of receiving an increase in educational funding for the city's schools from the state legislature, the Baltimore Teachers' Union, PSASA and BUILD shifted their attention from the issue of equity to restructuring the schools. Restructuring the schools, they hoped, would shift jobs and funds away from the central education bureaucracy to the schools themselves. By 1988, the three groups formed The Coalition for School Reform. After a series of meetings that year led by the Baltimore Teachers' Union President Irene Dandridge, along with Carol Reckling from BUILD and Arnett J. Brown, the president of PSASA, the Coalition published a report which called for a School-Based Management pilot program to begin in one high school, one middle school and one elementary school.

Mayor Schmoke looked favorably upon the Coalition's proposal. In fact, Schmoke's vision for the schools included both decentralization and the involvement of outside interests in educational policymaking in order to improve the performance of public school students. To accomplish these objectives, he selected Richard C. Hunter to replace Pinderhughes. Before coming to Baltimore, the 50 year old Dr. Hunter, who grew up in Omaha, Nebraska, was a tenured professor of education at the University of North Carolina. Previously he had served 11 years as superintendent of public schools in Richmond, Virginia. While in charge of the Richmond schools, Hunter had compiled an impressive record. He set up a massive busing plan with minimal controversy, raised reading and math scores, upgraded the teaching of basic subjects and instituted early childhood education programs. Hunter then moved on to Ohio to accept a position as the Superintendent for the Dayton public school system. But he left Ohio after nine months, to the considerable anger of Dayton's School Board.

Question's about Hunter's abrupt departure from Dayton initially kept the Board of School Commissioners from granting him the majority vote needed for approval to become the superintendent in Baltimore.[81] When the school board completed the final interviews, Dr. Hunter received only one vote, that of school board president, Mel Hollis. Hollis, a personal friend and Harvard acquaintance of the mayor's, moved himself and his family from Boston to Baltimore in the spring of 1987 with a promise of becoming part of the Schmoke administration.[82]

After considerable prodding by the mayor, the school board eventually hired Dr. Hunter despite their various reservations about his appointment. The mayor told school board members that he could work best with Hunter largely because Hunter expressed a desire to continue to build on the support of civic and business partnerships forged by outgoing Superintendent Alice Pinderhughes.

In 1988 when Hunter arrived in Baltimore, Baltimore Teachers' Union president Irene Dandridge, along with Carol Reckling from BUILD and Arnett J. Brown, the president of PSASA, spoke with the new superintendent regarding the Coalition's plan for restructuring the schools. Initially, Hunter agreed to set up School-Based Management in three schools. But as his administration progressed, Hunter began to impede the group's efforts. In general, Hunter resisted attempts to decentralize school programs. He made it clear to school activists that he was uncomfortable with outside involvement in school affairs.

He turned down a promising curriculum reform, for example, at the Barclay school, a public elementary school, serving mostly poor, minority students, when he told parents, teachers and the principal that they could not adopt the curriculum of the Calvert School, a private middle school with mostly white and well off students. Following the Barclay controversy, the Mayor Schmoke and supporters of School-Based-Management were skeptical about Hunter's commitment to a course of decentralization for the Baltimore City Public Schools.

The groundwork for the Barclay school proposal began during the Pinderhughes administration. A year prior to Hunter's arrival, Alice Pinderhughes had given Barclay's principal, Gertrude Williams, permission to work with Robert Slavin at the Johns Hopkins University Center for The Social Organization of Schools to adopt the Calvert School's curriculum. By 1988 Williams secured an informal commitment of a $250,000 grant from the Abell Foundation for teacher training and supplies. But the proposal languished for a year at the school system's central headquarters waiting for approval.

In addition to encountering resistance from Hunter, Barclay parents were also unable to secure support from the Baltimore Teachers' Union, even though Barclay teachers who were union members, supported the move to the new curriculum because it would increase their management responsibilities at the school. As the dispute progressed, it began to take on racial overtones. A white activist, JoAnn Robinson, who did not have a child enrolled in Barclay at the time, had become the chief spokesperson for the Calvert project so that Barclay's principal, Gertrude Williams, would not have to defy Superintendent Hunter in public. But some members of Baltimore's African-American community grew suspicious that Robinson was trying to start a private school for whites, even though Barclay was over 87 percent black. According to Dandridge, "Mrs. Robinson has one vision of the Baltimore City public schools, [and] I think her vision and my vision are totally different. My vision includes the worst child in the school system."

Despite the loss of support from the Baltimore Teachers' Union, parents at the Barclay school continued their effort. In January of 1989, they complained to Hunter that their proposal was still sitting at the school system's central bureaucracy. Hunter's immediate reaction, according to a former aide, was that no special interest group was going to push him around.[83]

In addition to asserting his authority over the curriculum, some city school observers perceived Hunter's decision on the Barclay proposal as an attempt to limit the influence of Robert C. Embry, Jr., the director of the Abell Foundation, which is the largest private-sector actor in school system affairs. Embry, a former school board president and member during the Schaefer administration, earned a reputation during his tenure on the Board of School Commissioners for contesting the leadership of Alice Pinderhughes. Dr. Hunter reportedly needed to show that he would not take orders from Embry.[84]

Hunter turned down the Barclay proposal and explained that individual schools seeking grants should go through a central clearing process. Martha Johnston, director of education programs for the Community Foundation of Baltimore City complained that the central clearing process was too time consuming, "We had to go through layers and layers of bureaucracy to get approval for projects, the process would take so long, many projects would die."[85]

Hunter repeatedly defended the operation. The central process would assure that an evaluation of all projects proposed from outside the school system would take place to see if they would help the system meet its priorities of higher pay for teachers, more textbooks and supplies, reduced class size and better school security. Those priorities, Hunter identified in the fall, when he met with community and school groups around the city. From those meetings, a "democratically arrived at list of priorities emerged."[86]

Initially, Mayor Schmoke deferred to the Superintendent's authority on the Barclay proposal. But the Barclay controversy would not go away. In June of 1989, Barclay parents and teachers arrived at City Hall for Taxpayers Night and requested that Mayor Schmoke intervene in the Barclay dispute. As a result of the parental opposition to Hunter's decision, the mayor ordered the superintendent to work out a solution with Barclay parents and staff. Hunter finally gave in to pressure from Schmoke and approved a plan for the Barclay school to carry out the Calvert School's curriculum, which gave Barclay parents an apparent victory after a two-year struggle with the city's Department of Education.

Hunter's actions caused him to loose the support of parents, the Abell Foundation, the Greater Baltimore Committee and BUILD. Although faulted as a lax administrator, Alice Pinderhughes won the support of the Baltimore community and cultivated a constituency throughout the city for the public schools. In her political role as superintendent, Pinderhughes received the support of Mayor Schaefer, parents, the Greater Baltimore Committee and BUILD. She was able to bring private sector programs to the schools that would provide more counselors, after school programs and field trips -- the types of enrichment programs that were lost during the budget cuts of the Schaefer administration.

Dr. Hunter, on the other hand, came to Baltimore with a constituency of one: Mayor Schmoke. By August of 1989, Hunter began to loose that constituency. As private sector involvement in the public school system remained static, public attention in Baltimore turned to Hunter's management of the Department of Education.

Hunter demanded unified control over the schools presumably because he sought more effective administration. But for almost a year, the issue of bureaucratic efficiency and responsiveness dominated the educational agenda of the city and by the time the school doors opened in the fall of 1989, the mayor began to complain publicly that Hunter was slow to bring changes to a system plagued by poor bureaucratic performance. The mayor criticized Hunter for his reorganization of the Department of Education. He found that problems of bureaucratic organization and response persisted in the central education bureaucracy despite the reorganization which the Superintendent promised would lead to greater administrative efficiencies.

Dr. Hunter reorganized the top staff of the department into five divisions and announced that the city school system would abolish 122 administrative jobs, including 22 top level appointed officials.[87] Hunter also eliminated another 100 managerial and clerical jobs at the middle management level, and 40 other employees, mostly curriculum experts who spent little time in schools, the superintendent transferred out of the central headquarters and into the schools.[88]

But the mayor said that the reorganization was never fully completed. One of the five associate superintendent positions remained unfilled for almost two years. In addition, Mayor Schmoke told Hunter that the reorganization did not produce the direction and leadership needed by the school system. As a result, administrative duties were left unattended by the central staff, which led to major embarrassments for City Hall and the Education Mayor.

The first was the discovery that a city warehouse was full of books while thousands of school children went to school each day without textbooks. After receiving complaints from parents, the mayor launched a public campaign to uncover textbook shortages in the schools. Schmoke started by visiting a middle school. The expressed purpose of the visit was to follow a typical book order through the system and to find the "breakdowns" that kept slowing down requests. With an entourage of reporters and television cameras following him, Schmoke went through the Baltimore school system trying to find out how the school system ordered and distributed textbooks. Schmoke's journey finally ended when he reached a textbook storage facility. There he found 100,000 textbooks waiting for distribution. An enraged mayor pointedly asked school administrators why some schools faced shortages when books were sitting in a warehouse. At the end of the tour Schmoke announced that he was bringing in a Baltimore Gas and Electric executive to make a month long study of what was wrong with the city's textbook system, a move that challenged Hunter's authority and control in the school system.

The second administrative embarrassment for City Hall was the discovery that the financially strapped Baltimore School system only recovered $15,000 of an estimated $1.3 million a year available in state

Medicaid funds because the Department of Education failed to properly bill the state of Maryland.[89] The money was to be collected under a new program to reimburse the city for medical examinations and treatments given to 18,000 disabled and special education students in the city schools. In May of 1989, the Mayor and Hunter approved the program, formerly known as the Third Party Billing Project. Under the program the city school system could bill Medicaid for services the city performed dating as far back as September 1988. The school system estimated that it would be eligible to recover 1.3 million for each nine month school year even if only 20 percent of the disabled children participated. But by March of 1990, only a fraction of that amount was collected. At that time, the city had not recovered the $50,000 it cost to set up the program.

The disclosure of the billing problem was coming at a time when the mayor was criticizing the central administration of the schools for bureaucratic inertia and lack of management. The billing problem angered members of the school board, who had been seeking an explanation from Dr. Hunter and the school administration for weeks. "I [do not] think he's really tuned in," remarked school board member Stellos Spiliadis, to a Baltimore *Sun* reporter. The school board began an investigation into the program following a meeting with Hunter. In the meeting, Hunter gave a bland response to their inquiries, telling school board members that his deputy, Herman Howard, was responsible for the program and that as superintendent he personally was unaware of any problems with the new billing project.[90]

Schmoke, Hunter and School-Based Management

Schmoke again challenged Hunter's authority in the school system when he forced the superintendent to reach a compromise with the Baltimore Teachers Union, the Public School Administrators and Supervisors Association (PSASA) and BUILD on the organizations collective restructuring efforts for the city's public schools. Hunter became an obstacle to the coalition's effort because he was not receptive to the idea of School-Based Management at all.[91] After almost a year of waiting for the superintendent to decide which three schools would participate in the Coalition for Reform's restructuring pilot project, Hunter made an abrupt departure from his initial position on the program and rejected the proposal in its entirety at the start of 1989.

Following Hunter's surprising actions, the teachers' union sought to formulate a school improvement plan independently of the office of superintendent or the mayor. Acting independently of both city offices would guarantee union members a voice in policymaking no matter whom the citizens of Baltimore chose to run the city. Even further, the Baltimore Teachers' Union looked for ways to guarantee that they would have a voice in policymaking no matter whom the mayor might choose to lead the school system.

During the 1989 negotiations with the mayor and school board, the Baltimore Teachers' Union decided to institutionalize the mechanism of voice by making the three school pilot program an integral part of their collective bargaining strategy. The Baltimore Teachers' Union brought in a School-Based Management facilitator from the American Federation of Teachers, Terry Mazzani, to assist them in their negotiations with the city. At the time Mazzani was working for the Center for Dispute Settlement in Detroit, a division of the American Federation of Teachers. During closed door sessions with the mayor, Union officials and the school board, Hunter continued to reject the restructuring program. Although the superintendent is not part of the negotiating process, the City Charter requires the superintendent's approval before the city can accept a contract with the teachers' union.

An angry mayor, however, instructed Hunter to reach a compromise with union officials. The year-long negotiations finally ended when Hunter achieved a settlement with the Baltimore Teachers' Union. He would permit School-Based Management to begin in Baltimore but a much weaker version than the one the union initially wanted. Instead of initiating the program at three schools, Hunter gave permission to the teachers' union, along with representatives from PSASA and BUILD, to write a school restructuring proposal for the city schools that the coalition would present to the Board of School Commissioners for approval. "We accepted that as a compromise" said Dandridge, "My sense is that the superintendent wanted as little as possible that he could get away with."[92]

Dandridge did, however, anticipate getting support from some members of the Board of School Commissioners. Following the contract negotiations, the Baltimore Teachers' Union began its efforts to train teachers for School-Based Management. The union took a teacher from each of the 177 city schools to a retreat in Hershey,

Pennsylvania, for two summers, in 1989 and 1990, for three days of training. Dandridge also invited all nine school board commissioners to attend the retreat. However, only two of the nine school board commissioners, Joseph Smith and Doris Johnson, agreed to attend. Following their return from the retreat in 1990, Dandridge received assurance from Smith and Johnson that they would help the union by caucusing with the Commissioners to get the majority voted needed to pass the plan. Following the retreat, the teachers returned to their schools to meet with the principal. The purpose of the meeting was to talk about their school becoming a pilot school in a School-Based Management program for the city's schools. If the principal agreed, then the next step for the teacher was to talk to the faculty in their particular school. If 90 percent agreed that they wanted to be a pilot school, then the teacher filled out a "Notice of Intent." Under the proposal, every school accepted into the program would receive $15,000 and a person released for half a day per week to guide the restructuring program. The union then trained the building representative in how to write the proposal. Proposals would be due by November 30, 1990, and pilot schools were selected in the beginning of 1991.

The Proposal is Released

By the fall of 1990, a School-Based Management proposal finally emerged from the union's efforts that would raise student achievement levels by increasing the involvement of principals, staff and teachers and parents in the management of the schools. Specifically, the plan called for 20 schools to experiment by establishing school restructuring teams with at least one PTA member, one union teacher, the principal and one BTU union paraprofessional. More members, up to 12, could be added at the team's discretion to attend monthly meetings during school hours. During those meetings, the teams would decide the specific aspects of school policy that would fall under the authority of the individual school rather than the central administration staff.

The participating schools would then report to Dr. Jeanette Evans, the director of restructuring for the city schools, and to a citizens board that is responsible for the schools undergoing restructuring. The citizens board would oversee the School-Based Management project and decide on the requests of additional schools to participate in the program. But the actual composition of the citizens board outlined by the Baltimore Teachers' Union proposal was deliberately vague.[93] According to the proposal, members on the board would be "stakeholders" in the city's educational system. The new board would be a policymaking apparatus that would not involve itself in the day to day operations of the schools. More important, however, the citizens board would provide a way in which the Coalition, particularly the Baltimore Teachers' Union, could set policy for the participating schools and presumably affect the distribution of resources to the union's advantage.

The Baltimore City Public Schools Adopt School-Based Management

The restructuring proposal became widely known within the city as the Baltimore Teachers' Union plan because restructuring had become an integral part of the union's contract negotiations with the city. When President Irene Dandridge presented their School-Based Management proposal to the Board of School Commissioners in September 1990, many parent and community groups expressed anger because they had been left out of the decentralization planning process. JoAnn Robinson, the former co-chair of the Pinderhughes School-Based Management Committee, voiced considerable opposition.

At the School board meeting, Robinson, representing the Western High School Parent Teacher Association, testified against the union plan, saying that parents did not have adequate representation in the Coalition's deliberations. Dandridge countered by saying that the BUILD organization represented parents. The need, Robinson replied, was to represent parents organized as parents so that their adequate representation was assured.

Despite its close association with the Baltimore Teachers' Union, the notion of decentralization still appealed to school constituents. Many community groups and activists, such as the League of Women Voters and the District Advisory Council, spoke in favor of some form of decentralization for the city's ailing public school system.

By October 1990 the Board of School Commissioners approved the plan -- at least in principle. First, however, the school board told the union to make significant changes to their proposal as a way of quieting opposition.   The first change would give parents and the community a more prominent role in the restructuring process by requiring that they comprise at least 40 percent of the council members.[94]

Second, the Board of School Commissioners directed the restructuring coalition to rework the proposal so that the citizens board would be advisory to the school board. In general, resistance to reform sometime comes from school boards who may be reluctant to share power or are concerned about delegating authority.[95]   This was the case with the Baltimore City Board of School Commissioners. School board members objected to the citizens board largely because they thought it would serve as a second school board that would infringe upon their authority in the educational policymaking process.

At the direction of the Board of School Commissioners, the Coalition revised the proposal so that the citizens board would be advisory to the school board and superintendent instead of setting school decentralization policy.   The new committee, called the Advisory Committee to Support Restructuring would also be a means of communicating back to its constituents information about restructuring.

The Advisory Committee would have at least 38 members representing a variety of organizations in the city, such the NAACP, the League of Women Voters, BUILD, the Citizen's Planning and Housing Association (CPHA) and the Fund for Educational Excellence. PSASA would have three members on the committee, Sheila Kolman, the association president who succeeded Arnett Brown after his death in 1991, and two principals, Elizabeth Turner, from Tench Tilghman Elementary School, and Sam Phillips from Walbrook Senior High School.   In addition, there were four school system staff members, including Dr. Jeanette Evans, Director of Special Projects for the Baltimore City Public Schools, and Patricia Speights, the facilitator for restructuring. The Baltimore Teachers' Union had four representatives, including its president, Irene Dandridge.

As interim convener of the Advisory Committee, Jerry Baum, the executive director of the Fund for Educational Excellence, worked with the superintendent to start the committee's deliberations. According to Baum, "Hunter was not particularly interested in the program or the Advisory Committee."[96]   He did show an interest, however, when it came to the appointment of a business community representative to the

Advisory Committee. In general, Hunter did not have a close working relationship with the Greater Baltimore Committee. The superintendent made it clear to Baum that he did not want the Greater Baltimore Committee on the Advisory Committee to Support Restructuring. When it came to the appointment of a business community member, Hunter picked Osbourne Payne, an African-American who owned a chain of McDonald's restaurants in Baltimore. What Hunter did not know, however, was that Payne was a member of the Greater Baltimore Committee's Education Committee and worked closely with Jeff Valentine. After Payne's appointment, he spoke with Valentine. "Osbourne agreed to do this," said Valentine, "although he did not really understand what [School-Based Management] was all about, and asked me to take his place on the committee."[97] From then on Valentine attended the Advisory Committee meetings, representing the Greater Baltimore Committee.

School-Based Management: An Incremental Reform Effort

In general Baltimore's movement to School-Based Management has been incremental, rather than a sweeping fundamental change. Proponents of School-Based Management in Baltimore wanted to avoid the initial pitfalls of an entire system undergoing restructuring like Chicago's. To date, Chicago, the nation's third largest school system, is the most extensive effort to carry out School-Based Management. In 1988, the entire Chicago public school system quickly moved to School-Based Management following the enactment of the 1988 The Chicago School Reform Act. Decentralization in Chicago entailed a significant amount of citizen involvement at the school building level. The new act sought to shift responsibilities from a hierarchical central education bureaucracy to 540 elected local school councils comprising parents, teachers, and community representatives. The result was chaotic, with school councils not knowing their respective duties and authority or how to run the schools.

Interest in the reform effort was significant. Over 17,000 candidates entered the first election. But the election of representatives to the councils has become a new source of patronage in Chicago's politicized school system.[98] Thus, it is prudent to conclude from the Chicago experience that incrementalism can be a highly prudent and often successful way of bringing about reform in a democratic society -

- indeed in most instances the only way in which real reform can come about.   Incrementalism on the other hand, allows established interests, the Baltimore Teachers' Union, for example, to capture and eviscerate reforms.   This has been the case with Baltimore's School-Based Management reform effort.   In sharp contrast to Chicago, Baltimore has moved too slowly.   The program was open to all 177 schools in its first year, however, only 22 schools applied.   Of those 22, only 14 schools met the criteria to join the restructuring program.   Douglass High School provides one example of a school that failed to meet the criteria for the program.   At that High School, the restructuring effort began with the principal, Shirley Hill, assigning a chairperson, assigning the teachers who were going to work on the proposal, and dictating the components of the school improvement plan.   Hill also refused to take a vote of her faculty to see if she had the support of 90 percent of the teachers.   Members of the Advisory Committee to Support Restructuring returned the Douglass proposal and told the principal she must have a vote in order to participate in program.   Hill refused.   Finally, some of the Baltimore Teachers' Union staff members conducted a vote at Douglass High School and found that only 50 percent of the faculty agreed to participate in restructuring. The Advisory Committee subsequently rejected the proposal because it did not have enough school-based staff support.

According to some school observers, the poor response by school faculties was also largely due to the manner in which the Baltimore Teachers' Union introduced the plan to city schools officials in the fall of 1990.   A quick response was necessary to become part of the School-Based Management effort. Marilyn Hunter, a UniServ Director for the rival teachers union, the Baltimore City Teachers' Association, agrees.   The National Education Association employs over 1,300 UniServ directors who live and work in the communities they serve. Their primary purpose is to provide staff support to local affiliates of the National Education Association, particularly in the area of education reform initiatives.   According to Hunter, "By November teachers [had] to vote and commit themselves to a pilot project they . . . were [not] familiar with.   No one understood exactly what School-Based Management would mean as far as additional working hours, additional responsibilities, because the plan was so vague." Hunter added that the decision to participate stemmed less from a thorough understanding of the process than from the fact that money came with participation in the project. "Schools are always looking for ways to find money to support various programs that they want to set into motion."[99]

Problems with the Restructuring Effort

Despite the possible benefits of an incremental reform there have been a number of problems with Baltimore's School-Based Management program. In the beginning of the project Rob Clark, the Education Director for CPHA, testified before the school board that the Advisory Committee to Support Restructuring was setting itself up to be another layer of bureaucracy.[100] In addition to reporting to the committee, Clark noted, the schools also had to report to Dr. Jeanette Evans.

The larger problem for the committee is that each representative or group brings diverse opinions and beliefs about how to run the schools to each meeting. The committee operates by consensus, and consensus on many issues has been difficult to achieve because of the variety of interests on the committee. The process had been so time consuming that the school system, upon the recommendation of Jeanette Evans, was forced to give committee members outside training to expedite the decision making process.

The issue of training has also been a constant source of conflict during committee deliberations. The lack of training has become a significant roadblock to restructuring at the local school site, largely because the principals and teachers were not prepared to accept new responsibilities. The principals have not received any training for their new roles and PSASA is unwilling to undertake any training efforts. Sheila Kolman maintains that training is the responsibility of the school system.[101]

The Baltimore Teachers' Union, on the other hand, did undertake some training. The teachers, however, did not have training in School-Based Management in general but in the proposal that the union and school officials wrote for Baltimore City. As a result, teachers had definite strong opinions about the direction School-Based Management in Baltimore City should take. In particular they wanted resources redistributed from the central administration to the schools and the teachers themselves. Their proposal originally introduced as a way to increase parental and neighborhood involvement evolved into a device for increasing the authority of teachers in relation to the central administration of the schools.

Despite their efforts, however, the teachers, as well as the principals did not feel that they had acquired any more authority and discretion than they had before the School-Based Management program began to run the schools. Mary Johnson, a committee member representing BUILD and a former principal at Montebello Elementary School, expressed reservations about the program. According to Johnson, restructuring should do what it purports to do. The schools should be able to adopt a sound curriculum, have staff development, and take part in the budgetary process. Instead, according to Johnson, many observers of the committee's deliberations were fearful that restructuring in Baltimore had come down to a struggle between labor, represented by the Baltimore Teachers Union, and management, the central headquarters located on North Avenue.[102]

Additionally, more problems occurred during committee meetings because the Advisory Committee to Support Restructuring did not have a clearly defined role. According to Jerry Baum, "the Committee is there to support restructuring." Baum added, "What that exactly means has been a problem during deliberations. For example, are we there to assess programs, provide benchmarks for achievements, or reward and punish schools not making these benchmarks?" The actual work of the committee, however, consisted of listening to schools give presentations to the committee about their activities. Following the March 1992 presentations, there was very little left for the Committee to do.[103]

The role of the Committee was clear to Dr. Jeanette Evans. Evans, who reports to the Board of School Commissioners and superintendent on the progress of the program, said that members of the Advisory Committee were policy influencers, not policymakers. They were to make suggestions and offer support to the schools participating in the School-Based Management program, but they were not there to set budgets or make changes in the curriculum.

Finally, the 14 participating schools removed themselves from the rest of the public school system. In the process, each individual school gained some authority to develop a school improvement plan and create partnerships with members of the Baltimore community. These partnerships in turn, would yield resources for the schools from the private sector to create distinctive programs in the schools participating in the program. Many community groups are involved with the schools in the pilot program. The Fund for Educational Excellence illustrates this point. Represented by its executive director Jerry Baum the Fund formed partnerships with four of the fourteen pilot schools. The Fund provided the schools with resources for training each school restructuring team and funding to help them identify effective models of School-Based Management as a way of increasing the individuality of the participating schools. In addition, the Fund is undertaking a project with a small grant to support staff development in all of the 14 pilot schools.

Although Rob Clark initially spoke out against the Advisory Committee to Support Restructuring, CPHA joined the restructuring effort. Created in 1941, CPHA had a broad membership including neighborhood, labor and charitable organizations as well as Chamber of Commerce boosters. CPHA turned its attention to the schools when Mayor Schmoke was elected and it became evident to Board members that education would be a number one priority for the city. CPHA, according to Clark, wanted to "provide the resources that the schools needed to be more autonomous."[104]   With the financial support from the Abell foundation, CPHA worked with six of the pilot schools -- Diggs Johnson, Roland Park, Harford Heights, Federal Hill, Robert Coleman and Garrett Heights.

In the long run, however, a series of incremental changes can eventually have a large cumulative impact. That was the hope of the new superintendent, Walter Amprey, chosen to replace Hunter. With the Advisory Committee firmly in place, Schmoke made an announcement in December 1990 that the city would not be renewing Dr. Hunter's contract. Schmoke's based his decision to dismiss Hunter at the end of 1990 more on political considerations than on dissatisfaction with the pace of educational improvement. By disposing of the superintendent when he did, Schmoke could prevent opponents in the upcoming Mayoral race from using Dr. Hunter's inept performance as a symbol of the Schmoke administration's failures. In November 1991, with a new superintendent in place, the citizens of Baltimore returned Schmoke to the Mayor's office.

Amprey, a Baltimore native and graduate of the city's schools, also taught in the Baltimore City Public Schools. He moved to the neighboring Baltimore County system in 1973. Amprey's 18-year career in Baltimore County Schools included positions as social studies teacher, school administrator, assistant principal, and principal. He finally rose to become a well-regarded Associate Superintendent.

His major initiative as Baltimore's superintendent, "enterprise schools," allowed school principals and "school improvement teams" to tailor education funds according to each school's needs. By 1994, 24 of the Baltimore City Public Schools 177 schools received this authority. The 24 schools included the original 14 School-Based Management schools that Amprey incorporated into his project. Amprey's avowed goal is to gradually make all the schools enterprise schools.[105]

Conclusion

By the beginning of the 1980's, the decline in student achievement in the Baltimore City public schools was beginning to have a profound effect on the city's economic well-being. To advance their economic development objectives, the Greater Baltimore Committee started the education reform debate by pushing education to the top of the city's agenda. The Greater Baltimore Committee initially introduced the notion of moving the Baltimore City public schools from a centralized system to School-Based Management to improve the schools. The reform movement gathered momentum when an alliance formed between the Greater Baltimore Committee and BUILD. The superintendent, Alice Pinderhughes, became one of the coalition's biggest supporters.

Dr. Richard Hunter, however, Pinderhughes' successor, obstructed the efforts of the Greater Baltimore Committee and BUILD. Eventually, the Baltimore Teachers' Union would co-opt their efforts. For their part, the teachers perceived School-Based Management as a device for increasing their authority in relation to the central administration of the schools. By 1989, the Baltimore Teachers' Union succeeded in capturing the city's School-Based Management movement when they negotiated a contract provision that called for a joint committee of administrators and teachers to work out a restructuring plan for the schools.

But the movement to School-Based Management has been slow and plagued by political conflicts between members of the Advisory Committee, the schools, and the central education staff. That is because restructuring proceeded from a political agenda, rather than an educational one. In both Minnesota and Baltimore City, the direction each school system would take is a response to political demands created by new interest groups in educational policymaking. Could the Baltimore City education system benefit from the use of the exit option in the public schools? It seems highly unlikely that there would be any benefit at all. Like other cities, Baltimore's educational system has already suffered enormously from the use of the exit option. During the 1970's and into the 1980's the more affluent segments of the population fled to the surrounding suburbs for jobs, better housing and, what is most important, better schools, leaving the poorest behind. Even the exodus to private schools and parochial schools has been highly damaging. Nearly 15 percent of the city's school age population attends private institutions.[106] It is, therefore, unlikely that use of exit would stop a system in decline.

One of the advantages of Minnesota's school system is that the private school tradition in that state is not so strong as in Maryland. With upper-to-middle income groups committed to the public schools in Minnesota, the education system benefits enormously from the power of support and criticism that comes from organizations like Public School Incentives, the Association of Metropolitan School Districts and state and local PTA organizations. In Baltimore, on the other hand, most of the public schools have been unable to sustain a Parent Teachers' Association.

The availability of exit can strengthen voice but so can the absence of this same option. In his analysis of exit and voice, Hirschmann draws attention to this dilemma. He cites the institutions trapped in cities because their physical plants are unmovable -- churches and department stores, for example. As a result, these institutions can become leading voices for reform in cities. The church-based organization BUILD and the Greater Baltimore Committee provide two examples of organizations drawing much of their strength from parties that are trapped in this way.

It is unlikely that an exit mechanism, like the Minnesota Public School Choice program, would emerge in Baltimore City as a method of recovery for the schools for two reasons. First, the minority enrollment is a significant factor. No doubt, white parents in the surrounding four counties that along with the City make up the Baltimore region would react strongly to a School Choice program. While minority enrollment in the city is more than 82 percent, the surrounding four counties have significantly lower levels -- Baltimore County, 21 percent, Howard County, 20 percent and Anne Arundel and Harford County, almost 18 percent and 15 percent respectively. In Minneapolis, on the other hand, where minority enrollment is almost

50 percent and relatively high compared to the rest of the state's 3 percent African-American enrollment, state monitored desegregation has effectively regulated and even stifled the movement of minority students.[107]

Secondly, the disparities in educational spending are much greater in Maryland than in Minnesota. In Minnesota, the state assumes almost 80 percent of the educational expense per student. In Maryland, on the other hand, a greater proportion of school budgets come from local sources and the state contributes only 64 percent. Because local property taxes fund a large portion of the budget for public schools, wide differences in per-pupil spending exist between wealthier counties and the state's less affluent inner-city and rural school districts. For example, per-pupil education spending totaled $4,614 in Baltimore City during the 1990-91 school year, maintaining its historically low ranking of 19th out of 24 school systems in the state and below the statewide school spending average of $5,814 per student. That compares with $7,590 per pupil in Montgomery County, the highest in the state, and $6,219 in surrounding Baltimore County. It is therefore unlikely that a statewide, interdistrict open enrollment plan would receive favorable consideration by the Maryland state legislature. Two rounds of census-driven redistricting since the 1970s have only increased the voting power of the relatively wealthier suburbs while reducing urban and rural representation.[108] Consequently, given the options of exit or voice, School-Based Management is the only available avenue of reform open to Baltimore City and perhaps a limited choice system in which a student transfer remains within the district.

Notes

[1] The Baltimore City Public Schools System is comprised of 177 public schools. There are 118 elementary, 27 middle, 14 senior high, 10 special education, 5 alternative, and 3 vocational/technical schools.

[2] Will Englund, "Baltimore Area Lowest in U.S. in Adults Finishing High School," *The Baltimore Sun*, 6 December 1987, 1(C).

[3] "Table 9. Years of School Completed by Persons 15 years Old and Over, by Age, Sex, Race and Hispanic Origin, for the 15 Largest Metropolitan Statistical Areas: March 1987." Kominski, Robert. *Educational Attainment in the United States: March 1987 and 1986*. Bureau of the Census, 1988.

[4]   *The Education Digest*, 126. See also Suzanne P. Kelly, "City, State are Among the leaders in School Suspensions," *The Baltimore Sun*, 13 December 1988, 1(A).

[5]   Suzanne P. Kelly "10% in city school are learning disabled, Poll Finds," *The Baltimore Sun*, 13 December 1988, 1(A).

[6]   "Baltimore City, Student Performance, Baseline Data -- School Year 1989-90." *Maryland School Performance Program Report, 1990: State and School Systems*. Maryland State Department of Education. Baltimore: 1991.

[7]   Kelly, 1(A).

[8]   Sandy Banisky, "Promotion of Tourism Helped City Turn From Manufacturing." *The Evening Sun*. 8 January 1987, 1(B).

[9]   Marc Levine, "Downtown Redevelopment as Urban Growth Strategy," *Journal of Urban Affairs* 9 (1987) 114.

[10]   M. Gittell & E.T. Hollander. *Six Urban School Districts: A Comparative Study of Institutional Response*. (New York: Praeger Publishers, 1968), 179.

[11]   Former Superintendent of Public Instruction, Baltimore City, Alice Pinderhughes, interview by Author, 25 February 1992, tape recording.

[12]   *Baltimore City Charter* Article VII, Section 59. Department of Budget, Salaries, 117.

[13]   The Abell Foundation, "A Growing Inequality: A Report on the Financial Condition of the Baltimore City Public Schools." (Baltimore: The Abell Foundation, 1989), 9.

[14]   Abell, 9.

[15]   *Who Negotiates for the Children?: The Importance of Teacher Union Agreements in the Quality of Education in Maryland's Public Schools*. (Baltimore: Advocates for Children and Youth, 1991), 89.

[16]   Szanton, Peter. *Baltimore 2,000: A Choice of Futures: Report to the Morris Goldseker Foundation* (Baltimore: Goldseker Foundation, 1986).

[17]   Szanton, 2.

[18]   *Education Digest*, Table 88: Selected Statistics for Public School Districts Enrolling More Than 20,000 Pupils by State: 1989-90: 97.

[19]   In constant 1970 dollars. See Marc Levine, "Economic Development to Help Underclass," *The Baltimore Sun*, 10 January 1988, 1(E).

[20]   Szanton, 12.

[21]   Baltimore City Department of Planning. *Poverty in Baltimore: Data and Indicators*. (Baltimore: Baltimore City Department of Planning, 1987).

[22]   Sandy, Banisky, "The Schaefer Legacy," *The Baltimore Sun*, 18 January 1987, 1(E).

[23]   "Economic Outlook to 1990." *The Economic Review*. 26 February 1986: 18.

[24]   Szanton, 5.

[25] According to figures released by the Regional Planning Council, in 1975 there were 459,914 in Baltimore City. By 1985, there were 460,580.

[26] *Employment Trends in the Baltimore Region: 1970-1990*, 16.

[27] *Commuting in The Baltimore Region: Historical Perspectives and Current Trends*. (Baltimore: The Regional Planning Council), 18.

[28] *Maryland Statistical Abstract 1986-1987* (Annapolis: Maryland Department of Economic Development, 1988), 114.

[29] Szanton, 6.

[30] *Commuting in the Baltimore Region*, 18.

[31] *Employment Trends in the Baltimore Region: 1970-1990*. (Baltimore: The Regional Planning Council), 12.

[32] "Employment Trends in the Baltimore Region, 12.

[33] Szanton, 6.

[34] Will Englund, "Baltimore Area Lowest in U.S. Adults Finishing High School," *The Baltimore Sun*, 6 December 1987, 1(C).

[35] Levine, 1(E).

[36] Sandy Banisky, "Race Made Mayor Fret -- At First, " *The Baltimore Sun*, 15 September 1983: 1 (A).

[37] O'Keefe, Kevin. *Baltimore Politics 1971-1986: The Schaefer Years and The Struggle for Succession*, The Georgetown Monograph in American Studies, 3, (Washington, D.C.: Georgetown University, 1987), 92.

[38] O'Keefe, 96.

[39] Sandy Banisky, "Mayor Begins 4th term with School Pledge," *The Baltimore Sun*, 7 December 1983, 1 (D).

[40] ibid.

[41] See Paul Peterson, *City Limits*, 33. Peterson also notes the importance of autonomous institutions to promote and achieve development objectives. Peterson, however, finds that because conflict is so insignificant in the making of developmental policies, it becomes acceptable to delegate decision making to small independent elites.

[42] Sandy Banisky, "City Trustees Going Out of Business, Schaefer Says," *The Baltimore Sun*, 7 March 1986, 1.

[43] Antero Pietila, "Patterson: From Crisis to Crisis," *The Afro-American*, 11 August 1974, 13.

[44] Bowler, 14.

[45] Elkin, *City and Regime in the American Republic*, 58.

[46] Marion Orr, *Urban Politics and School Reform: The Case of Baltimore City*. Draft. (Department of Political Science: Duke University, 1994), 9.

[47] DiConti, Veronica Donahue. *The Impact of the Bureaucratic Interest on Policymaking: The Case of Education Reform in Baltimore City*. Unpublished Masters Thesis. (Baltimore: Johns Hopkins University), 1992.

[48]   William Boyd & Florence Seldin, "The Politics of School Reform in Rochester, New York." *Education and Urban Society*, 7 (August 1975): 439-463.

[49]   Bowler, 24.

[50]   Englund, 1(A).

[51]   Will Englund, "Tightly Knit Group of Survivors Controls Power," *The Baltimore Sun*, 3 May 1988, 1(A).

[52]   Alice G. Pinderhughes, interview by Author.

[53]   Wirt, 165.

[54]   Alice G. Pinderhughes, interview by Author.

[55]   Kathy Lally, "Schools Told to Overhaul Budgeting." *The Baltimore Sun*. 19 April 1983, 1(D).

[56]   Senior Officer, The BUILD Organization, Carol Reckling, interview by Author, 17 March 1992, tape recording.

[57]   Former Principal, Montibello Elementary School, BUILD member. Mary Johnson, interview by Author, June 19, 1992, tape recording.

[58]   Carol Reckling, interview by Author.

[59]   Neal R. Pierce, "The Boston Compact-An '80's School Model." *The National Journal*. 1 February 1986: 284.

[60]   Carol Reckling, interview by Author.

[61]   Thomas, Kevin "Thousands of 12th graders Forfeit BUILD Jobs." *Evening Sun*. April 21 1986, 1(A).

[62]   Szanton, 18.

[63]   The foundation has paid the SAT fees for more than 1,000 students and the application fee for more than 500 students.

[64]   Robert J. Hilson, "Fund to Help City High School Students Attend College Raises $12.8 million." *The Baltimore Sun* 15 April 15, 1992, 6(B).

[65]   Sara Grey could not be reached for an interview in February and March of 1992.

[66]   Will Englund, "Schools Face High Expectations, Continued Problems," *The Baltimore Sun*, 12 June 1988, 1(D).

[67]   Kathy Lally, "Pinderhughes Response to Schaefer Wins Praise." *The Baltimore Sun*, 19 April 1987, 1 (B).

[68]   Will Englund, "Huge Bureaucracy Drifts Without a Plan," *The Baltimore Sun*, 1 May 1988, 18(A).

[69]   Eileen Canzian, "Welfare Tie to Schools Considered: Panel Ponders Aid Cuts in Fighting Absenteeism." *The Baltimore Sun*, 5 May 1986, 1 (D).

[70]   Kevin Thomas, "School Plans A Foot Before Schaefer," *The Evening Sun*, 19 April 1987, 1(A).

[71]   Gwen Ifill, "Mayor Criticizes School Management," *The Evening Sun*, 10 May 1984, 1(A).

[72] Community Activist, Morgan State University History Professor, JoAnn Robinson, interview by Author, 5 March 1992, tape recording.

[73] JoAnn Robinson, interview by Author.

[74] Mike Bowler, *The Lessons of Change*, (Baltimore: The Fund For Educational Excellence, 1990), 8.

[75] At that time, the BTU had fewer than 200 dues paying members, but 1,200 teachers, most of them in secondary schools, stayed out for two days. The strike was ignored by the 6,000 member rival PSTA, and its parent bodies, the Maryland State Teachers Association and the National Education Association, but Mayor Thomas D'Alessandro 3rd interceded and granted bargaining rights to teachers. See Bowler, *Lessons of Change*, 10.

[76] Baltimore Teacher's Union President, Irene Dandridge, interview by Author, 11 March 1992, tape recording.

[77] ibid.

[78] Jay Merwin, "Chapter One Changes? None Yet." *The Evening Sun* 9 May 1990, 1(A).

[79] *Guidelines: Chapter 1 Program Improvement Plan*. Maryland State Department of Education. Baltimore: July 1992. In 1988, under a new law that passed by Congress, the federal government begin to demand that school systems show measurable progress for Chapter One expenditures, or in the long run risk losing those funds altogether.

[80] Merwin, 1(A).

[81] Will Englund, "The Ordeal of Richard Hunter." *The Baltimore Sun Magazine*, 3 June 1990, 15.

[82] Michael Ollove, "Schmoke Picks Savvy Newcomer to Lead School Board," *The Baltimore Sun*, 12 December 1987, 9 (A).

[83] Will Englund, "Foundation Rejects Hunter Proposal," *The Baltimore Sun*, 2 May 1989, 3 (D).

[84] ibid.

[85] Director of Education Programs, The Community Foundation of Baltimore City, Martha Johnston. Interview by Author, 13 March 1992, tape recording.

[86] Will Englund, "Rebuffs by Hunter Leave School Parents, Charities, Unsure of Role," *The Baltimore Sun,* 20 March 1989, 1(A).

[87] Suzanne P. Kelly "City Schools to Abolish 122 Jobs," *The Baltimore Sun*, 6 January 1989, 1 (A).

[88] Kathy Lally, "Schools Chief Praised for Pruning Staff: Systems Critics See Hope at Last," *The Baltimore Sun*, 8 October 1989, 1 (A).

[89] Martin C. Evans, "City's Schools Fail to Collect from Medicaid," *The Baltimore Sun*, 25 March 1990, 1 (B).

[90] Evans, B(1).

[91] Irene Dandridge, interview by Author.

[92]   ibid.

[93]   ibid.

[94]   Will Englund, "City Board Shifts Power to Schools." *The Baltimore Sun.* 12 October 1990, 1(A).

[95]   Hill, Wise, and Shapiro, 21.

[96]   Executive Director, The Fund for Educational Excellence, Jerry Baum, interview by Author, March 16, 1992, tape recording.

[97]   Deputy Director, the Greater Baltimore Committee, Jeff Valentine, interview by Author, 7 March 1992, tape recording.

[98]   G. Alfred Hess, Jr. *School Restructuring, Chicago Style.* Newbury Park, California: Corwin Press, Inc. 1991.

[99]   UniServ Director, Baltimore City Teachers Association, Marilyn Hunter, interview by Author, 18 March 1992, tape recording.

[100]   CPHA, Education Director, Rob Clark, 10 March 1992, interview by Author, tape recording.

[101]   Shelia Kolman, interview by Author.

[102]   Former Elementary School Principal, The Baltimore City Public Schools, Education Team for Baltimoreans United In Leadership Development, Mary Johnson, 19 June 1992, Interview by Author, tape recording.

[103]   Jerry Baum, interview by Author.

[104]   Rob Clark, interview by Author.

[105]   Orr, 21.

[106]   "Table 58. - Enrollment, Teachers, and High School Graduates in Private and Elementary and Secondary Schools, by State: Fall 1980 and 1979-1980." *Education Digest*, 69.

[107]   Total minority enrollment in Minnesota is 8.8 percent: African-American, 3.1 percent, Hispanic, 2.1 percent, Asian, 2.9 percent, Native Americans, 1.6 percent. See Table 44, "Enrollment in public elementary and secondary schools, by race or ethnicity and State: Fall 1986 and Fall 1989" *Education Digest*, 58.

[108]   Bowler, 18.

Chapter Five

Conclusions and Implications for the Future

During the 1980s, the education reform debate proceeded from a public consensus reached by a diversity of interests in the policymaking arena. Business leaders along with politicians first launched the reform movement at the start of the decade. Following the release of *A Nation at Risk* in 1983 by the Reagan Administration's National Commission on Excellence, the efforts of business and politicians to reform the nation's schools intensified. The "excellence movement," as the reform effort became popularly known, followed almost two decades of dramatic nationwide declines in student achievement levels.

Excellence in education was an essential ingredient for greater economic productivity, business and political leaders argued, because it would help meet the needs of an increasingly technological society. Initially, this powerful coalition succeeded in enacting numerous reforms in states that were designed to raise educational standards. By elevating educational standards, reformers hoped that students and teachers would be forced to work hard to improve their performance.

But as the excellence movement progressed, the interest of the education establishment in general and the school system's bureaucracy in particular could not be engaged in the coalition's efforts. As a result, after several years of increased monitoring and accounting activity, student performance remained stagnant. By 1986, the education discussion shifted away from the goal of improving student performance to the mechanism of how to reach that goal. Restructuring, reformers argued, would be the mechanism to reach that goal. As the popularity of restructuring increased, two proposals became prominent in the reform debate. Both proposals sought to minimize or eliminate the potential for bureaucratic interference with new educational policies by shifting functions away from the central administrators down to the students and schools themselves.

Choice proposals, restructuring proponents argued, would change the incentive structure of public schools from an essentially bureaucratic model to one more closely attuned to client preferences, while School-Based Management models propose ways to reform the existing bureaucratic structure of schools by decentralizing some functions as a way of making school programs more responsive to the communities the schools should be serving.

The proposals, Public School Choice and School-Based Management, gained widespread application and popularity in the United States. Although it is difficult to say with certainty how many of the nation's 15,000 school districts moved toward restructuring, a careful examination of numerous state education documents, business reports, newspaper accounts and journal articles reveals that in almost every state, several schools districts did in fact undergo some form of restructuring.

Despite the popularity of restructuring, reform minded business leaders and politicians encountered resistance to their efforts, once again from the public school bureaucracies themselves -- the school boards, the central administration staff, and in many instances, the school superintendent. Instead of joining the restructuring reform effort, the education establishment became an interest group in its own right and continued to pursue protectionist policies.

But as the popularity of restructuring increased in reform debates across the country, the nation's teachers deserted the education establishment and joined the effort to improve the schools. Their interest stemmed from the fact that several reports from 1986-1988 strongly emphasized the value of decentralizing functions from the central education bureaucracy to the schools themselves as a way of giving teachers an expanded role in decision making and increasing their professional status.[1]

All three interest groups -- business leaders, political officials and teachers -- did reach a consensus on the need to increase school autonomy as a way to achieve higher levels of academic achievement. In fact, during the restructuring movement, the business community, politicians and educators not only provided most of the fuel that generated school reform but the balance of power among them went far in explaining the political settlements shaping educational policy.

Although reform advocates achieved a consensus on the need to restructure the schools, reformers disagreed on whether an increase in opportunities for exit, as provided by School Choice, or an increase in the use of voice, as provided by School-Based Management, would be the more successful reform strategy to pursue. For example, politicians and educators significantly shaped the restructuring debate, in both Minnesota and Baltimore, private sector involvement in general and the business community in particular, became a significant element in stimulating and creating an environment in which educational improvement would occur. In each case, the business community, acting through an organization of business leaders, stimulated the education debate by placing their agenda in the center of the policymaking arena, and becoming recognized players, for the first time, in education reform.

Although the business community influenced the reform debate, nonetheless, the influence each of the interest groups brought into the policymaking arena explains why a deterioration in some school systems generated a demand for the exit option offered by the schools of Choice concept while deterioration in other school districts led to pressure for School-Based Management systems that would in turn strengthen the use of voice.

Reformers, however, do not necessarily need to make a choice between the two reform strategies, largely because School Choice and School-Based Management are not incompatible. Used together judiciously exit and voice mechanisms can serve the cause of reform. The disagreement on which type of restructuring effort to pursue, however, stemmed from the intentions of reformers. Politicians were more closely aligned with Choice because it promised fundamental reform at a minimal cost. Teachers, on the other hand, feared School Choice because the resulting competition threatened both the security of their jobs and their collective bargaining positions. Instead, teachers supported School-Based Management as a way to direct reform efforts to their advantage. In the process the teachers sought to gain authority and resources from central education bureaucracies. In essence, the group that acted as the chief catalyst for reform strongly influenced the kind of reform that was adopted.

The case studies presented in chapters three and four highlight the ability of interest groups to capture and redefine a public institution based on the mechanisms of exit and voice. The research also provides an examination of the political context of recent decentralization efforts and the acceptable exit and voice models for reform that emerged. In both cases, a model emerges that explicates the techniques of reformers in the policymaking process. Reformers encountered numerous problems in the policymaking arena when competing interests tried to carry out either Choice or School-Based Management as strategies for improving the performance of school systems. From their initiatives and efforts, several general patterns appear in the policymaking arena that also emerged in other states and school districts that began to debate the merits of Open Enrollment and School-Based Management.

In terms of Public School Choice, Minnesota Governor Perpich advanced a reform model that would remove two of the most contentious features from the exit option that had previously stymied acceptance of this strategy at the national and state levels. The first was the cost of the program. School Choice woulu satisfy the demands of both lawmakers and the business community by requiring minimal expenditures. -- $50,000 per year for the transportation of low-income students. The second issue concerned the flow of public dollars to sectarian as well as other types of private schools. Unlike previous exit option programs, School Choice remained within the public school system. This was essential in a state like Minnesota where strong teachers organizations viewed the competition introduced by vouchers as an arrangement that would weaken their collective bargaining position.

Although Perpich eliminated these two controversial elements from his initiative, it still took almost a decade to create sufficient support to set up Public School Choice in Minnesota. After Perpich presented his reform proposal, "Access to Excellence," significant compromises reached in the Governor's Discussion Group, such as making the program voluntary for the first two years, smoothed the way for the bill's passage in the state legislature. By the end of the 1980s, the idea of Public School Choice became acceptable to members of the education community, particularly the most vocal opponents, the

Minnesota Education Association and the School Boards Association. This acceptance was due in large measure to the fact that nearly all the policy formulations that emerged from the Governor's Discussion Group had been a part of the political debate in Minnesota since 1980. The Choice concept grew substantially from the original initiative sponsored in 1980 by State Legislator Conni Levi to the 1991 Charter School Law. As School Choice became more acceptable to opponents, it became possible to put it into effect on a limited basis in the state. Finally, by 1990, the Open Enrollment law became mandatory for all Minnesota school districts.

In general, elected officials across the country began the dialogue for Public School Choice and looked to set up the Minnesota model in their states. The is true of four of the five states -- Arkansas, Idaho, Utah, Iowa and Nebraska -- that followed Minnesota's lead and implemented Open Enrollment plans by 1990. In Arkansas, for example, then former Governor William Clinton saw the opportunity to embrace one piece of the Republican platform that would endear him to more conservative voters as he began his quest for the presidency. Idaho State Legislator Herm Steger and Utah State Legislator Richard Bradford, both Republicans, also became the main spokesman for Open Enrollment even though their states already had intradistrict transfer policies in effect for public school students. For many years Idaho law was such that there was voluntary open enrollment throughout the state and about half the school districts were engaged in allowing students to transfer across district lines. Under the old open enrollment plan, students were paying tuition. After passage of the 1990 law, students were no longer required to pay tuition in the new district. In Utah, on the other hand, the state had a general statute statement since the 1940s that permitted students to transfer between all 40 school districts. The 1990 law in Utah merely codified an existing practice. Both Steger and Bradford wanted to gain recognition for their states during the education reform movement while at the same time showing solidarity for the National Republican Platform.

The second pattern for change is the need for coalitions to either support new initiatives or acquiescence in the policymaking arena. A review of the evidence suggests that enacting Open Enrollment Plans depends on public officials deliberately building supportive coalitions. But the acquiescence of coalitions is equally important. For example, the consent of education groups like the Minnesota Education Association and the Minnesota School Boards Association was an important element in the passage of Open Enrollment. This was also true in other states. In Iowa and Nebraska, for example, the Iowa Education Association and the Nebraska Education Association along with the School Boards Associations did not oppose Open Enrollment as long as the program was voluntary and did not include vouchers.

Finally, the implementation of Choice programs has been successful largely for two more reasons. First, in each of the five states that replicated the Minnesota Open Enrollment Plan, it was attractive to reformers and legislators because it did not require a new set of appropriations to become operational.

Second, each of these states has a relatively low minority enrollment in the public schools, with white enrollments above 75 percent.[2]   In places like Little Rock, Arkansas, where minority enrollment stands at 64 percent and is the highest in the state, limits are placed on the movement of students by court-ordered desegregation plans.[3]

Education reform in Minnesota demonstrates the power of interest groups in the policymaking systems. The same is true for Baltimore. As different as Minnesota is from Baltimore City, their reform efforts resembled one another in several aspects.   Like Minnesota, questions of accountability and effectiveness surrounded the day to day operations of the Baltimore City public school system. In Minnesota, the Business Partnership sought to change a system in decline. In Baltimore, on the other hand, the Greater Baltimore Committee sought ways to help an education system in genuine crisis. In both cases, the business community pushed education reform to the top of the public agenda.   The Greater Baltimore Committee, however, took a less controversial position on school reform than its Minnesota counterpart.

In Minnesota, business leadership for education reform started at the state level as part of a new coalition for education reform spearheaded by governors and legislators. This contrasts sharply with the coalitions that were formed at the local level.   In Baltimore City, business involvement began as supportive services, and, in fact, much of their involvement in the schools remained on the periphery of educational policy.

For example, the Greater Baltimore Committee began by pursuing policies and programs that were administered directly by the individual schools.   In this way, reformers hoped to develop and effectively increase the mechanisms of voice in the educational policymaking arena and remain distant from political battles brewing at the city's central administration. But without any force behind their recommendations, programs, such as the 1983 Site-Based Budgeting program, just faded away.

Although the pilot project did not receive the support necessary from the central education bureaucracy to become fully operational, the program did signal an important change in the direction that educational policymaking would take in Baltimore City. Site-Based Budgeting began a ten-year incremental movement toward School-Based Management because reformers, along with a weak superintendent, were hoping to decrease the authority of the school system's central administration.

This shift in authority would accelerate with the creation of programs such as the Partnership Agreement, the Baltimore Commonwealth and Project CollegeBound began in the schools. Initiated by the Greater Baltimore Committee, BUILD and other members of the private sector, these programs should have provided local area businesses with more qualified employees, provided a guarantee that more of Baltimore's minority youth could take advantage of the opportunities created by economic development and brought more resources and better organization into the school system.

In addition, the Partnership program, Commonwealth and Project CollegeBound increased the role of the individual school in the policymaking process. By setting up programs directly at the school site, each school would receive the resources tailored to its specific needs. In the process, individual schools, as well as the groups they served, would participate in policymaking.

But Commonwealth and CollegeBound did not have the backing from school personnel to become fully effective or operational. In the policymaking arena in general, it is important to obtain bureaucratic consensus on ends and means in order to achieve the desired outcome.[4]

Although the private sector had the support of Superintendent Pinderhughes, the programs encountered hostility from the administrators at the central headquarters.

The next superintendent, Dr. Richard Hunter, was also hostile to outside interest groups. Hunter began his administration by closing down arrangements with interest groups that the outgoing Superintendent Alice Pinderhughes had spent years in developing. Conflict and the pursuit of bureaucratic autonomy became characteristic of the policy process as Hunter resisted attempts to decentralize school programs and decisions.

Hunter also attempted to stop School-Based Management from beginning in the city's schools. School-Based Management, however, finally emerged when the Baltimore Teacher's Union, in cooperation with PSASA and BUILD, successfully negotiated a provision for this arrangement in its contract. Like collective bargaining, School-Based Management became a part of bilateral decision making: the participation of management and employee representatives in decision making about conditions of work and professional practice. In Baltimore as in other cities, the school board and city hall officials remained dependent on the teachers for information, policy recommendations and policy implementation. School-Based Management, originally introduced as a way to increase parental and neighborhood involvement, evolved into a device for increasing the authority of teachers in relation to the central administration of the schools.

In general, the catalyst for School-Based Management has been the collective bargaining position of the union, particularly members of the American Federation of Teachers. Union leaders were interested in School-Based Management as a way to diminish the authority of a central education bureaucracy and advance their members interest. In Dade County, Los Angeles, New York City, Cincinnati, Rochester, Toledo, Hammond, Albuquerque, San Francisco and Pittsburgh, it was the leadership of the Union that pressed the school district for School-Based Management as part of their contract.

The actual implementation of School-Based Management, however, remains an elusive goal. In fact, school observers identify eight barriers to successful implementation: resistance to changing roles and responsibilities, fear of losing power, inadequate or inappropriate resources, lack of definition and clarity, lack of skills, lack of trust, lack of hierarchical support, and fear of taking risks.[5] All eight elements were present in the Baltimore case study and have been found in other School-Based Management reform efforts. For example, in Chicago, the district created individual councils for the city's 545 public schools to increase local control. Each locally elected council, composed of six parents, two teachers and two community representatives, had broad budgeting and governing powers including the authority to hire the principal, establish performance standards, develop the schools budget and prepare a school improvement plan.

But the Chicago school reforms, legislated in the face of resistance from the school system, were unable to become effective or even begin at all. Council members could not get information from the central headquarters necessary to make proper decisions, in the areas, for example, of budget and curriculum.

Implications for the Future

It is difficult to argue that either the possibility or the practice of exit or voice has made a positive contribution to the cause of education reform in America's big cities. Moreover, it has been quite clear for some time that neither Public School Choice nor School-Based Management is capable of addressing the major problems facing U.S. education and neither of the reforms is capable of bringing about the massive structural changes reformers were seeking. The poor performance of Choice and School-Based Management as catalysts for change is largely due to the fact that much of the debate in reform circles had very little to do with teaching and learning or educational philosophy and the functions of schools beyond their contributions to economic development and employment. Although education reform touched upon certain important systemic issues, in general it has remained peripheral to what goes on in the classroom. In fact, the proposals for structural reform were not serious attempts to improve the quality of education. Instead, the proposals served educationally extraneous interests that sought to weaken a central administrative authority.

For example, Public School Choice, or Open Enrollment, did not become a significant catalyst for change in Minnesota. Less than 1 percent of the state's school population took advantage of the program, and most of them for reasons of convenience, not education. Minnesota's last attempt at increasing the exit and voice option, Charter schools, is a minuscule initiative in a state with 700,000 school age children. In Baltimore City, on the other hand, there was even less change. Out of 177 schools, only 14 schools applied to become part of the School-Based Management effort in its first year. The result was that School Choice and School-Based Management never successfully threatened the hegemony of the public schools.

Privatization

In fact, the failure of Public School Choice and School-Based Management to achieve any measurable improvement in the schools has prompted new ways of diminishing the role of the central education bureaucracy and has even led to private companies running public schools in Minnesota and Baltimore City. In Minneapolis the City's School Board voted in November 1993 to turn over management of all city schools to Public Strategies, Inc., to manage its 75 schools and $220 million dollar budget while the city's school board would continue to set policy. Minneapolis's attempt to change school management is the most sweeping to date.[6] Public Strategies Inc., is the only company to manage an entire school district. In Minneapolis the school system consists of 82 schools, 45,000 students and 4,000 teachers. This takeover, however, leaves the district budget, teachers and facilities up to the control of the school system. Instead, Public Strategies assumed control of the Superintendent's office and Minneapolis paid the company for its leadership services, $250,000 in 1994. Peter Hutchinson, designated as the superintendent, works with school district and Public Strategies professionals assembled solely to produce the results specified in the contract.

Public Strategies, Inc., has worked with a variety of clients across the country including municipalities, state agencies, school districts, county agencies and even zoos. In Minneapolis, the company receives payment only if it produces specific results, including safer schools, higher student achievement and curriculum reform.[7] The company re-invests any savings generated along the way. This contract arrangement is different from privatization. Privatization involves turning over part of the school system to a private company that operates the schools for profit which the firm captures from running the schools more efficiently.[8] Minnesota's effort to hire a private company has been much less controversial than Baltimore's because Minnesota differs significantly from Baltimore City in two ways.

To begin with, in Baltimore, Education Alternatives Inc. (EAI), a small Minneapolis firm, guaranteed that it would improve student's skills and raise attendance while at the same time it also guaranteed investors that it will make a profit. These two goals, opponents argue, collide with one another. Secondly, school privatization has meant handing over control of district budget, teachers and facilities.

In Baltimore the move to privatize some of the city's schools began during the summer of 1990. During this period, Mayor Schmoke lost confidence in Superintendent Hunter and was frustrated with the slow pace of restructuring, a plan which some critics called vague and too timid.[9] John Golle, chief executive officer of EAI contacted Robert Embry, the Abell Foundation Director, after receiving a feeble response from Hunter. Embry then brought the idea of a private company running some public schools to Schmoke's attention.

For the 1993-1994 school year, the city contracted with EAI to run eight elementary schools and one middle school, all situated in poor, inner-city communities. Later, the company started to provide support services to three schools, known as consulting schools. In the first nine schools, the Minneapolis company used a new education model it developed, called Tesseract, after a fictional dimension in the book *A Wrinkle in Time*.

The Tesseract model relies on low student-teacher ratios, the use of computers and other technology. EAI also provided facility maintenance services to the schools while its partner, Johnson Controls, handled repairs, landscaping, and janitorial services. Finally, KPMG Peat Marwick, an accounting and consulting firm, provided managerial and financial expertise to the management of the schools.

The five-year contract covered more than 5,100 students and included provisions to allow expansion beyond the nine initial schools. Under the Baltimore agreement, Education Alternatives should have received the same average cost per student, $5,415, which the city spends in its other schools.

Controversy, however, started almost immediately after EAI's takeover. For example, EAI's decision to replace $12-an-hour with $8-an-hour college educated "interns" at the company's Tesseract schools triggered opposition from the Baltimore Teachers' Union. The BTU, which represents the paraprofessionals and its parent American Federation of Teachers, launched a national campaign against EAI.[10]

But in March, 1996 Baltimore ended the three-and-a-half year experiment in school Privatization. In addition to requiring more money than the average per pupil expenditure, an independent evaluation by the Center for Educational Research at the University of Maryland Baltimore County showed that test scores did not improve. Other experiments in the city, however, such as the partnership with the Barclay and Calvert school showed improvement. Mr. Schmoke said the Tesseract agreement must require better student performance at no greater cost to the city.[11] The city decided to terminate its five-year contract with EAI in December when the firm appeared unwilling to accept $7 million in cuts this school year. The school system expects to save about $3 million gross this year by terminating the contract, though after the extended leases and contracts, the savings will be closer to $1.25 million.[12]

Political considerations no doubt dominated the mayor's position on privatization. Many school observers credited the mayor's move as a way to defuse what was likely to become one of the most significant election-year issues. City Council President Mary Pat Clarke, who challenged Mr. Schmoke's bid as the Democratic nominee for a third term, was an outspoken critic of the EAI venture.

EAI, in fact, has lost several contracts. Although the company successfully runs two of its own private schools in Minnesota and Arizona, the same has not been true for its public school operations. For example, in 1991, EAI brought its Tesseract method and classroom materials to South Point Elementary, a new public school. At the end of 1994, the company's role at the school ended because scores on standardized tests increased at about the same rate at those of a nearby comparison school. But Dade County school officials did not walk away from privatization. Instead they agreed in December 1995 to work with EAI's main rival, the Edison project financed by entrepreneur Christopher Whittle. The City of Hartford, Connecticut, provides another recent example. In September 1994, EAI began managing the entire 32-school district, which has an enrollment of about 24,000 pupils and a $171 million budget. By 1995, however, after several disputes with the company, the city canceled the contract.

The New Politics of Decentralization

Whether the decision to remove EAI was politically motivated or based on sound educational decision making, it looks like privatization is likely to continue in the public schools. In fact, many private contractors are handling public schools services for Baltimore. At a news conference announcing the city's plan to cancel the contract, Dr. Amprey said the lesson is not to shun for-profit school management. Rather, he said, the lesson is to build a better contract.[13] In addition to EAI, Baltimore has other private vendors in the public schools, like the Sylvan Company. The Sylvan Learning Systems best-known for supplementary academic instruction, now does Chapter One instruction at 10 centers in Baltimore, 3 more in the Eastern Shore area of Maryland, and 2 schools in Pasadena, Texas.[14] At Sylvan's 29 centers in Baltimore schools, when students do not met agreed-upon achievement goals, the company loses profit because it must continue to tutor the children at no extra cost to the school system.

More examples in Baltimore City include the Efficacy Institute of Massachusetts, which trains teachers and other school staff to raise expectations of children, and a contract started in 1994 with the Marriott Corporation to run cafeterias in almost 30 schools.

Private management of public schools and the trend toward privatization both demonstrate a need to decentralize large public school systems. Decentralization, at least for quite some time in the future, will continue to gain popularity with reformers for two reasons.

First, faced with disparate groups -- each with its own notion of which ideas and values are important, it is easier to abandon the idea of collective purpose. It is perhaps more comfortable to settle into smaller communities like those offered by School-Based Management or even the smaller circle of family or individual that Public School Choice can provide. It is this urge to retreat that ultimately accounts for much of the popular appeal of both forms of decentralization, exit and voice, and also accounts for much of the appeal of privatization.[15]

Secondly, decentralization will continue to be popular because it promises some relief for potentially explosive school problems. In a highly centralized system, conflict at any point in the school system -- at a particular school for example -- becomes a problem for the center, especially when disturbances ripple throughout the system. Decentralizing authority not only relieves the center's burden of responding to the problem, but, what is more important, it increases the probability of containing a conflict within a specific neighborhood.[16] Therefore, reforms that strengthen exit or voice will continue to be attractive to reformers in the future and perhaps even to school administrators themselves.

Notes

[1]   Carnegie Task Force. The National Governors Association. *Time For Results, Investing in our Children*, 1985 and *Children in Need*, Committee For Economic Development, 1990.

[2] Using 1989 figures, the year the Open Enrollment Plans were debated or enacted, Arkansas is 74.8 percent white, Idaho, 92.6 Utah, 93.7 percent white, Iowa, 94.5 percent white, and Nebraska, 90.3 percent white. *Education Digest,* Table 44 - "Enrollment in Public Elementary and Secondary Schools, by Race or Ethnicity and State: Fall 1986 and 1989.

[3] In a state like Maryland, however, it is unlikely that the parents or state legislators would even consider an Open Enrollment Plan. The percentage of minorities is much greater than in other states and concentrated in a few counties. Statewide out of the nine largest school districts, Baltimore City and Prince George's County have the highest minority enrollments, 82 percent and 71 percent respectively. The other seven all have substantially less minorities, ranging from almost 37 percent in Montgomery County to 8 percent in Frederick County. *Education Digest,* Table 88 - Selected Statistics for Public School Districts Enrolling More than 20,000 pupils by State: 1989-1990, 97.

[4] Graham Allison, *Essence of Decision: Explaining the Cuban Missile Crisis,* (Boston: Little, Brown and Company, 1971), p. 112.

[5] The problems encountered when changing from a traditional organizational structure to one based on School-Based Management were explored by the Southwest Educational Development Laboratory through contacts with educational practitioners currently implementing the strategies. See "Insights on Educational Policy and Practices." July 1990, Number 21, Austin, Southwest Educational Development Laboratory, 3.

[6] "Private Company Agrees to Run Baltimore Schools. *Wall Street* 1 *Journal,* 10 June 1992, 6(B).

[7] Linda Kanamine, "School Operations Fails for Profit Test," *USA Today,* 24 November 1995, 3(A).

[8] Sharon L. Jones, "School-operating Business Chalks Up Mixed Grades," *The San Diego Union-Tribune,* 13 November 1993, 1(A).

[9] Orr, 31.

[10] Jean Thompson, "School Board Urges Mayor to Drop EAI," *The Baltimore Sun,* 22 November 1995, 1(A).

[11] Jean Thompson and JoAnna Daemmrich, "Schmoke's Intervention In Schools Stirs Questions," *The Baltimore Sun,* 20 March 1995, 1(B).

[12] Mary Maushard, "Contract with EAI Ends Today," *The Baltimore Sun,* 4 March 1996, 3(B).

[13] Jean Thompson, "Officials Assess Lessons of EAI," *The Baltimore Sun,* 26 November 1996, 1(C).

[14] Dennis Kelly, "In Business to Education," *USA Today,* 17 October 1994, 1(D).

[15] Henig, 9. Henig's argument is based on the specific segment of the education reform movement that draws on market models for inspiration. I

take Henig's argument one step further and say this also applies to another form of decentralization, School-Based Management.

[16] Paul Peterson, "Afterward: The Politics of School Decentralization," 475.

APPENDIX

INTERVIEWS

Anderson, John, Vice President, Education Initiative for International Business Machine, Chairman, Education Task Force, the Business Roundtable, 1987-1990. Interview by Author, 6 March 1992, Washington. Tape recording.

Armstrong, Malethia, UniServ Director, Baltimore City Teachers Association. Interview by Author, 18 March 1992, Baltimore. Tape Recording.

Baum, Jerry, Executive Director, The Fund for Educational Excellence. Interview by Author, 16 March 1992, Baltimore. Tape recording.

Barrett, Joan, Executive Director, Arizona Business and Education (ABLE). Interview by Author, 7 August 1992. Tape Recording.

Bates, Douglas, Coordinator of Utah School Law and Legislation. Interview by Author, 11 August 1992. Tape Recording.

Billirakis, Michael, Vice President, Ohio Education Association. Interview by Author, 13 August 1992. Tape Recording.

Blair, Nancy, Arizona Department of Education. Interview by Author, 6 August 1992. Tape Recording.

Bliegh, Robert, Legal Counsel, Nebraska Association of School Boards. Interview by Author, 11 August 1992. Tape Recording.

Bradford, Richard J., Utah Republican State House Representative, 1982-1992. Interview by Author, 19 August 1992. Tape Recording.

Burningham, Dee, Director of Governmental Relations, Utah Education Association. Interview by Author, 17 August 1992. Tape Recording.

Bussey, Phil, Vice President, Washington Roundtable. Interview by Author, 17 August 1992. Tape Recording.

Butts, Robert, Research Analyst, Washington House of Representatives. Interview by Author, 17 August 1992. Tape Recording.

Cairns, John, Director, Public School Incentives. Former President, Minnesota Business Partnership, 1979-1984. Interview by Author, 24 September, 1992. Tape Recording.

Camp, Kenneth, R., Director of Governmental Affairs, Arkansas State Chamber of Commerce & Association Industries of Arkansas. Interview by Author, 14 August 1992. Tape Recording.

Chilcote, Richard, President, Idaho Education Association. Interview by Author, 17 August 1992. Tape Recording.

Clark, Rob, Education Director, Citizen's Planning and Housing Association. Interview by Author, 10 March 1992, Baltimore. Tape Recording.

Collins, Lester, Executive Director, Council on Black Minnesotans. Interview by Author, 27 August 1992. Tape Recording.

Condie, Betty, Executive Director, Utah Education Association. Interview by Author, 17 August 1992. Tape Recording.

Cross, Christopher, Former Executive Director, Education Project, The Business Roundtable. President Maryland State Board of Education. Interview by Author, 26 February 1992, Washington. Tape Recording.

Dandridge, Irene, President, the Baltimore Teachers Union. Interview by Author, 11 March 1992, Baltimore. Tape Recording.

Davis, Kim, Research Analyst, Nebraska State Senate. Interview by Author, 11 August 1992. Tape Recording.

Drees, Jan, Program Coordinator, Iowa Business and Education Alliance. Interview by Author, 6 August 1992. Tape Recording.

Evans, Dr. Jeanette, Director of Special Projects, Baltimore City Public Schools. Interview by Author, 16 March 1992, Baltimore. Tape Recording.

Falconer, Mark, Public Affairs Manager, Hewlett Packard, Boise, Idaho. Interview by Author, 19 March 1992. Tape Recording.

Fallin, Deborah, Director of Public Relations, Colorado Education Association. Interview by Author, 19 August 1992. Tape Recording.

Freiland, Carolyn, Iowa Business and Education Roundtable. Interview by Author, 10 August 1992. Tape Recording.

Friend, Mike, Idaho Association of School Administrators. Interview by Author, 7 August 1992. Tape Recording.

Gannon, Mary, Iowa Association of School Boards. Interview by Author, 7 August 1992. Tape Recording.

Ginsburg, Tru. President, Metropolitan Education Coalition. Interview by Author, 18 March 1992, Baltimore. Tape Recording.

Gleave, Winston, Executive Director, Utah School Boards Association. Interview by Author, 17 August 1992. Tape Recording.

Green, Richard, Dr., Director of Education Affairs, Honeywell Corporation, Minneapolis. Interview by Author, 24 September 1992.

Hammond, Utah PTA Officer, Utah Parent Teacher Association. Interview by Author, 17 August, 1992. Tape Recording.

Hanaker, Sue, Administrator, Minnesota Senate Education Committee. Interview by Author, 18 September 1992. Tape Recording.

Hartley, Ed, Boise Education Administration, Boise, Idaho School District. Interview by Author, 21 August 1992. Tape Recording.

Harris, Larry, Former Director of Legislative and Community Relations, Minneapolis Public Schools, 1967-1988. Interview by Author, 8 September 1992. Tape Recording.

Hay, Janet, Chairman, Idaho House Education Committee, 1984-1990. Interview by Author, 17 August 1992. Tape Recording.

Helvick, Don, Consultant, Iowa Bureau of School Administrators and Accreditation. Interview by Author, 7 August 1992. Tape Recording.

Henderson, Mike, Policy Analyst, Washington House of Representatives. Interview by Author, 21 August 1992. Tape Recording.

Hermanson, Rose, Director of Legislation, Minnesota Federation of Teachers. Interview by Author, 17 September 1992. Tape Recording.

Hoskyn, Jim, Committee Administrator, Minnesota Education Finance Committee. Interview by Author, 15 September 1992. Tape Recording.

Hunter, Marilyn, UniServ Director, Baltimore City Teachers Association. Interview by Author, 18 March 1992, Baltimore. Tape Recording.

Hutchison, Richard, Government Relations Director, Arkansas Education Association. Interview by Author, 21 August 1992. Tape Recording.

Jenni, Phil, Finance Director, The Citizen League. Interview by Author, 24 August 1992. Tape Recording.

Jensen, Dale, Executive Director, Minnesota Association of School Administrators. Interview by Author, 26 August 1992. Tape Recording.

Johnson, Carl, Director of Legislative Services, Minnesota School Boards Association. Interview by Author, 3 September 1992. Tape Recording.

Johnston, Martha, Program Director, Community Foundation of Baltimore. Interview by Author, 13 March 1992, Baltimore.

Johnson, Mary, Former Elementary School Principal, The Baltimore City Public Schools, Education Team for Baltimoreans United In Leadership Development. Interview by Author, 19 June 1992. Tape Recording.

Johnson, Verne, Vice President, General Mills, Former Executive Director, Citizen's League, Minneapolis. Interview by Author. 18 September 1992. Tape Recording.

Kawimura, Lani. Former Commissioner of Minnesota State Planning Agency. Chief Policy Advisor to Governor Rudy Perpich, 1983-1991. Interview by Author. Tape recording.

Keating, Van, Staff Attorney, Ohio School Board Association. Interview by Author, 13 August 1992. Tape Recording.

Kemble, Eugenia, Director of Education Issues. American Federation of Teachers. Interview by Author, 24 September 1992. Tape Recording.

Kerr, David, Project Coordinator, Indiana COMMIT. Interview by Author, 13 August 1992. Tape Recording.

Kirkpatrick, David, Executive Director, Reach Alliance. Interview by Author, 12 June 1992. Tape Recording.

Koch, Elbert, Executive Director, Minnesota Elementary School Principals Association. Interview by Author, 3 September 1992. Tape Recording.

Kolderie, Ted, Analyst. The Humphrey Institute, University of Minnesota Minneapolis Campus. Interview by Author, 11 September, 1992. Tape Recording.

Kolman, Shelia, President, Public School Administrators and Supervisors Association. Interview by Author, 23 March 1992. Tape Recording.

Levi, Connie, Former Minnesota State Representative, (R) 1979-1986, House Majority Leader, 1984-1986, Education Committee Member, 1979-1986. Interview by Author, 14 September 1992. Tape Recording.

Lindgren, Steven, Minneapolis Public Affairs Consultant. Interview by Author, 14 September 1992. Tape Recording.

Loritz, Daniel, Deputy Chief of Staff to Governor Rudy Perpich, 1989-1991, Minnesota Governor's Lobbyist 1987-1988, Director of Government Relations, Minnesota Department of Education, 1985-1986, Minnesota Assistant Education Commissioner, 1983-1984. Interview by Author, 10 September 1992. Tape Recording.

Luehr, Paul, Assistant to the Director of the Arkansas Department of Education. Interview by Author, 3 September 1992. Tape Recording.

Lundy, Marilyn, Michigan State Board of Education Member. Interview by Author, 14 August 1992. Tape Recording.

Lyon, Marina, Program Officer, McKnight Foundation Minneapolis. Interview by Author, 11 September 1992. Tape Recording.

McDermott, James. Minnesota Federation of Teachers, Union Representative. Interview by Author, 8 September 1992. Tape Recording.

McKnew, Mary, Executive Policy Assistant to Governor Booth Gardner, Washington State. Interview by Author, 11 August 1992. Tape Recording.

Mahony, Jodie, Arkansas Democratic State Representative, 1970 -, Education Committee Member. Interview by Author, 14 August 1992. Tape Recording.

Mammingay, Eugene, Former Minnesota Commissioner of Education 1990-1993, Director of Governmental Relation, 1987-1990, Chief Lobbyist, Minnesota Education Association, 1974-1984. Interview by Author, 30 September 1992. Tape Recording.

Mattheis, Duane, Executive Director, Association of Metropolitan School Districts, Minneapolis. Interview by Author, 8 September 1992. Tape Recording.

Meyer, Neil, Former President, Minneapolis Citizens Committee for Public Education (MCCPE). Interview by Author, 11 September 1992. Tape Recording.

Miller, Sally, Trustee, The Community Foundation of Baltimore. Interview by Author, 13 March 1992, Baltimore.

Murphy, Larry, Iowa State Senator (D), 1984-. Interview by Author, 10 August 1992. Tape Recording.

Nathan, Joe, Education Consultant, University of Minnesota. Interview by Author, 10 September 1992. Tape Recording.

Nelson, Tom, Former Minnesota Education Commissioner, 1989. Former Minnesota State Senator (DFL), 1977-1986. Interview by Author, 8 September 1992. Tape Recording.

Northcutt, Wanda, Arkansas Democratic House Representative, Education Committee. Interview by Author, 14 August 1992. Tape Recording.

Otterson, Ron, President, Minneapolis Citizens Committee for Public Education (MCCPE). Interview by Author, 10 September 1992.

Peterson, Judge Randolph W., Former Minnesota State Senator, 1981-1990. Chairman of the Education Funding Committee, 1987-1990, Education Committee Member, 1981-1990. Interview by Author, 24 September 1992. Tape Recording.

Pinderhughes, Alice, Former Baltimore City Superintendent of Public Instruction, Interview by Author, February 25, 1992, Baltimore. Tape Recording.

Plato, Cathleen, Executive Director to the Washington State Superintendent of Public Instruction. Interview by Author, 18 August 1992. Tape Recording.

Poppe, Ken, Consultant for School Restructuring and Alternatives, Denver, Colorado. Interview by Author. 21 August 1992. Tape Recording.

Price, Leonard, Educator & Minnesota State Representative, 1982-. Interview by Author, 4 September 1992. Tape Recording.

Prince, Dr. Julian, Executive Director, The Public Education Forum. Former Dean of Education, Samford University, School of Education, Advisor to the Governor, the Hunt Commission, Alabama Education Study Committee. Interview by Author, 10 August 1992. Tape Recording.

Putnam, Douglas, Deputy Director of Legislative Services, Ohio School Boards Association. Interview by Author, 19 August 1992. Tape Recording.

Quie, Al, Speaker and Consultant. Former Governor of Minnesota, 1978-1982. Former Minnesota Congressman. 1956-1978. Interview by Author, 15 September 1992. Tape Recording.

Randall, Ruth, Former Minnesota Education Commissioner. Interview by Author, 27 August 1992. Tape Recording.

Reckling, Carol, Senior Officer, Baltimoreans United In Leadership Development. Interview by Author, 17 March 1992, Baltimore. Tape Recording.

Reichgott, Ember, Minnesota State Senator. Interview by Author. 7 September 1992. Tape Recording.

Renicke, Janet, Lobbyist, Iowa Education Association. Interview by Author, 10 August 1992. Tape Recording.

Robey, Barbara, Director of Governmental Relations, Arizona School Boards Association. Interview by Author. 6 August 1992. Tape Recording.

Robinson, JoAnn, Community Activist, Professor of History, Morgan State University. Interview by Author, 5 March 1992 & 11 March 1992, Baltimore. Tape Recording.

St. Clair, Robert, Executive Director, Minnesota Association of Secondary School Principals. Interview by Author, 3 September 1992. Tape Recording.

Salinas, Elaine, Education Program Officer, Minneapolis Urban Coalition, 10 September 1992. Inrerview by Author. Tape Recording.

Sandhofer, Richard. Director for Open Enrollment, Minneapolis Public Schools. Interview by Author, 4 September 1992. Tape Recording.

Schneider, Jeffrey, Senior Policy Analyst, The National Education Association. Interview by Author, 15 September 1992. Tape Recording.

Short, Al, Michigan Education Association. Director of Governmental Affairs. Interview by Author, 11 August 1992. Tape Recording.

Speights, Dr. Patricia. Facilitator of Restructuring. Interview by Author, March 16, 1992, Baltimore. Tape Recording.

Steger, Herm, Idaho Republican State Representative 1986-1992. Interview by Author, 17 August, 1992. Tape Recording.

Strickland, June, Executive Director, Maryland Business and Education Roundtable. Interview by Author, 5 March 1992, Baltimore. Tape Recording.

Sullivan, Barry, Minnesota Department of Education. Interview by Author, 11 September 1992.

Teasley, Kevin, Executive Director. Excel Group, California. Interview by Author, 12 June 1992. Tape Recording.

Thomas, Kathryn, Vice President, Education Alternatives. Interview by Author, 9 September 1992. Tape Recording.

Tilman, Fred, Idaho Republican State House Representative. Interview by Author, 20 August 1992. Tape Recording.

Triplett, Tim, Executive Director. The Minnesota Partnership. Former Minnesota Finance Commissioner. Interview by Author. 11 September 1992.

Valentine, Jeff, Former Deputy Director of Public Policy, the Greater Baltimore Committee. Interview by Author, March 9, 1992, Baltimore. Tape Recording.

Van Laningham, Kathy, Assistant to the Vice Chancellor for Academic Affairs. Former Assistant to Governor William Clinton for Education. Interview by Author, 24 August 1992. Tape Recording.

Van Zanzt, Mark, Director of School Laws, Missouri Department of Elementary and Secondary Education. Interview by Author, 10 August 1992. Tape Recording.

Vinters, Tommy Roger, Dr., Executive Director, Arkansas School Board Association. Interview by Author, 10 August 1992. Tape Recording.

Walz, Deborah, Special Assistant for Education, Office of Former Governor William Clinton. Interview by Author, 24 August 1992. Tape Recording.

Whalen, Tommy, Vice President, Human Resources, Valmont Industries, Nebraska. Interview by Author, 26 August 1992. Tape Recording.

Wilson, Jim, Staff Attorney, Legisltaive Research and General Counsel, Utah State Legislature. Interview by Author, 13 August 1992. Tape Recording.

Wise, James, Director of Board and Community Relations, Des Moines Public Schools. Interview by Author, 10 August 1992. Tape Recording.

Zohn, Barbara, Former Resolutions Chair Minnesota Parent Teacher Association. Interview by Author, 8 September 1992. Tape Recording.

BIBLIOGRAPHY

Abell Foundation, "A Growing Inequality: A Report on the Financial Condition of the Baltimore City Public Schools." Baltimore, Maryland, January 1989.

Achilles, W.H., Payne and Z. Lanford. "Strong State-Level Leadership for Education Reform: Tennessee's Example." *Peabody Journal of Education* 63,4 (Summer 1988): 23-44.

Alexander, Lamar. "Time for Results: An Overview." *Phi Delta Kappan* 68 (November 1986): 202.

Allison, Graham. *Essence of Decision: Explaining the Cuban Missile Crisis*, Boston: Little, Brown and Company, 1971.

Arons, S. "The Peaceful Uses of Education Vouchers." edited by La Noue, G.R. *Educational Vouchers: Concepts and Controversies.* New York: Teachers College Press, 1972, 70-97.

Areen, J., C. Jencks. "Education Vouchers: A Proposal for Diversity and Choice." edited by La Noue, G.R. *Educational Vouchers: Concepts and Controversies.* New York: Teachers College Press, 1972, 49-57.

Asayesh, Gelareh. "Amprey Tells City Principals: My Door is Open." *The Baltimore Sun* 5 November 1991, 1(D).

Ascher, Carol. "Urban School-Community Alliance." *Trend and Issues* 10, Institute for Urban Minority Education: December 1988.

"Baltimore Looks to Region's talent for Schools Chief." *The Baltimore Sun* 12 January 1991, 3(B).

Bacharach, S. B, ed. *Education Reform: Making Sense of It All.* Boston: Allyn and Bacon, 1990.

Bailey, S.K., R.T. Frost, P.E. Marsh, and R.C. Wood. "Schoolmen and Politics: A Study of State Aid to Education in the Northeast." Kirst, M.E. *The Politics of Education at the Local, State and Federal Levels.* Berkeley: McCutchan Publishing Corporation, 1970: 220-250.

Baltimore City Department of Planning. *Poverty in Baltimore:Data and Indicators.* Baltimore: Baltimore City Department of Planning, 1987.

Banisky, S. "City Trustees Going Out of Business, Schaefer Says." *The Baltimore Sun* 7 March 1986, 1(A).

_____. "Embry Will Head Abell Foundation." *The Baltimore Sun* 30 May 1987, 8(A).

_____. "Embry Resigns School Job, Considers Mayoral Bid." *The Baltimore Sun* 23 November 1986, 1(A).

_____. "Mayor Begins 4th Term with School Pledge." *The Baltimore Sun* 7 December 1983, 1(A).

_____. "The Schaefer Legacy," *The Baltimore Sun* 18 January 1987, 1(E).

_____. "Promotion of Tourism Helped City Turn From Manufacturing," *The Evening Sun* 8 January 1987, 1(B).

_____. "Race Made Mayor Fret -- at First." *The Baltimore Sun* 15 September 1983, 1(E).

_____. "Schools Post Goes to Embry." *The Baltimore Sun* 4 August 1985, 1(A).

_____, S. "Schmoke Style Wears Well in 18 Months" *The Baltimore Sun* 5 June 1989, 1(A).

Barber, Benjamin, R. *An Aristocracy of Everyone: The Politics of Education and the Future of America.* New York: Ballantine Books, 1922.

Bendt, Bruce. "Much of Minnesota's Brainpower is Being Exercised Elsewhere." *Minneapolis Star and Tribune* 19 July 1987.

Berger, J. "Eighty Schools to Join Principals in Program." *New York Times* 19 July 1990, 1(A).

Berke, Richard, "Schaefer to Business leaders" More Efforts for the City." *The Evening Sun* 23 January 1985, 1(H).

Berkowitz, Bernard. "Rejoinder to Downtown Redevelopment As an Urban Growth Strategy: A Critical Appraisal of the Baltimore Renaissance." *Journal of Urban Affairs* 9, (1987):125-132.

Berman, Paul, Weiler and Associates. *The Minnesota Plan: The Design of A New Education System.* 1, Berman Weiler and Associates: Berkeley: November, 1988.

_____. Clugston, R."A Tale of Two States, the Business Community and Education Reform in California and Minnesota." 121-149.

Berry, Jeffrey M. *The Interest Group Society.* Boston: Little Brown and Company, 1984.

Bowie, Liz. "Embry Gets Mixed Grades as President: Novel Ideas Failed to Solve Chronic Problems." *The Baltimore Sun* 23 November 1986, 1(C).

Bowler, Mike. *Lessons of Change.* Baltimore: The Fund For Educational Excellence, 1990.

Bowles, Samuel and Herbert Gintis, *Schooling in Capitalist America: Educational Reform and the Contradictions of Economic Life.* New York: Basic Books, Inc., 1976.

Boyd, William L. & Florence Seldin. "The Politics of School Reform in Rochester, New York." *Education and Urban Society* 7 (August 1975): 439-463.

Boyd, W.L. "The National Level: Reagan and the Bully Pulpit." ed. S.B. Bacharach, *Education Reform: Making Sense of it All.* Boston: Allyn and Bacon, 1990: 42-51.

Boyd, W.L. and D.A. O'Shea. "Theoretical Perspectives on School District Decentralization." *Education and Urban Society,* 7, (August, 1975): 357-376.

Boyd, W.L. and F. Seldin. "The Politics of School Reform in Rochester, New York." *Education and Urban Society* 7, (August, 1975): 436-463.

Boyer, E. *High School: A Report on Secondary Education in America.* The Carnegie Foundation for the Advancement of Teaching. New York: Harper & Row, 1983.

Bridge, R.G. & Blackman, J. *A Study of Alternatives in American Education Volume IV: Family Choice in Schooling.* Santa Monica: The Rand Corporation, 1978.

The Business Roundtable, B*lueprint for Action.* The Business Roundtable Ad Hoc Committee on Education. New York: The Business Roundtable, 1988.

_____. The Business Roundtable, *The Business Roundtable Participation Guide: A Primer for Business on Education.*

Developed by the National Alliance of Business. New York: The Business Roundtable, 1990.

_____. *The Business Roundtable Directory of Education Initiatives.* New York, New York: 1990.

_____, *1991 Status Report on the Business Roundtable Education Public Policy Agenda.* Pre-publication Draft. Washington: The Business Roundtable, 1991.

Callahan, Raymond. *Education and the Cult of Efficiency.* Chicago: University of Chicago Press, 1962.

Canzian, Eileen, "City Still Struggles with Problems of Poverty." *The Baltimore Sun* 8 January 1987, 1(C).

Carnegie Forum on Education and the Economy. *A Nation Prepared: Teachers for the 21st Century.* New York, New York: May, 1986.

Carnegie Foundation for the Advancement of Teaching, *TeacherInvolvement in Decisionmaking: A State-by-State Profile.* New York: September 1988.

Celis, W. "Oregon Considers Tax Credits to Aid Private Schooling." *New York Times* August 22, 1990, 1(A).

Chubb, John, E. "Why the Current Wave of School Reform Will Fail." *The Public Interest* 90 (Winter 1988), 28-49.

Chubb, John E. T. Moe. *Politics, Markets, & America's Schools.* Washington, D.C.: Brookings Institution, 1990.

_____, "Politics, Markets and the Organization of Schools" *The American Political Science Review* 82 (December 1988): 1065-1087.

Cibulka, J.G. "School Decentralization in Chicago." *Education and Urban Society* 7 (August 1975): 412-438.

_____. "State Performance Incentives for Restructuring, Can they Work?" *Education and Urban Society* 21 (August 1989): 417-435.

Cistone, P.J., J. Fernandez, and J.A. Tornillo. "School-Based Management/Shared Decision Making in Dade County (Miami). *Education and Urban Society.* 21 (August, 1989): 393-402.

Citizens League. *Chartered Schools=Choice for Educators + Quality for All Students.* Minneapolis: The Citizens League, 1988.

_____. *Issues of The 80's: Enlarging Our Capacity to Adapt.* Minneapolis: The Citizens League, 1980.

_____.*Linking A Commitment to Desegregation with Choices for Quality Schools.* Minneapolis: The Citizens League, 1979.

_____.*Rebuilding Education To Make it Work.* Minneapolis:The Citizens League, 1978.

_____. *Remaking the Minnesota Miracle: Facing New FiscalRealities.* Minneapolis: The Citizen's League, 1990.

Clewell, B.C. & Joy, M.F. *Choice in Montclair New Jersey.* Princeton: Educational Testing Service Policy Information Center, 1990.

Cohen, D.K. "Reforming School Politics." *Harvard Educational Review* 48 (November 1978): 429-447.

_____ and E. Farrar. "Power to the Parents?- The Story of Education Vouchers." *Public Interest.* 48 (Fall/1977): 72-97.

Cohen, M. "State Boards in an Era of Reform." *Phi Delta Kappan* 69 (September, 1987): 60.

Coleman, James S. et al. *Equality of Educational Opportunity.* Washington: U.S. Office of Education, 1966

Colopy, Kelly W. & Tarr, H.C. *Minnesota's Public School Choice Options.* Washington: U.S. Department of Education, 1994.

_____, & Funkhouser, J.E. *Minnesota's Open Enrollment Option: Impact on School Districts.* Washington: U.S. Department of Education, 1994.

Committee for Economic Development, *Investing In Our Children.* New York: Committee For Economic Development, 1985.

_____. *Children in Need.* New York: Committee for Economic Development, 1990.

Congressional Budget Office, Congressional Budget Office Study, *The Federal Role in Improving Elementary and Secondary Education.* Washington: Government Printing Office, May 1983.

Conley, S.C. "Who's on First? School Reform, Teacher Participation, and the Decision making Process." *Education and Urban Society.* 21 (August, 1989) 366-379.

Coons, J.E., S. Sugarman. *Education By Choice: The Case for Family Control.* Berkeley: University of California Press, 1978.

Cooper, B.S. "Bottom-up Authority in School Organization: Implication for the Administrator." *Education and Urban Society* 21 (August, 1989): 380-392.

Corbett, D.H., J. A. Dawson, and W.A. Firestone. *School Context and Social Change: Implications for Effective Planning* New York: Teachers College Press, 1984.

Cremin, Lawrence A. *The Transformation of the American School: Progressivism in American Education* New York: Alfred A. Knopf, 1961.

_____. *Traditions of American Education.* New York: Basic Books, 1977.

Crenson, Matthew. "Urban Bureaucracy in Urban Politics Notes Toward A Developmental Theory," in J. David Greenstone *Public Values and Private Power in American Politics*. Chicago: University of Chicago Press, 1982: 209-245.

Cubberly, E.P. *The History of Education.* Boston: Houghton Mifflin, 1920.

Dahl, Robert. *Who Governs?* New Haven: Yale University Press, 1969.

Dentler, R.A. "Vouchers: A Problem of Scale." *Teachers College Record* 72 (February 1971): 383-387.

Dewey, John. *Democracy and Education*. New York: The Free Press, 1966.

DiConti, Veronica Donahue. *The Impact of the Bureaucratic Interest on Policymaking: The Case of Education Reform in Baltimore City*. Unpublished Masters Thesis. Baltimore: Johns Hopkins University, 1992.

Doyle, D.P. "The Politics of Choice: A View From the Bridge." in *Parents, Teachers and Children*. San Francisco: San Francisco Institute for Contemporary Studies, 1977: 227-355.

_____. and C.E. Finn, Jr. "American Schools and the Future of Local Control." *National Affairs* 77 (Fall 1984): 77-95.

_____. and T.W. Hartle. *Excellence in Education: The States Take Charge.* Washington, D.C.: American Enterprise Institute for Public Policy Research, 1985.

Doyle, Pat. "Minorities Soon To Be Majority In Minneapolis Public Schools." *Minneapolis Star and Tribune* 24 May 1987, 1(A).

"Economic Outlook to 1990". *The Economic Review* The Regional Planning Council: Baltimore, 1986.

Education Commission of the States, Task Force on Education for Economic Growth. *Action for Excellence* Denver: Education Commission of the States, 1983.

Edmonds, Ronald. "Effective Schools for the Urban Poor." *Educational Leadership* 37 (October 1979): 15-42.

Elkin, Stephen. *City and Regime in the American Republic*. Chicago: University of Chicago Press, 1987.

Elmore, R.F. *Restructuring Schools*. San Francisco: Jossey-Bass Publishers, 1990.

Englund, Will. "A Reorganized Bureaucracy is Still A Bureaucracy." *The Baltimore Sun* 15 January 1989, 1(D).

_____. "Baltimore Area Lowest in U.S. in Adults Finishing High School." *The Baltimore Sun* 6 December 1987, 1(C).

_____. "Baltimore Leaders Huddle over Grand Plan for High School Graduates." *The Baltimore Sun* 27 January 1988, 1(B).

_____. "Baltimore School Board Flatly Turns Down Barclay Plan." *The Baltimore Sun* 7 April 1989, 1(E).

_____. "Barclay Parents Call Schools' Action Unfair." *The Baltimore Sun* 17 March 1989, 1(E).

_____. "Barclay School Wins Curriculum Fight With Mayor's Aid." *The Baltimore Sun* 23 March 1990, 1(D).

_____. "Bureaucracy Looks Too Big From Vantage of A Classroom." *The Baltimore Sun* 2 May 1988, 13(A).

_____. "City Board Shifts Power to Schools." *The Baltimore Sun* 12 October 1990, 1(A).

_____. "City Schools, GBC Unite to Help Graduates Get Jobs." *The Baltimore Sun* 25 April 1985, 1(E).

_____. "Coalition Formed to Fight Area Schools Problems." *The Baltimore Sun* 17 February 1987, 1(D).

_____. "Foundation Rejects Hunter Proposal." *The Baltimore Sun* 2 May 1989, 3(D).

_____. "Hollis Says Barclay Plan Needs Airing." *The Baltimore Sun* 15 March 1989, 1(D).

_____. "Huge Bureaucracy Drifts Without a Plan." *The Baltimore Sun* 1 May 1988, 18(A).

_____. "Hunter Gives Up School Chief's Role to Active Schmoke." *The Baltimore Sun* 7 January 1990, 1(A).

_____. "Hunter Outlines Highs Hopes, Goals for City Students." *The Baltimore Sun* 23 August 1990, 1(B).

_____. "Hunter Says He Will Stay on the Job." *The Baltimore Sun* 21 March 1990, 2(A).

_____. "Hunter to Re-evaluate National Science Project." *The Baltimore Sun* 3 March 1989, 1(A).

_____. "Hunter Requests $506 Million for Baltimore Schools." *The Baltimore Sun* 22 December 1989, 1(A).

_____. "Hunter Tells Officials He Will Stay Despite Those Out to Get Him." *The Baltimore Sun* 19 January 1989, 1(D).

_____. "Loosening Central Control is Next Step for Schools." *The Baltimore Sun* 23 October 1989, 1(B).

_____. "Mayor Bids School Principals Work Directly with Him." *The Baltimore Sun* 16 December 1989, 1(A).

_____. "Mayor Wants Hunter Out, Sources Say." *The Baltimore Sun* 20 March 1990, 1(A).

_____. "Rebuffs by Hunter Leave School Parents, Charities, Unsure of Role." *The Baltimore Sun* 20 March 1989, 1(A).

_____. "Schools Face High Expectations, Continued Problems." *The Baltimore Sun* 12 June 1988, 1(D).

_____. "Tightly Knit Group of Survivors Controls Power."*The Baltimore Sun* 3 May 1988, 1(A).

_____. "The Ordeal of Richard Hunter" *Baltimore Sun Magazine* 3 June 1990.

Evans, Martin C. "City's Schools Fail to Collect from Medicaid." *The Baltimore Sun* 25 March 1990, 1(A).

"Existing Business in the Baltimore Region: An Overview." The Economic Development Council. Baltimore: The Greater Baltimore Committee. Baltimore, 1987.

Everhart, R.B. *The Public School Monopoly* Cambridge, Massachusetts: Ballinger Publishing Company, 1982.

Ferguson, Tim W. "Executive Makes School Choice a Yes-or-No Proposition." *Wall Street Journal* 27 August, 1991, 13(A).

Finn, Chester, E. "Toward Strategic Independence: Nine Commandments for Enhancing School Effectiveness." *Phi Delta Kappa* April 1984.

Fiske, Edward B. "Retooling America's Schools by Shifting from the Factory Floor Model to the Power-Sharing One." *New York Times* 4 January 1987, 10(B).

Fosler, R.S. *The Business Role in State Education Reform.* New York: The Business Roundtable, Committee for Economic Development, 1990.

Friedman, Milton. *Capitalism and Freedom.* Chicago: University of Chicago Press, 1962.

_____ "The Role of Government in Education." edited by La Noue, G.R. *Educational Vouchers: Concepts and Controversies.* New York: Teachers College Press, 1972.

Fund, J. H., "Milwaukee's Schools Open to Competition." *Wall Street Journal* 4 September 1990, 14(A).

Gilbert, Patrick. "They Want the Schools Run By the Principals." *The Evening Sun* 27 January 1989, 1(A).

_____. Merwin, J. "Schmoke Rips Hunter - Again." *The Evening Sun* 8 March 1990, 1(D).

Gittell, M. and E.T. Hollander. *Six Urban School Districts: A Comparative Study of Institutional Response.* New York: Praeger Publishers, 1968.

Goodland, John L. *A Place Called School.* New York: McGraw Hill, 1983.

Graham, E. "Starting from Scratch: Rochester Wipes the Slate Clean, Gives Teachers New Responsibility," *Wall Street Journal* 31 March 1989, 4(R).

Greater Baltimore Committee, "A Concept Paper on the Organization and Management of the Baltimore City Public Schools." Baltimore: The Greater Baltimore Committee, 1982.

Greer, Colin. *The Great School Legend.* New York: Basic Books, 1972.

Guidelines: Chapter 1 Program Improvement Plan. Maryland State Department of Education. Baltimore: 1992.

Gunter, Katie. "Neighborhood Trends." *The Baltimore Sun* 19 July 1983, 1(A).

Guthrie, J.W. "School-Based Management: The Next Needed Education Reform." *Phi Delta Kappan,* 68 (December 1986), 305-309.

Gutmann, A. *Democratic Education.* Princeton: Princeton University Press, 1987.

Hall, Wiley A. "Educational Statistics Paint a Picture of Harshness, A Mosaic of Misery." *The Baltimore Sun.* 13 December 1988: 1(A).

Hamilton, Alexander, J. Madison and J. Jay. *The Federalist Papers.* New York: Bantam Book, 1982.

Hammond, Linda Darling, S.N. Kirby. *Tuition Tax Deductions and Parent School Choice.* Santa Monica: Rand Corporation, December 1985.

Hanson, Royce. *Tribune of the People.* Minneapolis: University of Minnesota Press, 1989.

Henig, Jeffrey R. *Rethinking School Choice: Limits of the Market Metaphor.* Princeton: Princeton University Press, 1994.

Hess, Alfred G., Jr. *School Restructuring, Chicago Style.* Newbury Park, CA: Corwin Press, 1991.

Hill, Paul T., A.E. Wise, L. Shapiro. *Educational Progress: Cities Mobilize to Improve their Schools.* Santa Monica, California: Rand Center for the Study of the Teaching Profession, January 1989.

Hirschmann, Albert O. *Exit, Voice and Loyalty.* Harvard University Press: Cambridge 1970.

Hrebenar, Ronald J., R.K. Scott. *Interest Group Politics in America.* Englewood Cliff: Prentice-Hall, 1982.

Iannaccone, L. "Changing Political Patterns and Governmental Regulations." edited by Everhart, R. B. *The Public School*

Monopoly. Cambridge, Massachusetts: Ballinger Publishing Company, 1982.

_____. *Politics in Education*. New York: The Center for Applied Research in Education, 1967.

Ifill, Gwen. "Schaefer Sworn in 4th Time." *The Evening Sun* 6 December 1983, 1(A).

_____. "Mayor Criticizes School Management," *The Evening Sun* 10 May 1984, 1(A).

Jessup, Dorothy K. *Teachers, Unions and Change: A Comparative Study*. Greenwood: Praeger, 1985.

Jones, Charles O. *An Introduction to the Study of Public Policy*. Belmont: Duxbury Press, 1984.

Kaufman, H. "Administrative Decentralization and Political Power." *Public Administration Review* (Jan/Feb, 1969): 3.

Katz, Michael. *The Irony of Early School Reform: Educational Innovation in Mid-Nineteenth Century Massachusetts*. Cambridge: Harvard University Press. 1968.

Katznelson, Ira and M. Weir. *Schooling for All: Class, Race, and the Decline of the American Ideal*. New York: Basic Books, 1985.

Kirst, M.W. "The Crash of the First Wave." Edited by S.B. Bacharach, *Education Reform: Making Sense of it All*. Boston: Allyn and Bacon, 1990: 20-29.

_____. *The Politics of Education at the Local, State and Federal Levels*. Berkeley: McCutchan Publishing Corporation, 1970.

Kelly, Suzanne P. "46% of Baltimore 9th-graders Drop Out Before Graduation." *The Evening Sun* 8 February 1988, 5(A).

Lally, Kathy. "City Schools to Abolish 122 Jobs." *The Baltimore Sun* 6 January 1989, 1(A).

_____. "City/State Are Among the Leaders in School Suspensions." *The Baltimore Sun* 13 December 1988, 1(A).

_____. "10% in City School are Learning Disabled, Poll Finds." *The Baltimore Sun* 13 December 1988, 1(A).

_____. "Hunter Outlines His Goals for City's School System." *The Evening Sun* 7 July 1988, 1(A).

_____. "UNC Professor said to be Semifinalist to Replace Pinderhughes." *The Evening Sun* 26 May 1988, 15(D).

_____. "Unruly Students Sent Home By City Schools." *The Evening Sun* 26 October 1988, 1(A).

_____. "City to Cut 197 Teachers, Hire 224 in Critical Fields." *The Baltimore Sun* 28 June 1989, 1(A).

_____. "Are the Schools Failing? There is both Good News and Bad," *The Baltimore Sun* 13 May 1984, 1(A).

_____. "GBC Issues call for Renaissance in School System," *The Baltimore Sun* 21 May 1987, 1(D).

_____."Maryland Schools Ranked 4th Most Segregated in Survey." *The Baltimore Sun* 30 January 1987, 1(A).

_____. "Mayor Consults School Board About Hunter." *The Baltimore Sun* 1 April 1990, 4(B).

_____."Mayor's School Fund Sets 1st Project," *The Baltimore Sun* 18 May 1984, 1(A).

_____. "Minimal Fallout Seen From Schmoke-Hunter Conflict." *The Baltimore Sun* 13 April 1990, 1(E).

_____. "October is a Cruel Month for City Schools Chief." *The Baltimore Sun* 20 November 1988, 1(A).

_____. "Pinderhughes Response to Schaefer Wins Praise." *The Baltimore Sun.* 19 April 1987, 1(B).

_____. "Schmoke Says School Chief Will Keep Job." *The Baltimore Sun* 12 April 1990, 1(A).

_____. "Schmoke Taps Lawyer to Run School Board: Harvard Colleague, New to Baltimore, Replaces Fine." *The Baltimore Sun* 12 December 1987, 1(A).

_____. "Schools Chief Praised for Pruning Staff." *The Baltimore Sun* 8 January 1989, 1(A).

_____. "Schools Told to Overhaul Budgeting." *The Baltimore Sun* 19 April 1983, 1(D).

_____. "Schools Chief Praised from Pruning Staff: Systems Critics See Hope at Last." *The Baltimore Sun* 8 October 1989, 1(A).

_____. "Schools Haven't Responded to the Mayor's Touch," *The Baltimore Sun* 18 January 1987, 5(E).

_____. "Schmoke Asks School Officials for Master Plan," *The Baltimore Sun* 14 August 1989, 1(A).

_____. "Schmoke Say School Chief Will Keep Job" *The Baltimore Sun* 12 April 1990, A1.

_____. "$60 Million Boost Sought For Baltimore Schools." *The Baltimore Sun* 20 January 1989, 1(A).

_____. "22 Top Jobs to be Cut from Baltimore Schools." *The Baltimore Sun* 6 January 1989, 1(A).

_____, & LoLordo, Ann. "Pinderhughes Plans to Retire as Schools Chief." *The Baltimore Sun* 11 December 1989, 1 (A).

Lamar, Alexander, "Time For Results: An Overview" *Phi Delta Kappan* 68 (November 1986): 202-204.

La Noue, G.R. *Educational Vouchers: Concepts and Controversies.* New York: Teachers College Press, 1972.

LaPointe, Archie E., N. A. Mead, G.W. Phillips. *A World of Differences: An International Assessment of Mathematics and Science.* Report Number 19-CAEP-01: Princeton: Educational Testing Service, January 1989.

Levin, Harry M. *Community Control of Schools.* Washington, D.C.: Brookings Institution, 1970.

Levine, Charles. *The Politics of Retrenchment: How Local Governments Manage Fiscal Stress.* Beverly Hills: Sage Publications, 1981.

Levine, Marc V. "Downtown Redevelopment as an Urban Growth Strategy: A Critical Appraisal of the Baltimore Renaissance." *Journal of Urban Affairs* 9 (1987): 103-123.

_____. "Economic Development to help Underclass," *The Baltimore Sun* 10 January 1988, 1(E).

_____. "Response to Berkowitz, Economic Development in Baltimore: Some Additional Perspectives." *Journal of Urban Affairs* 9 (1987): 133-138.

Lieberman, Myron. *Beyond Public Education.* New York: Praeger, 1986.

Lindquist, K.M. and J.J. Muriel. "SBM, Doomed to Failure?" *Education and Urban Society* 21 (August, 1989): 403-416.

LoLordo, Ann. "A Smaller, Poorer City in the Future," *The Baltimore Sun* 18 January 1987, 1(E).

Lowi, Theodore J. "Machine Politics Old and New" *The Public Interest* 9 (Fall 1967): 83-92.

Lukas, Anthony J. *Common Ground: A Turbulent Decade in the Lives of Three American Families.* New York: Alfred A. Knopf, 1985.

Maddus, J. "Parental Choice of School: What Parents Think and Do." *Review of Research in Education* 16 1990: 267-295.

Malen, Betty. "Enacting Tuition Tax Credit Deduction Statutes in Minnesota." *Journal of Education Finance* 11 (Summer 1985): 1-28.

Malken, B., Ogawa, R.T. "Community Involvement." Edited by S.B. Bacharach, *Education Reform: Making Sense of it All.* Boston: Allyn and Bacon, 1990: 52-66.

March, J.G. and J.P. Olson. "Organizing Political Life: What Administrative Reorganization Tells us about Government." *American Political Science Review.* 77, (1983): 281-293.

Maryland Statistical Abstract, 1986-1987. Anapolis: Maryland Department of Economic Development, 1988.

Mazzoni, Tim L. "Bureaucratic Influence in the Formation of State School Policy." *Planning and Changing.* 16 (Summer 1985): 77-78.

_____. "State Policymaking and Public School Choice in Minnesota, from Confrontation to Compromise." *Journal of Education* 63 (1986):45-69.

_____. and B. Malen. "Mobilizing Constituency Pressure to Influence State Education Policy." *Educational Administration Quarterly* 21 (Spring, 1985): 91-116.

McGiveny, J. H. and J.H. Hawght. "The Politics of Education: A View from the Perspective of the Central Office Staff." *Educational Administration Quarterly* 8 (Winter, 1972):18-38.

McKenzie, William P. "Is George Bush A Progressive Republican?" *Ripon Forum Magazine,* September, 1991. 13.

McManus, Susan. "Linking State Employment and Training and Economic Development Programs: A 20 State Analysis," *Public Administration Review* (November/December 1986).

Merwin, J. "Chapter One Changes? None Yet." *The Evening Sun* 9 May 1990, 1(A).

_____. "Hunter's Pace is criticized Halfway into His Term." *The Evening Sun* 7 February 1990, 1(A).

_____, J. "Mayor Said To Hurt Hunter Credibility." *The Evening Sun* 5 April 1990, 1(B).

_____, J. and Gilbert P. "Mayor Wants Hunter to Get a No. 2." *The Evening Sun* 22 March 1990, 1(D).

_____. "Schmoke to Help Grade Hunter." *The Evening Sun* 21 March 1990, 1(D).

_____. "We Delivered, Mayor Says, on the Vow to Provide Student Aid." *The Evening Sun* 26 September 1989, 4(B).

Minnesota State House of Representatives, House of Representatives Research Department, *Minnesota Charter Schools: A Research Report.* Minneapolis: December, 1994.

Minnesota Business Partnership, Task Force on Education, *An Education Agenda for Minnesota: The Challenge to Our Communities and Schools.* Minneapolis: The Minnesota Business Partnership, 1990.

"Minnesota's Experiment With Choice Could Be A Wave of The Future." *National Journal* 19 October 1985: 2370-2371.

Minnesota House Research Department *Minnesota Charter Schools: A Research Report.* Minneapolis: 1994.

Mullis, Ina V.S., L.B. Jenkins. *Science Learning Matters: The Science Report Card: An Interpretive Overview* Report Number 17-S-02. Princeton, N.J.: Educational Testing Service, 1988.

Murnane, R.J. "Family Choice in Public Education: The Roles of Teachers, Students, Parents and other Designers." *Teachers College Record* 88 (Winter:1986):169-189.

Muth, R., J. Azumi. "The District Level" *Education Reform: Making Sense of it All.* Boston: Ally and Bacon, 1990 52-66.

_____. Wayne Jennings, *Access to Opportunity: Experiences of Minnesota Students in 4 Statewide School Choice Programs, 1989-1990.* Minneapolis: Center for School Change: Hubert H. Humphrey Institute of Public Affairs: University of Minnesota, 1990.

_____. "Helping All Children, Empowering All Educators: Another View of School Choice." *Phi Delta Kappan* (December 1989): 304-307.

National Assessment of Educational Progress, Executive Summary, *Mathematics: Are We Measuring Up? The Mathematics Report Card.* Report Number 17-M-02. Princeton: Educational Testing Service, 1987.

National Center for Education Statistics. *Digest of Education Statistics, 1991.* Washington: Government Printing Office, 1991.

National Commission on Excellence in Education, "A Nation At Risk: The Imperative for Educational Reform." Washington, D.C.: Government Printing office, April 1983.

National Education Association, Internal Document. *Listing of AFT Local Affiliates Where they Represent Employees in Bargaining.* Washington: National Education Association, September 1992.

National Education Association, Special Committee on Restructuring, "Final Report of the National Education Special Committee on Restructuring Schools: Toward Restructured Public Schools" *Restructuring Issues* 6 Washington, D.C.: National Education Association, December 1988.

National Governor's Association. *Time For Results.* Washington, D.C.: The National Governor's Association, 1986.

O'Keefe, Kevin. *Baltimore Politics 1971-1986: The Schaefer Years and The Struggle for Succession.* The Georgetown Monograph in American Studies, 3 Washington, D.C.: Georgetown University, 1987.

O'Shea, Christine M., Ernest Kahane, Peter Sola. *The New Servants of Power: A Critique of the 1980's School Reform Movement.* New York: Greenwood Press, 1989.

Ollove, M. "CollegeBound Fund Drive Seeks to Aid City Youth." *The Baltimore Sun* 27 January 1988, 1(B).

_____. "Hollis faulted Over Job Offer To Hunter." *The Baltimore Sun* 25 June 1988, 1(A).

_____. "Schmoke Picks Savvy Newcomer to Lead School Board." *The Baltimore Sun* 12 December 1987, 1(A).

Opinion Dynamics Corporation, "Public Attitudes Toward Education Issues," *MassInsight Survey* Study Number 3271, Cambridge: Opinion Dynamics Corporation, 1990.

Orr, Marion. *Urban Politics and School Reform: The Case of Baltimore City.* Draft. Department of Political Science: Duke University, 1994.

Peddie, Sandra and Kahn, A. "Minnesota Gets Fired Up for the Task." *St. Paul Pioneer Press* 3 March 1985, 1.

Peterson, P.E. "Afterward: The Politics of School Decentralization." *Education and Urban Society* 7 (August, 1975): 464-484.

_____, P. E. "Analyzing Developmental Politics: A Response to Sanders and Stone." *Urban Affairs Quarterly* 22, (June 1987): 540-547.

_____. *City Limits.* Chicago: The University of Chicago Press, 1981.

_____. *The Politics of School Reform.* Chicago: The University of Chicago Press, 1985.

_____. *School Politics Chicago Style: Bargaining and Unitary Policy Making Models.* Chicago: University of Chicago Press: 1976.

Pilo, M.R. "A Tale of Two Cities: The Application of Models of School Decentralization to the Cases of New York City and Detroit." *Education and Urban Society.* 7 (August, 1975): 393-411.

Pierce, Neal R. "Reforms to Make Teachers Accountable." *National Journal* 17 November 1990, 2819.

_____. "The Boston Compact - An '80s School Model," *National Journal* 1 February 1986, 284.

_____. & Sagen, Deborah, "Business Increasingly Sees Quality Education As Vital to Its Interests," *National Journal 15* October 1983, 2109-2113.

Pietila, Antero. "Patterson: From Crisis to Crisis," *The Afro-American.* 11 August 1974, 13.

"Poverty In Baltimore: Data and Indicators," Baltimore: Baltimore City Department of Planning. Policy Research Section., 1987.

Provenzo, E.F. Jr. "School-Based Management and Shared Decision making in the Dade County Public Schools." edited by Rosow, J. and R. Zager. *Allies in Educational Reform.* San Francisco: Jossey-Bass, 1989, 146-163.

Quarterly Review of State Choice legislation, Washington, D.C. Center for Choice in Education, U.S. Department of Education, February 1992.

_____. Geiger, K. *School Choice: Issues and Answers.* Bloomington, Indiana: National Education Service, 1991.

Ravitch, D. *The Great School Wars.* New York: Basic Books, 1974.

_____. *The Revisionist Revised: A Critique of the Radical Attack on the Schools.* New York: Basic Books, 1974.

Raywid, M.A. "Rethinking School Governance." edited by Elmore, R.F. *Restructuring Schools.* San Francisco: Jossey-Bass Publishers, 1990.

_____. "Schools of Choice: Their Current Nature and   Prospects." *Phi Delta Kappan* 64 (June 1983): 684.

Rebell, M. A. "Overview: Education and The Law: Schools, Values and the Courts." *Yale Law and Policy Review* 7 (1989): 275-342.

The Regional Planning Council, "Commuting in the Baltimore Region: Historical Perspectives and Current Trends." Baltimore: The Regional Planning Council, 1985.

_____. "Economic Indicators: Baltimore City, 1981-1982." Baltimore: The Regional Planning Council, 1983.

_____. "Economic Outlook to 1990." *Economic Review.* Baltimore: The Regional Planning Council, 1986.

_____."Employment Trends in the Baltimore Region: 1970-1990." Baltimore:The Regional Planning Council, 1988.

"Remarks by the President to Distinguished School Principals." The White House Office of the Press Secretary. October 18, 1989, 13.

Roberts, N.C., and King, P.J. "The Process of Public Policy Innovation." Eds. A.H. Van de Ven, H.L. Angle & M.S. Poole,

Research on the Management of Innovation. New York: Harper and Row, 303-335.

Rogers, D. *110 Livingston Street.* New York: Vintage Books, 1969.

Rosenthal, A. "New Voices in Public Education." edited by Kirst, M.E. *The Politics of Education at the Local, State and Federal Levels.* Berkeley: McCutchan Publishing Corporation, 1970: 101-110.

Rosow, J. and R. Zager. *Allies in Educational Reform.* San Francisco: Jossey-Bass, 1989.

Ross, Leonard and R. Zeckhauser. "Education Vouchers." *Law and Contemporary Problems48*:451.

Rossell, C.H. and C.L. Glenn. "The Cambridge Controlled Choice Plan." *Urban Review* 20 (1988): 75-93.

Rourke, Francis E. *Bureaucracy, Politics and Public Policy.* Boston: Little Brown and Company, 1984.

Rubenstein, Michael C. & R. Hamar, N.E. Adelman. *Minnesota's Open Enrollment Option.* Washington, D.C.: U.S. Department of Education, 1992.

Rubinson, Richard. "Class Formations, Politics, and Institutions: Schooling in the United States." *American Journal of Sociology* 92 (1986): 519-548.

Salganik, L.H. "The Fall and Rise of Education Vouchers." *Teachers College Record.* 83 (Winter 1981): 263-283.

Samuelson, Robert J. "From Crisis to Crisis," *National Journal* July, 9, 1983, 1426.

Sandler, A. B. and D.E. Kapel. "Educational Vouchers: A Viable Option for Urban Settings?" *The Urban Review* 20 (1988): 267-282.

Schiff, M. "The Educational Failure of Community Control in Inner-City New York." *Phi Delta Kappan,* 57 (February, 1976): 375.

Schulman, Paul R. *Large-Scale Policy Making.* Westport, Ct: Greenwood Press, 1980.

Selden, D. "Vouchers- Solution or SOP?" *Teachers College Record.* 72 (February 1971): 365-371.

Sheisty, Ted. "Schools Are Top Priority, says GBC Report." *The Baltimore Sun* 12 April 1987, 1 (C).

Smetanka, Mary Jane. "Liberated Learning: Minnesota is First to Give Teachers, Parents." *Minneapolis Star and Tribune* 26 May 1991.

_____. "Report Questions Whether Means Jjustify Ends for Charter Schools." *Minneapolis Star and Tribune* 18 January 1995: 1(B).

Smith, C. Fraser. "As Shadow Government Grows Stronger, its Accountability to the Public Lessens." *The Baltimore Sun* 20 April 1980, 1(A).

_____. "Baltimore's Trustees Play High Finance on a Tightrope; Gambles Sometimes Lose." *The Baltimore Sun* 14 April 1980, 1(A).

_____. "City Trustees Are Not Hampered By Checks Ruling Other Officials." *The Baltimore Sun* 13 April 1980, 1(A).

_____. "Two Trustees and a $100 Million 'Bank' Skirt the Restrictions of City Government." *The Baltimore Sun* 13 April 1980, 1(A).

Snider, William. "Minnesota Backs Nation's First Choice System." *Education Week* 7 (May 1988): 13.

Spring, J. *Conflict of Interests: The Politics of American Education.* New York: Longman, 1988.

_____. *Education and the Rise of the Corporate State.* Boston: Beacon Press, 1972.

Stewart C. Purkey, and M. S. Smith, "School Reform: The District Policy Implications of the Effective Schools Literature." *The Elementary School Journal* (1984).

Stoker, Robert P. "Baltimore, the Self-evaluating City," in Sanders, Heywood and Stone, Clarence N. *The Politics of Urban Development.* Lawrence, Kansas: University Press of Kansas, 1987: 244-266.

Stone, Clarence & Sanders, Heywood, "Reexamining A Classic Case of Development Politics: New Haven, Connecticut, *The Politics of Urban Development*: 159-181.

_____. "Developmental Politics Reconsidered." *Urban Affairs Quarterly* 22: 521-539.

Stone, Nathan. "Does Business Have any Business in Education?" *Harvard Business Review*: 52.

Sullivan, Barry. *Draft: Selected Education Reforms and Policy Trends Since 1983.* Minnesota Government Relations Office: Minnesota, 1992

Szanton, Peter. *Baltimore 2,000: A Choice of Futures: Report to the Morris Goldseker Foundation.* Morris Goldseker Foundation. Baltimore, Maryland: 1986.

Teaford, John. *The Rough Road to Renaissance.* Baltimore: The Johns Hopkins University Press, 1990.

Thomas, Kevin. "Thousands of 12th graders Forfeit BUILD Jobs." *Evening Sun* 21 April 1986, 1(A).

_____. "School Plans A Foot Before Schaefer." *The Evening Sun* 19 April 1987, 1(A).

Thompson, M.D. "Sun Loses Its Plea to Open School Interviews." *The Baltimore Sun*.18 June 1988, 1(A).

Timer, Thomas. "The Politics of School Restructuring," *The Education Digest.* (May 1990): 7-10.

Timpane, Michael, L.M. McNeill. *Business Impact on Education and Child Development Reform: A Study Prepared for the Committee on Economic Development.* New York: Committee for Economic Development, 1991.

Toch, Thomas. *In The Name of Excellence: The Struggle to Reform the Nation's Schools, Why its failing and What Should be Done.* New York: Oxford University Press, 1991.

_____. "Plugging the School Tax Gap in Education: Courts Nationwide are Challenging Funding." *U.S. News & World Report,* 26 June 1990, 58.

Traub, James. "Fernandez Takes Charge." *The New York Times Magazine,* 17 June 1990, 23.

_____. "Separate and Equal." *The Atlantic,* September, 1991, 24.

Tweedie, J. "Parental Rights and Accountability in Public Education: Special Education and Choice of School." *Yale Law and Policy Review,* 7 (1989): 396-418.

Tyack, David B. *The One Best System: A History of American Urban Education.* Cambridge: Harvard University Press, 1974.

Urbanski, A. "A Teacher Reports From Rochester: Choice Works Now!" in Bacharach, S. B, ed. *Education Reform: Making Sense of It All.* Boston: Allyn and Bacon, 1990.

Verhovek, Sam Howe. "Legislature in Texas Send School-Aid Plan to Voters." *The New York Times* 12 (A).

West, E.G. "An Economic Analysis." edited by Everhart, R. B. *The Public School Monopoly.* Cambridge, Massachusetts: Ballinger Publishing Company, 1982: 369-391.

_____. "An Economic Rationale for Public Schools: The Search Continues." *Teacher's College Record* 88 (Winter 1986): 152-168.

White, Paula A. "An Overview of School-Based Management: What does the Research Say?" *NAASP BULLETIN* September, 1989, 2.

"Who Negotiates for the Children?: The Importance of Teacher Union Agreements in the Quality of Education" in Wiles, D.K.

"Community Participation Demands and Local School Response in the Urban Environment." *Education and Urban Society* 6 (August, 1974): 451-468.

Wirt, F.M. and Kirst, M.W. *The Political Web of American Schools.* Boston: Little, Brown and Company, 1972.

_____. *Schools in Conflict.* Berkeley: McCutchan Publishing Corporation, 1982.

Wohlstetter, Priscilla and Karen McCur "The Link Between School Decentralization and School Politics." *Urban Education* 25 (January 1991): 391-414.

Index